ACTIVE
TUTORIAL WOR...

Active Tutorial Work

SIXTEEN TO NINETEEN

Programme Editor
HARRY WELLS

Programme Directors
JILL BALDWIN
ANDY SMITH

BASIL BLACKWELL · PUBLISHER

Active Tutorial Work Development Project
The dissemination of the materials and associated training
programme is funded by the Health Education Council.

Printed and bound in Great Britain

FOREWORD

In the years since I was privileged to write a short foreword to the earlier Active Tutorial Work books, a great deal of progress has been made. The first five books are in use nationwide, and overseas, and this additional '16–19' book has been added to the series in response to widespread requests. Serving teachers have been seconded to the project as field officers, for a year each, and we have developed a highly competent team of teacher-trainers to support the work in our schools. Jill Baldwin has had a long period of secondment to the Health Education Council in order to provide in-service training courses on the Active Tutorial Work process to education authorities throughout England and Wales, and Harry Wells has retired but has returned, unofficially, to contribute to the production of this sixth book. They and the whole of the County's writing and training teams, over the last six years, deserve thanks and congratulations.

Few can now doubt that pastoral work in schools and colleges should have positive aims. Life and social skills have become increasingly recognised as essential elements in the development of young people to prepare them for a rapidly changing world. Active Tutorial Work with its emphasis on developing education in human relationships offers a major contribution to this vital task.

The sixth form or college ethos can be a potent influence in a young person's life; sometimes this exerts as much influence as that which we set out to achieve through the curriculum itself. Active Tutorial Work, with its emphasis laid as much on approach as on content, can be a sensitising agent. It is concerned with feelings and with awareness, and may throw into sharp relief the pressures which surround the pupil in his or her daily life.

This carefully thought out series places the group/personal tutor in his rightful place at the heart of pastoral work. I hope that it will be both stimulating and helpful to tutors in their efforts to engage their students actively in their personal growth and development, and I commend it to you.

A. J. Collier
Chief Education Officer, Lancashire

ACTIVE TUTORIAL WORK

This project was set up in response to the growing demand for worthwhile things to do in the form tutorial period. The aim has been to produce a coherent programme in which the approach is as fundamental and as important as the material.

A more direct approach to pastoral work began within the Lancashire authority in 1972 with the appointment of Ken David as specialist adviser for education in personal relationships (EPR). From this there developed a growing range of courses under the heading of Pastoral Care/EPR, concerned with enhancing skills such as counselling, interviewing and group dynamics and with broadening horizons. Within many schools the allocation of time for tutorials began to be increased slowly and some schools even allocated EPR 'slots' on the time-table. There followed a phase when teachers, seeking tutorial materials, adapted commercially produced resources from other areas of the curriculum to this education for personal growth and development.

It became apparent, however, that there was a need to devise a teaching programme aimed at facilitating the pupil's personal growth and development through his own active participation.

In order to initiate such a programme a group of teachers was recruited, mainly from East Lancashire; they were invited to participate in an extensive practical course in developmental group work, so that programme writing could be started from a basis of common experience. A number of teachers had previously been trained in Developmental Group Work on courses run for the Authority by Dr Leslie Button of Swansea University, on which this programme of tutorial work for six years of secondary education is based. This programme was to be essentially practical and based heavily on the developmental group work approach. There would be 'threads' running through all the years, for example self-picture, self-respect, and the development of learning and study skills, as well as themes which the team deemed to be particularly applicable to specific years. In putting these ideas into practice the project team are grateful to Douglas Hamblin of Swansea University, another of our mainsprings of inspiration, for allowing us to adapt some of his materials.

It is important to emphasise that the resulting programme is not an *ad hoc* collection of materials; there has been a determined effort to create a rationale for the work, i.e. that it is developmental and has clear aims and objectives stated in small simple steps wherever possible so that teachers and pupils can observe for themselves that something is being achieved.

Training in the acquisition of certain key skills, and continued support for teachers who are attempting to train their colleagues in school, have been central parts of the project. This means that teachers have not only access to materials, with accompanying guide-lines, but also the opportunity to participate in in-service training focused on close work with young people. This has been aimed at developing social skills by meeting people, skills of listening and conversation, step-by-step discussion, coping with relationships with authority figures, with family and peer group relationships and with feelings about self and the ability to make friends.

It is 'teacher style' which makes even the most carefully documented programme unique in every classroom situation. It is mentioned here because it is of paramount importance, when working in the field of interpersonal relationships, to be aware of what we, as teachers, bring to the situation; i.e. to know ourselves, our mannerisms, our beliefs, attitudes, prejudices, and the signals which we give. In short, to be sure that our 'being' is in accord with what we are saying and what we are trying to do.

To sum up, this tutorial programme is not concerned with the administrative side of a teacher's pastoral role, nor with crisis counselling. Instead, it is concerned with assisting young people with their normal growth and development, with developing their social competence, and with weathering the passing 'storms' of growing up to gain increasing control of their own destiny.

J. Baldwin and A. Smith
Project Directors

WRITING TEAM

Mrs Sheila Clay
St Hilda's High School, Burnley

Mr Alec Mackie
The Castle County Secondary
School, Lancaster

Mr Alan Scholes
Barden High School, Burnley

Miss Kathleen Smith
St Wilfrid's High School, Blackburn

Mr Tony Bryant
Skelmersdale College

Mrs Marion Hunt
St Wilfrid's High School, Blackburn

Mr David Neville
Skelmersdale College

Miss Joyce Bentley
St Wilfrid's High School, Blackburn

Programme Editor:
Mr Harry Wells,
(former Curriculum Development Officer, Burnley)

Project Directors:
Mrs Jill Baldwin,
Health Education Council

Mr Andy Smith,
S. Martin's College, Lancaster

Active Tutorial Work Development Project
Training project now based at
S. Martin's College,
Lancaster, LA1 3JD

TRIALS OF THE DRAFT MATERIALS

The following institutions tested the materials as they were written, and provided invaluable feedback and constructive criticism, for which the team are very grateful:

St Wilfrid's High School, Blackburn
Hesketh High School, Fleetwood
Skelmersdale College, Lancashire
Nelson & Colne College, Lancashire
Walton High School, Staffordshire
Dr Challoner's Grammar School, Amersham
Bilston Sixth Form Centre, Wolverhampton
King Edward VI High School, Stafford
Blue Coat School, Oldham

Pelsall Comprehensive School, Walsall
Princess Margaret Royal Free School, Windsor
Wilnecote High School, Tamworth
Our Lady and Pope John School, Corby
Altwood C.E. School, Maidenhead
Finham Park School, Coventry
Foxford Comprehensive School, Coventry
Chichester Girls' High School
Pembroke School, Dyfed

CONTENTS and PLANNING GUIDE

LIST OF APPENDICES

TO THE TUTOR

This book was initiated in response to requests for sixth-form material. It soon became evident that the post-16 demand was for a range far wider than the traditional sixth-form and much of the material can be used equally well with students in Colleges of Further Education (e.g., Higher Nationals, Block Release, etc.), Colleges of Industry and Agriculture, and even in the training of teachers and nurses. Do not be put off by references to 'First Sixth' and 'Second Sixth' etc. This is simply a convenient way of indicating that some materials may be more appropriate to earlier or later stages of a two/three year course, or the desirability of bringing new students into contact with more experienced students from time to time.

The '16–19' programme presupposes a time allocation of about an hour per week with the tutor group. Even so, there is a great deal to work through. The writers hope that you will try to tackle all the themes, for most of which a variety of approaches and strategies have been suggested, to allow for differing situations and your own preferences. We hope, however, that you will not choose only the 'safe' topics and approaches, but will branch out and tackle those which may be more demanding and problematical for you.

Beware of labelling the activities as too simple or 'childish'. We ask sincerely that activities be *tried* before being condemned as too simple or inappropriate for your particular group. You may be surprised by the group's responses.

The programme is not intended to be followed rigidly, step-by-step, week-by-week, from page 1 to the end. After careful consideration we felt that certain topics were useful early in the first term, perhaps as an induction programme.

Furthermore, the programme is certainly not intended to be a 'Definitive Guide to Tutorial Work'. We hope you will continue to use your own strategies and approaches where these have proved to be successful for a particular purpose. We would ask, however, that you keep 'one eye' on your objectives to ensure that all are being given equal status.

Finally, we don't expect miracles! A single session on many of the themes can, obviously, have only a limited effect. Therefore, we hope that you will be able to return to them, recapitulating and building on what has gone before. Above all, we hope that both you and your students will enjoy your Active Tutorial Work together.

THE MAIN AIMS FOR TUTORIAL WORK WITH THE 16–19 AGE GROUP

To develop in the student:

- the ability to embrace life and accept its challenges

- the ability to assess his/her future life pattern

- the ability to prepare for independence

- to begin to develop and be aware of a personal philosophy of life

- an ability to facilitate integration within the immediate peer group (tutor group), within the year as a whole, and contribute to a corporate group identity

- an understanding of human relationships and what is involved in dealing with people in school/college

- an understanding of human relationships and what is involved in dealing with people outside school/college

- a sense of belonging to a group

- a realisation of the specific demands of Advanced Level work

- the ability to assimilate knowledge effectively

- an understanding of what is involved in independent and non-directed study

- a recognition of one's own limitations and the consequent/possible necessity to modify aspirations

- political awareness and an understanding of one's rights at 16+, 17+ and 18+

- an understanding of economics

- an ability to recognise the need to reconcile the expectations of parents and the demands of school with personal goals

- an ability to accept that, after the fifth form, he/she is in a different mental and physical environment

- critical faculties

- the ability to evaluate one's own potential with regard to skills, abilities and interests, and develop and utilise creative powers.

ABOUT AIMS AND OBJECTIVES

It is useful for us, as teachers, to have a fairly wide range of objectives which are clearly and precisely expressed, in order to plan the learning opportunities for the students and devise means of assessing the extent to which the students have achieved the stated objectives. It is fairly common to find a list of objectives carefully and precisely stated at the beginning of subject syllabuses, integrated projects and the like. These have been thought out in terms of cognitive/learning and the type of responses which will demonstrate the learning, usually some form of examination or test.

Stating objectives is another matter, however, when it comes to 'affective' and 'emotional' learning, the values and attitudes which are part of the educational process.

We tend to speak in general terms when referring to the 'pastoral' side of education, and to use words and phrases rather loosely. This leads us to feel that there is general agreement about the purposes of education, that we all know what we are trying to do, so we do not need to spend time discussing it or writing it down. In fact, when terms are defined and discussion pursued, agreement is not so widespread.

The members of this project feel that it should be possible to state clear objectives for affective education, and put forward the following propositions:

(a) That the personal development of the students is equally as important and should be as carefully planned and organized as their cognitive development.

(b) That a planned scheme for personal development will enhance and underpin all the cognitive learning planned by the school or college.

(c) That objectives for personal development should include, where possible, the type of behaviour to be observed so that, some attempt can be made to measure the change and, therefore, assess whether objectives are being achieved.
It should not be assumed that they are being achieved.

(d) The objectives should be stated in terms of what the student can achieve in observable behavioural terms. There will be different levels of achievement, as a member of the class, group, and as an individual, and the student himself should be central to the process of keeping the objectives under review.

(e) Objectives should be unambiguous, should communicate to others a clear intention, and give an indication of content. A simple but important criterion is 'What will the student be doing?'

WORKING IN GROUPS

WHY HAVE GROUPS?

The project's approach to tutorial group work is based on Leslie Button's expressed belief that such work is 'about helping children in their growth and development, in their social skills, their personal resources and in the kind of relationships they establish with other people. Social skills can only be learnt in contact with other people.'[1] It is the purpose of active tutorial work to provide pupils with practical situations in which they are in constant interaction with others, can try new approaches, experiment in new roles, develop insights, come to know and to help themselves and seek to establish personal goals.

WHAT KIND OF GROUP?

To most secondary school teachers, group work usually suggests half-class groups or groups of ten to sixteen pupils. The usual reaction to this is that 'It's impossible to have half-classes or groups of a dozen in our school', and that group work is thus a non-starter in their situation.

Whilst some schools have managed to create a climate in which pastoral group sessions of twelve to sixteen have become a norm, the writing team believed that it would be unrealistic to plan a programme of active tutorial work for each of the years from eleven to sixteen on the supposition that this would become the norm in all schools. Thus, we based our programme on the premise that the form teacher would be working with the whole class, or large groups, which would then break down into small groups – sometimes of three or four, sometimes five or six, sometimes based on the friendship patterns in the class, and sometimes based on other criteria which are applicable to a particular situation or activity.

These small groups have something in common with the buzz group, embrace something of the discussion group, and are often particularly concerned with the exploration of feelings. What we seek is maximum participation and inter-action for each student, even though we may be faced with a large group situation. Therefore, we require more than two, but preferably not more than five or six youngsters in our small groups if we are truly to achieve active tutorial work for all.

Tutors of the 16–19 age group will probably have more opportunity for working in small groups than their counterparts in the 11–16 age range, and will quite often find it necessary to make up the number of small groups needed to operate some activities successfully.

STEP-BY-STEP DISCUSSION

It is not difficult to stimulate discussion within a large group, when it is broken down as suggested above, by posing a series of questions. After a question has been discussed in small groups for a few minutes, the tutor may call for the attention of the whole tutor group so that they may report to one another interesting points which have arisen in their small groups. These exchanges usually lead quite naturally into the next question which is then fed back to the small groups. This is referred to as 'step-by-step discussion'[2]. The important skill for the tutor lies in being able to foresee a series of questions, each of which represents a small step forward. The ability to foresee possible outcomes, and thus to arrange a programme of questions, has to be balanced by a genuine openness to change and to unforeseen responses, if real dialogue is to ensue.

Many lower ability students may be unable to discuss abstract concepts (e.g. relationships), and one has to begin at the level of simple recall:

> 'Who were the first two people you met this morning?' (Groups then work at this together.)

> 'Who else did you meet?'

[1] L Button, *Developmental Group Work in the Secondary School Pastoral Programme*, p. 1, Department of Education, University College of Swansea, 1978

[2] This technique has been developed by Leslie Button and described by him as 'Socratic Group Discussion' in L Button, *Discovery and Experience*, pp. 120–126, OUP, and L Button, *Developmental Group Work With Adolescents*, pp. 151–161, Hodder & Stoughton, 1974

'Who did you think was the most important person you met?' (More small group discussion. Perhaps – What do we mean by important?)

'How did you behave towards each other?'

'Who spoke first?'

'How did you feel?'

Then, perhaps, move on to a more general discussion on relationships, difficulties experienced in meeting other people, and so on. The early stages of their discussion will last only a few minutes and are not meant to be exhaustive, but rather to open up discussion, stir ideas, encourage participation.

This type of group work is an effective way of involving and activating young people, leading them step-by-step into deeper understanding, accelerating exploration and involving everyone in active participation in new experience. It is not formalised, is easy to initiate, and seems to have the effect of allowing individual students to formulate tentative ideas and rehearse statements which they then feel better able to bring forward to the whole tutor group – often with the support of their small group behind them.

The tutor's role is to encourage contributions from one group after another, to move in close to the groups from time to time, to intervene, to suggest points missed, add emphasis, crystallise, support and draw out the timid and the soft-spoken, and yet demonstrate that everyone is included in the general exchanges. The tutor's sense of pace is important – more often moving things forward in a lively way, yet allowing pauses for introspection or a greater depth of contemplation. Sensitivity to feelings and an ability to convey warmth and encouragement are essential.

USING VISITORS

This technique was introduced initially as a 'social technique' with youngsters in their first year of secondary education.[1] It was put to wider use in succeeding programmes because, in our experience, it had proved an invaluable tool for learning. We have found it equally valuable with adult groups and therefore can with confidence commend its use with the 16–19 age group. As some tutors may not have used this method of involving visitors before, we cannot do better than repeat the notes printed in earlier volumes even though the language may need to be modified for use with older pupils.

As the tutorial work programme progresses, ways in which the visitor technique can be usefully employed often arise naturally out of the work. In the first place, however, it usually arises from direct suggestions by the tutor. So let's start from there.

The question is put: *Shall we have a visitor to the group?* This is followed by: *Who shall it be?* A short but lively session ensues, with questions such as: *Who will invite the visitor? How will it be done? When will it be? How long will it last?* These are discussed until the broad details are decided.

The next consideration is: *What do we want to know, or find out, from our visitor?* Ideas may flow freely, or may have to be initiated by strong prompting from the teacher. You may wish to jot the random ideas down on the blackboard, or the group might wish to appoint a scribe. Next, the group sifts through the ideas: *Which can we use? What might make the best opening question? Who's going to ask the second question?* and so on, until the opening stages of the session are beginning to take shape. The group might then consider: *Is there anything special we want to tell the visitor?* and after that: *Will the visitor want to ask any questions? Who's going to ask this?* etc.

By now we're turning to: *Who's going to greet the visitor? You, Ian? How are you going to do it? Come on, show me! Right, now let's try it again. Is that OK?* and so on. Then might follow questions and short role plays about how the visitor will feel, how he will be put at ease and made to feel welcome, until everyone is quite sure about what will happen and what is to be said. This knowledge, this detail, this sureness, engenders confidence and a sense of security.

Then, on again: *Where will the greeting take place? Will it be at the door of the tutor room, at the school/college entrance? Come on, Ian, show me. Imagine I'm your visitor. Oh, by the way, what are you going to talk about as you walk through the school/college with the visitor? Come on, the rest of you, help him!* These are very active stages, with many interruptions, questions and short snatches of role play. *Stop! Show me! Good, now let's try again,* etc. *Now we've reached the room, are you going to introduce everyone? You are? Go on, then, show me! Where do we sit? How do you want the room arranged? Come on, then, let's do it like that. Now, who's going to ask the first question? Right, fire away!* And so on to the next and the next.

Then: *Fine, that's going nicely, so let's go back and start all over again. First, who's going to play the part of the visitor? Gordon? Good! Off you go to the main entrance. Ready, Ian? Ready, everybody? Off we go again!*

Work through the whole situation again, stopping, prompting, questioning, involving the whole group in a corporate wish to do something well. You might find, additionally, that the group wishes to discuss and sort out the organisation of tea and biscuits.

Preparation of the visitor is as important as the preparation of the group. The visitor will need to know a little about the nature of the group and the work you're doing, as well as about the situation and the kind of questions he can expect to meet. The visitor must anticipate a certain stiltedness about the first few questions and be briefed not to talk at length or to rush to fill in the small silences which might arise, in case he cuts

[1] J Jordan, *The Role and Contribution of the Visitor in Developmental Group Work*, Department of Education, University College of Swansea; and L Button, *Developmental Group Work*, pp. 86, 110, 163, Hodder & Stoughton, 1974

across some of the questions which your young people have so carefully prepared. *Very important*: ask your visitor to be punctual to the minute, if possible. The group builds up to a point of keen anticipation and a late arrival can kill the spontaneity which will be present in the situation, despite its having been carefully rehearsed.

It is not unusual for teachers/tutors to 'put off' the first visitor session saying: 'My group isn't ready yet.' Don't delay: experience has shown this to be a most unifying exercise and is often the point at which the group takes off. Your hardest job, as a tutor, is to sit back, shut up and leave it all to the group when your visitor arrives. One of your most rewarding moments comes when they gather round afterwards, bursting to talk about the experience, sharing a corporate sense of 'Didn't we do well?' and quite sure that they can do even better next time.

To summarise: certain basic questions need to be considered in preparing for the occasion, and procedures need to be well rehearsed so that everyone may feel confident about their own contribution, e.g.

- Who do we invite and for what purpose?
- What do we talk about?
- Who asks the questions? In what order?
- Can we make sure everyone says something, even the shy members? How do we help them to do this?
- How do we prevent certain members dominating the occasion?
- Can we ask personal questions? Dare we ask about . . .?
- Where would be the best place to meet?
- Do we provide refreshments? If so, who looks after these?
- How do we greet the visitor on arrival? What do we say/do?
- Where should he sit when he arrives? What about us?
- Who will actually extend the invitation? Do we do this in writing or in person?

ABBREVIATED EXTRACTS FROM A REPORT BY PRACTISING COLLEAGUES

In preparing a group for a visit, the teacher will be concerned that it should:

offer them the opportunity for practising their social and conversational skills, and developing these further;

prove useful to those who have difficulty in social exchanges with adults and strangers, especially any shy and withdrawn members;

be an opportunity for group members to support those who are in difficulties, and increase support generally in the group;

be a rewarding occasion for the visitor.

The range of possible visitors is almost endless: other members of staff, including all ancillaries – students might even get to understand why the caretaker doesn't like it when things are put down the toilets! Also parents, who may be asked to talk about their occupation, interests or their role as parents; medical personnel and public figures e.g. police, careers advisers, vicars; elected members of councils and trade union representatives; official representatives of industry, public relations officers, etc.

Not all visitor occasions are successful, for a number of reasons, but often because of lack of preparation with the group or with the visitor. One or two members, or the visitor himself, may have dominated the situation. Some groups can be so overcome by their own self-consciousness that they are unable to carry through what they have practised. It is important that the first visitor to such a group is sensitive to their difficulties and can help to overcome them.

Surprisingly, experience has shown that it is often the young people who would seem to be the least likely to appear socially competent, who come forward as the most able in meetings with visitors, whilst the apparently more competent ones seem often to become tongue-tied and self-conscious. Young people have been surprised and delighted at carrying off the occasion. They gain significance in their own eyes through the willingness of an adult to speak freely with them, and are often eager for the next visit to take place. In this way, the contribution of the visitor to learning can be considerable.

NOTES ABOUT STUDY SKILLS

The study skills section extends 'care' to caring about the students' progress and their ability to work and study efficiently.[1] In bringing this concern into the area of pastoral care and active tutorial work, there is not a deep-laid plot to usurp the functions of other departments or interfere with the requirements or philosophies of other subject areas. Indeed, in this programme we suggest approaches to teachers in various departments for co-operation and assistance. The study skills section is seen – as with all the other sections – as being *active* tutorial work.

HOMEWORK, LEARNING, REVISION
Can your students:

- pick out key points, produce their own key cards, identify key questions?
- distinguish the salient from the peripheral?
- produce 'skeleton' frameworks relating to essays, etc., and diagram summaries?
- think in terms of head-lines and identify logical connections between item one and the next?
- demonstrate clear, logical structure in essays?
- develop reasoned and coherent arguments?
- organise their own study retrieval systems?
- use teacher comments constructively, set targets for themselves – and keep to them?
- organise their own study; take notes; understand and answer questions, i.e. have a technique for tackling examination questions?

Are they flexible enough to discard unprofitable approaches and develop better ones?

Have they effective techniques of study and self-evaluation?

How do they read? Can they 'scan' at speed? What is their recall like? Do they comprehend what they read? Does reading generate new ideas?

[1]See also D Hamblin, *The Teacher and Pastoral Care*, ch. 3, Basil Blackwell, 1978

Are they rigid or flexible? Do they stick to the known? Are they convergent or divergent thinkers?

Do they ask why? Can they discern motive or intention in a passage, an act, or an article?

Are they rendered ineffective/inefficient by their inability to cope with examination anxiety?

Study is hard work for most students. For the unsuccessful student this is even more so. Sucess is necessary, not only as a reward for past endeavours, but also as a stimulant for continuing effort. Consequently, the understanding and development of techniques and skills for the profitable use of study periods, homework, revision and exam preparation is an integral part of sixth-form life. Even this may not be enough unless examination anxiety is acknowledged and dealt with constructively.

People differ in their innate susceptibility to anxiety and the degree to which they need to avoid stressful situations, and there is a minority who require individual help and counselling. Most people, however, feel anxiety from time to time in reaction to specific situations, and one such situation is the examination. In our tutorial periods it is possible to bring students to examine for themselves those situations which cause them anxiety, and help them to develop strategies for coping with these situations which will give them the feeling of being in charge of, and of shaping situations, rather than being shaped and controlled by them. It is more helpful for them to get down to facing facts about situations and tasks than to continue with patterns of avoidance.

RIGIDITY AND FLEXIBILITY (Convergent and divergent thinking)
Some people have more difficulty in integrating new thought, whether fact or philosophy, into existing thought. They also have difficulty in breaking through to the formation of new concepts and are rigid rather than open-minded in their approach to problem-solving. This rigidity seems to have more to do with feelings than

intelligence and, despite attainment and ability, there is a tendency to resist change and lean towards conformity; there is a preference for concrete rather than abstract thinking.

Thus we might see in some students:

- a tendency to approach a problem from only one angle, i.e. inability to define the nature of a task or problem, allowing acquired habits to govern thinking and approaches to problems
- a tendency to accept rather than ask why, i.e. not to think about the intention or motive behind an article, a passage, an act or a question.

There is a tendency to suppress doubts and alternatives; a preference for simplifying issues and accepting quick and easy solutions. Therefore, there is a preference for sticking to known and perhaps limited techniques and convergent approaches when in-depth study through divergent approaches would be more profitable.

NOTES ABOUT LISTENING

The development of listening skills is central to the personal growth of students taking part in the Active Tutorial Work programme, and the team would hope that tutors are constantly aware that, alongside the stated objectives for each activity or theme, other objectives are also being pursued.

The objectives, when we listen to people, are both basic and simple:

1 We want people to talk freely and frankly.

2 We want them to cover matters and problems that are important to them.

3 We want them to get greater insight and understanding of their own values and attitudes (problems) as they talk about them.

4 We want them to try to see a situation clearly from where they themselves stand.

In the course of this work, we hope to encourage students to be aware of themselves as listeners, and to avoid:

1 hasty interruption or argument

2 passing judgement too quickly, or in advance

3 jumping to conclusions, or making assumptions on too little evidence

4 allowing the speaker's sentiments to react too directly on their own.

In addition, we hope that the students will not allow their feelings about a person or a situation to colour their judgement.

These points are easy to understand intellectually, but the real problem is in applying them effectively in our relationships with other people. This requires practice, repetition and awareness.

NOTES ON BRAINSTORMING

As a process for drawing out an agenda from the group, brainstorming is used frequently in this programme. Most people will be familiar with the process, but it is worthwhile highlighting the main principles.

1 It should be carried out quickly and vigorously, without allowing too much time for reflection and consideration.

2 Everyone's contribution should be noted in some way, e.g. jotted on a blackboard. The skill lies in finding a short way to note down what someone has tried to articulate in a rambling way. The precis should encapsulate the main essence of the longer statement.

3 The tutor may add some suggestions if the ideas which he or she has planned for are not forthcoming. However, a better route to meeting objectives may emerge from the group's own suggestions.

4 Start in broad, general terms, narrowing the topic down to achieve more depth.

Example: a discussion about friendship, its importance, difficulties, making new friends, etc., will have more meaning if it arises from the students' own insight and experience. Thus, an initial question, posed to students working in pairs or small groups may be: *What does friendship mean to you?* or *What is involved in making and keeping friends?*

After a few minutes' discussion, all the ideas are drawn from different groups and written on the board at random, e.g.

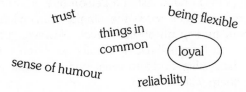

From the above concepts, one of the ideas may be chosen for further discussion, according to the emphasis and direction which the tutor may wish to pursue *or* according to the amount of interest and discussion it has produced. a ring may be placed around it on the board and the groups asked to discuss that particular concept, e.g. *What do you understand by the word 'loyal'?*

Other concepts may be treated in the same way, although some topics lend themselves more readily to brainstorming than others.

Brainstorming is a way of stimulating thought and producing a wide range of ideas on a topic, or approaches to a problem, in a very short space of time. It produces ideas almost completely at random; free association, as used in the latter part of Study Skills – 'Planning and Sequencing' (d), is a refinement of this process with links between the last word/idea and the next.

PRACTICAL TRUST ACTIVITIES

These activities can be used to introduce the ideas of trust, concern and support which are difficult concepts to explain. Actually experiencing putting one's trust in a person or a group of people is much more meaningful than talking about trust at an abstract level. However, the activities for trust-building require quiet, reassuring leadership, and tutors may find it valuable to try them with a group of their own colleagues before using them with students. This will have the benefit of increasing confidence and allowing the tutor to experience the activity for himself, thus increasing his understanding of the feelings which the students may experience. An alternative or further step would be to lead the activities in a smaller group with whom the tutor has a comfortable relationship.

Tutors may feel that students will react adversely to this kind of activity by being noisy and silly. This does sometimes happen, of course, in which case it is important to stop the activity and discuss why they are reacting in this way. If the tutor is able to treat the topic of 'trust' seriously and naturally without embarrassment, the students can be encouraged to try again, overcoming the awkwardness and embarrassment which they may feel. Quite often they respond to the activity quite seriously, and will gain a great deal from it, and the discussion about their feelings, which follows, will be serious and constructive.

EXAMPLES

1 Blind Trust

The students are asked to find a partner, one of whom will keep his eyes closed as a 'blind' person. His partner will lead him round the room, negotiating furniture and other people and, if possible, continue outside the room, where the 'blind' person becomes more disorientated and, therefore, more dependent. After about six or eight minutes, the partners are asked to change roles, so that each has a turn at leading and being led.

The 'leaders' are encouraged to hold their partners comfortably and securely and, at the same time, describe the textures, colours and shapes which are encountered. The leader in this way helps the 'blind' person to 'see' through his (the leader's) eyes.

The tutor will encourage thoughtfulness and a concern for helping the 'blind' person to feel safe. Discussion afterwards would be about how far this was achieved, styles of leading, what happened when other people were encountered, and so forth.

2 Supporting Someone

In pairs, roughly of equal height and weight, one person stands with eyes closed, with his back to his partner. The other person places his hands comfortably on his partner's shoulders and supports the weight of his partner, who leans gently backwards. As this person relaxes, the partner has to support more weight and take care to make his partner feel 'safe'. Partners then change over to experience supporting and being supported.

3 Supporting in Threes

As above, but the person in the middle now has someone in front as well as behind, and is pushed gently between them leaning first on one, then the other. This usually helps to make people relax more easily as they lose their fear of falling forwards. Each person should have a turn in the middle, whilst the tutor circulates, encouraging a relaxed feeling.

4 Supporting in Groups

A volunteer stands, with eyes closed, in the centre of a group of five or six people. They stand close together and support the person in the centre, who sways gently from one to another. A feeling of group concern for the person in the middle is generated, and silence and concentration should be encouraged. The group can then lift the person gently to shoulder height and sway him backwards and forwards before lowering him to the floor, or placing him back on his feet again. Other people are then encouraged to take a turn in the middle.

This is a real opportunity to *feel* what being

cared for is like, if the activity has been led quietly and purposefully. It is important to focus on how easy or difficult it feels to place one's trust in the hands of others, as well as how trustworthy one allows oneself to be when responsible for someone else.

These kinds of activities are not ends in themselves and should be repeated on different occasions to continue the process of building trust and a caring atmosphere within the tutor group. This atmosphere is especially important when dealing with aspects of relationships, such as friendship, family and feelings of self-worth.

If such an atmosphere is carefully nurtured, there will be a wonderful opportunity for members of the tutor group to help each other to grow and develop in self-esteem and personal responsibility.

NOTES ABOUT ROLE-PLAY

We have avoided using the term 'role-play' in the 16–19 programme as far as possible. It is a term which seems to 'put off' so many people! Nevertheless, there are many situations within this programme, and in group work generally, where enacting or re-enacting a situation is helpful. This may produce initial laughter and silliness to cover embarrassment, but students normally respond and enjoy the physical action, which seems to relax the situation and bring discussion to life. By acting out how they think someone would behave in a situation, they can be encouraged to consider what it is like to be in someone else's shoes.

Role play should arise spontaneously in response to a need to communicate 'what it was really like'.

Therefore, it may arise out of discussion or contribute to it, and may help less secure youngsters in the group to 'rehearse' whatever is the next little step forward for them. It may help, for example, to prepare for meeting strangers, carrying out conversations and meeting people in authority. It will help them to become used to the idea of the new experience before the actual event, and have confidence in their own participation.

Thus role-play is not seen as something special, a 'big production' for which a specialist is needed, but as an essential part of active tutorial work, flowing in and out of the events as they occur, e.g. 'Don't tell us – show us!'

NOTES ABOUT ACTION RESEARCH

It is a fundamental principle of this tutorial programme that the students should become actively engaged in making their own discoveries about themselves and their relationships. A matter of outstanding importance is the degree to which the students are committed to, and engaged in, their own learning. This work sets out to encourage this commitment by using a process which Leslie Button has called Action Research[1]. Thus, if the pupils are actively engaged in finding out for themselves, either what it is like to be in someone else's shoes or to take on some responsibility on another's behalf, then their discoveries can have a strong impact on them and stir a determination to take some action about the situation which they have uncovered. Moreover, through their enquiries the students will have already begun to affect the situation which they are examining.

Action Research may be seen as a series of developing steps:

1 A line of enquiry which has stirred the group to want to take some action, is identified.

2 Some of the group may be 'commissioned' to carry out a pilot enquiry. For example, the topic may be anything from an enquiry into people's problems of getting to school/college, to an examination of loneliness, arising out of a friendship study, or an enquiry about the world of work or life after the fifth form.

3 The main enquiry is then undertaken and it is important to guide the group in an examination of the possibility of their taking some action.

Objectives for action should be limited, as it is vital that the youngsters should feel that there is a possibility of bringing about some change in the situation under review. Similarly, the plan of action decided upon should be well within the time span that the students are likely to be able to sustain.

The value of Action Research lies in the central part played by the students themselves. They are involved from the beginning in diagnosing the problem, discussing in small groups different strategies for action, preparing enquiry forms and articulating the plan for themselves, with the help and guidance of the tutor.

Action Research is a valuable tool in helping to foster an individual's own growth and development, particularly where personal difficulties impede his growth. It is a way of helping a person to see beyond himself, so that he becomes not merely aware of the needs and problems of other people, but is moved to make a personal contribution.

---

[1]L Button, *Developmental Group Work With Adolescents,* Hodder & Stoughton, 1974

THEMES

Books 1 to 5 were divided into three sections – Autumn, Spring and Summer Terms. The units were arranged in what the writing team deemed to be a logical order within this framework whilst, at the same time, leaving teachers the flexibility to ·rearrange this order in response to their specific needs.

This arrangement does not appear to fit quite so easily into the 16–19 structure, and consequently there is no pattern to the order in which the units are presented in the book. Whilst all units have their own specific objectives and most of them can 'stand alone', it would be possible to group them loosely under thematic headings as shown below.

INDUCTION
Who we are and what we are like
What we have in common
What's in a word?
Learning from others
Master plan

GROUPS AND GROUP ACTIVITIES
News line
What is a family?
Planning a day's outing to London
Take a card
Rules and rights
Community concerns
Looking at groups

STUDY SKILLS
What's in a word?
Learning from others
Study skills – Coping with anxiety
         – Planning revision
         – Key facts/Active reading
         – Rigidity and flexibility
         – Using diagrams
         – Logical sequencing
         – Sequencing
The life of a robin
Help!
Questions and answers
A teaching–learning exercise
Time in your hands

LEADERSHIP AND AUTHORITY
Leadership
An exploration of authority
Rules and rights
Looking at groups

PERSONAL IDENTITY AND PHILOSOPHY
School career (Understanding the system)
Pairs
I've got a . . .
Famous people
Anyone can join
All you need is understanding
Taking it all on board
Dreaming
This is me
Starting from scratch
Labelling and stereotyping
Prejudice

FAMILY AND COMMUNITY
What is a family?
Take a card
Understanding the system – School career
What next?
Community concerns
Community responsibility
Organizing opinion (parties, protest and pressure
Parents and adults
Negotiating
Town development

COMMUNICATION
Truth
Give us a clue
Verbal and non-verbal communication
Negotiating
Town development

TRUST AND FRIENDSHIP
Trust   Friendship

FUTURE LIFE
Dreaming   Job forum
Dr Who   Living away

ADDITIONAL MATERIALS IN BOOKS 1 TO 5

Trial schools have found the programme beneficial both with the traditional and the newly developing 'open' sixth forms. There have been requests to add further materials for the latter. The Project Team feels that the inclusion of additional material would make this volume too unwieldy and too expensive. Instead, they have reviewed Books 1–5 and list below units which they feel may be suitable for adaptation for use with 16–19 group.

YOU MAY FIND THE FOLLOWING BOOKS USEFUL SUPPLEMENTARY READING

K Blackburn, *The Tutor,* Heinemann, 1975

L Button, *Discovery and Experience,* OUP, 1971

L Button, *Developmental Group Work with Adolescents,* Hodder & Stoughton, 1974

L Button, *Group Tutoring for the Form Teacher: 1 Lower Secondary School,* Hodder & Stoughton, 1981

L Button, *Group Tutoring for the Form Teacher: 2 Upper Secondary School,* Hodder & Stoughton, 1981

D Hamblin, *The Teacher and Pastoral Care,* Basil Blackwell, 1978

D Hamblin, *Problems and Practice in Pastoral Care,* Basil Blackwell, 1981

D Hamblin, *Study Skills,* Basil Blackwell, 1981

Health Education Council Project 12–18: *Living Well,* Cambridge University Press, 1977

Hopson & Scally, *Lifeskills Teaching,* McGraw-Hill, 1981

Hopson & Scally, *Lifeskills Teaching Programme No. 1,* Lifeskills Associates, 1981

Hopson & Scally, *Lifeskills Teaching Programme No. 2,* Lifeskills Associates, 1981

M Marland, *Pastoral Care,* Heinemann, 1974

Priestley & McGuire, *Social Skills and Personal Problem Solving,* Tavistock, 1978

Schools Council project, *Health Education 5–13 Think Well,* Nelson, 1977

NOTE: Ideally, this unit is intended for use at an early tutor meeting when students have just entered the sixth-form or are commencing a new training initiative. If the students are new to one another, more direct action needs to be taken by the tutor in the early part of the unit. If the students feel that they already know each other well, challenge this assumption – encourage them to talk to someone they do not know so well. If they have come from schools or classes where *Active Tutorial Work* has been carried out, they will be familiar with this 'opening activity'. If they express boredom at having to go through it yet again, then they have missed the point!

Student Objectives	Activities	Organisation and Method
To take an active part in developing tutor-group identity, by showing interest in and concern for its members.	*WHO WE ARE AND WHAT WE ARE LIKE* Getting to know the group. Talking and listening. Making an agreement and 'shaking' on it – encouraging the students to shake hands as an act of goodwill and an affirmation of their agreement to work together. It could be explained that, in the world at large, 'shaking on it' is seen as a concrete symbol of people's good faith and goodwill towards each other.	The teacher's introduction will depend on how well the students already know one another. The reasons for this activity are obvious if the students are all new to each other. However, those who are familiar to each other can be challenged to check out how much they really do know about other tutor-group members. Invite everyone to move around the room, shaking hands and exchanging greetings with everyone, including the teacher. Say: 'If we are to help and support each other for two years, and if the tutor-group is to mean something to us, we have to make sure that we know one another, that we feel a part of the group, and also show that we are prepared to put something into it as well as take something out.'

To become aware of a tutor-group identity by being aware of the importance of everyone's contribution, including his/her own.	The students should be challenged with questions such as:
	
	Did your handshake convey anything?
	
	Why are some people embarrassed by handshaking?
	
	How do people usually greet each other
	  in this country?
	  in other countries?
	
	How do we convey feelings, e.g. warmth, in our greetings?
		NOTE: Give vigorous encouragement to this mingling and continue it as long as possible. It usually helps considerably if the tutor participates (briskly) in this introductory 'mingling' activity.

Student Objectives	Activities	Organisation and Method

To show a willingness to make a positive contribution to the activities of the group, at the same time ensuring equal opportunity for everyone to take part.	*In twos*
	NOTE: Encourage the pairs to exchange basic information about one another – even if they think they already know it. Ask them to test their knowledge, e.g.:
	  Where does your partner live?
	  What is his/her family background, former school experience, hopes, aspirations. (Why is your partner here?)
	What are you particularly interested in at the moment?
	What has made you happy/upset/concerned/pleased during the last two weeks?
	(Allow about one or two minutes for an exchange between each item.)
		'Now sit with someone you don't know very well or have only just met.'
		Encourage the students to be honest about not sitting with friends. If they persist, *stop* the activity and discuss the objectives – have they *any* meaning for the students? Return to the activity at the next meeting.
		Encourage the pairs to go a little *deeper* in discovering what kind of person they are talking to. Use the agenda suggested opposite.

To develop and demonstrate listening skills and a degree of self-confidence in challenging situations.	*In fours*
	How well did you listen?
	My name is .... etc.
	I live at...
	At the moment I like..
	I am pleased about ....
	I am concerned about...............................
	Have you learned anything
	  about your partner?
	  about yourself?
		Ask each pair to join with another pair nearby, making a group of four. Each person introduces his partner to the other three *as if he is talking about him/herself,* remembering the details of their conversation (opposite).
		
		The teacher may need to demonstrate the idea of speaking about someone else in the first person, and then move around, encouraging the students to help each other to remember details.
		(See introductory note on Step-By-Step Discussion, page viii.)
		
		When all have had a turn, ask a general question about their listening skills.

Student Objectives	Activities	Organisation and Method

Long-term aim:
 	
To begin to accept that, in the sixth-form, he/she is in a different mental and physical environment.
 	
To begin to understand what the sixth-form tutor can do for the students in his group, and how they can help him to function most effectively, and know the role and function of other members of staff.
 	
To examine the role of sixth-formers in relation to the school or college community.
	Step-by-step discussion using APPENDIX 1, The Lower Sixth-Form.
	Which statements do you think are particularly appropriate to sixth-form life?
	
	(Conduct the discussion vigorously. Encourage everyone to respond, within their small group, but do not allow too much time between each statement.)
	
	Finally, the whole class considers:
	1 What will be the most important features of sixth-form life?
	
	2 Refer back to the objectives for this work.
	
	    Are they valid?
	    Can they be achieved?
		You will need
		APPENDIX 1: The Lower Sixth-Form, one per pupil
		
		Now that the students are in fours, this establishes a way of working which will be used many times in tutorial work. Working in small groups should be emphasised, i.e. that it is *work* and that they have a good deal to learn from each other as well as from their academic subjects.
		
		Use APPENDIX 1 as an agenda for initiating a discussion about the students' understanding of sixth-form life.
		
		Close the whole tutor-group discussion, drawing out interesting (overheard) items from different groups for consideration by the whole tutor-group, and compare some of these with the objectives for the work.
		
		The students may be encouraged to list their own 'feature list' and keep it for future reference.

3

'Worked well – a good "mixer"; gave a sense of commonality and reinforced the self-confidence of weaker members. Good preparation (gets them talking) for the next unit.' Quote from a trial school.

Student Objectives	Activities	Organisation and Method
To take an active part in developing tutor-group identity by being aware of everyone's contribution.	*WHAT WE HAVE IN COMMON* An introductory activity for increasing inter-action and organising random groups of four. 1 'Things' in common may range from superficial items such as hair or eye colour, through interests or studies in common, to beliefs and ambitions.	1 Ask the students to move around the room exchanging a few words of greeting. Then ask each person to turn to the person nearest to them and to talk about things which they might have in common. Suggest that a list of at least five things be produced after five minutes. This method avoids friends always pairing up, possibly leaving some individuals out.
To become aware of a tutor-group identity by showing interest in its members.	2 The second part of the activity involves 'negotiating' and discovering more things that people have in common, in order to make larger groups.	2 When everyone has paired up and discussed their 'commonality' for a few minutes, the pairs are asked to make fours with other pairs who have the same thing(s) in common. This may need some discussion and a need to find other common factors. The tutor may need to help and intervene to make sure that everyone fits in somewhere. Some pairs may need to split up in order to fit in. The tutor can help the dynamic by joining in, finding things in common with some of the students.
To show a willingness to make a positive contribution to the activities of the group, at the same time ensuring equal opportunity for everyone to take part.	*Guessing what the common factor is* Has this activity given us more information about one another? How much information do we get about people on first impression? How much do you know about each other now?	When all the groups are seated again, a guess may be made at what various groups have chosen. Some will be obvious, others not, in which case clues may be needed. Some discussion may follow about how well the students feel they know each other, according to how long they have been together.

4

Student Objectives	Activities	Organisation and Method
To recognise what the tutor can do for the group and help to develop the 'climate' of the tutor group.	3 *What do you think I did?* Set the scene – who are the characters involved besides yourself? Draw the first episode (pinmen suffice). Draw each turn of events, leaving out the crucial part, i.e.: 'and I said . . .' or 'I did . . .' or 'What happened was . . .'	3 With the students sitting in the groups formed by the last activity, the tutor introduces this section by using an incident which has happened to him/her recently, and drawing it as a serialised story on the board, leaving the last frame empty. The students are encouraged to ask questions to clarify the story and help to build in background details. Artistic ability is not important. Matchstick men or cartoon figures are most effective.
To develop a firmer understanding of the uniqueness of the individual with respect for the individuality of others.	Ask the class: 'Are you thinking about what you personally would have done in this situation, or can you put yourself in the other person's shoes (in this case mine) and envisage what I would have done?' *NOTE:* Drawing the story seems to help in communicating the feelings and emotions which may have been involved in the incident, as well as the factual events.	Finally, they are encouraged to suggest what happened. Hilarity, within reason, need not be suppressed, but a serious and practical solution should eventually be arrived at. In their groups, students are asked to think about something which has happened to them and volunteer to share it, in the same way, with their group. The tutor should move around and perhaps ask a student to share his/her story with the whole group in the next section. Failing this, the tutor may need to use another story of his/her own.
	4 *Understanding what you mean, listening with understanding* Spotting the words and emotions which give clues to the feelings underlying what is said – sometimes called 'feeling' words.	4 The same story which has been drawn may, in fact, be used, as it is being listened to from a different angle, as suggested opposite.

Student Objectives	Activities	Organisation and Method
To demonstrate listening skills.	Sometimes our choice of words give us away when we are trying to be cool and unemotional, e.g. is there a difference between: 'I didn't say anything' and 'I kept quiet'? or: 'I wished it was time to go' and 'I looked at the clock to see what time it was'? or: Is it sometimes to do with the way (intonation) in which we say things? How easy is it to hear the 'hidden' message when we are engrossed in the story?	The student, or tutor, tells about an incident which has happened to him/her, in as straightforward and factual manner as possible. Two other students are asked to tap with pencils every time they think that there is more behind the words. Everyone else listens to see if they agree with the taps, or whether they would have tapped earlier or in different places. The 'story' should be fairly brief and when this has been discussed, i.e. whether taps came in the right places, etc., the tutor will need to be prepared to share a bit more of the 'story', i.e. feelings and emotions involved. The groups can then do the same exercise.
To develop an understanding of human relationships and what is involved in dealing with people.	*Agenda for discussion* Did you make your 'taps' in the right places, or did you forget to tap altogether? Did you tell the 'storyteller' what you thought was behind the story? Did he/she agree? 5 What have we learned from this session?	A student in each group – a different person from the one who did the 'drawing' activity, tells a story about him/ herself, with the others listening for the 'feeling' words and tone. 5 This is an important part of the session, and time should be allowed for it. It is important not to put words in the students' mouths, but for them to articulate what the session was about. More may need to be done, and these activities could be repeated at a later date in order to achieve the objectives.

6

NOTE: This unit requires tutors of groups in first and second-year sixth forms to co-operate in achieving the objectives. The terms 'first year' or 'second year' (1/6th, 2/6th) are used to cover lower- and upper-sixth forms and students in sixth-form colleges.

'First-year sixth got considerable reassurance from second-year sixth students. Sharing of experiences appreciated.' (A trial school.)

Student Objectives	Activities	Organisation and Method
To assess his/her own progress and compare it with the assessment of others.	*LEARNING FROM OTHERS* Giving students an opportunity to find out more about other students. Encouraging thinking about themselves as a result.	The 2/6th tutor is doing preliminary work with the students in preparation for question/answer session with 1/6th students.
To identify personal limitations and identify goals.	*Agenda for students in 2/6th* Each student to complete very quickly the following statements: a) My time in the first-year sixth was . . . . b) When I came into the sixth-form I found . . . very worrying. c) I wish someone had warned me about . . . d) If only I had realised the importance of . . . . e) What I now realise is . . . . f) When I leave here I will . . . g) I have chosen this career because . . . . h) If I don't get the grades I need I will . . . . i) To prepare for this I have . . . j) I am a different person from last year because	2/6th students in pairs. Tutor to feed in questions from agenda opposite as a basis for discussion. Feed in questions quickly, each student answering spontaneously. Each student to choose the three most interesting or controversial answers given by his/her partner, and discuss these in more detail. *NOTE*: Students could possibly have a paper and pen to jot down their partner's replies in order to remember more easily what has been said.

Student Objectives	Activities	Organisation and Method
To assess his/her own progress and compare it with the assessment of others.	*Conversations in pairs: 1/6th with 2/6th* 'Who is following the same or similar course to me, and has only just started (or has completed a year already)?'	When two groups are brought together, an introductory exercise is essential to 'break the ice'. Thus, the students are first encouraged to find out the names of people from the other group, and the courses they are following.
To examine personal limitations and identify goals.		
To generate an atmosphere within which sixth-form students feel they can relate and communicate their problems.		They then find a partner from the *other* group who is following a course of study similar to their own.
To help to reduce possible friction between first- and second-year sixth-form groups.		
To recognise and cope with the freedoms and responsibilities of sixth-form life.	*The Three-Minute Rule* 1 'Each person speaks in turn for three minutes without interruption.'	The tutor explains that the conversations the students will have in their pairs will be strictly guided, and they must not break the three-minute rule (see opposite).
	2 'Time for thought (silence) is allowed.'	
	3 'When it is not your turn to speak, listen and do not interrupt until it is question time.'	

Student Objectives	Activities	Organisation and Method
To demonstrate listening and communication skills.	*Agenda for first speaker (2/6th to 1/6th in each pair)* Tell your partner: a) Why and how you decided to come into the sixth-form. b) Whether or not you have decided what you want to do when you leave. If YES – What helped you to decide? If NO – What are your doubts, uncertainties?	The tutor gives the agenda for the first three minutes (see opposite). The agenda may be given a step at a time, with the tutor interrupting every 30 seconds or so to give the next step. *NOTE*: Interrupting at the most appropriate time is difficult, and may make the flow disjointed, but some students may need this structure. However, if students are able to talk freely, the whole agenda can be given at once and the students then talk for three minutes around it.
Show a willingness to make a positive contribution to the activities of the group, at the same time ensuring equal opportunity for everyone to take part.	c) Whether you think you are different now. d) What you think of the first year in retrospect. e) Who was the most important person for you.	
To become aware of a tutor-group identity by showing interest in and concern for its members.	*Any questions?* *Agenda for 1/6th to 2/6th* Tell your partner: a) Why you have decided to come into the sixth-form. b) Whether you feel different now and whether it is what you expected. c) What you feel about the kind of work/ responsibility you are expected to undertake.	The listening partners are encouraged to ask questions to clarify or enlarge on what they have heard, before they embark on their own three-minute agenda.

Student Objectives	Activities	Organisation and Method
To develop an ability to manage and organise time effectively between work and leisure.	d) Whether older students could help you and how. e) What has been the high spot of sixth-form life so far. f) What has been the low spot.	The tutors involved will be circulating, encouraging students who may be finding it difficult to sustain three minutes' worth of information about themselves; ensuring that partners are listening and not interrupting; noting any comments or points from individual students which may need to be raised at a later date. At the end of the three-minute period 2/6th partners now asks questions to clarify and enlarge.
To demonstrate an ability to listen and interpret meaning accurately.	*Any questions?* *Final three minutes – 'Free for all'* A chance to add to, or change what you have said. A chance to check up on the information you have been given in readiness for the next stage, which will be a test of how well you have listened to your partner. *NOTE*: Discretion in what partners pass on about each other is an important skill. Students should be alerted to the need for it.	The next three minutes are open for normal conversation in the pairs, to ask each other any questions they might have thought of whilst their partner has been speaking. It is also a chance to recap, since students will be asked to select items from the information which they have been given by their partner to tell others in a larger group.
To be aware of the needs and problems of others in the group, by showing a willingness to provide and receive support and share experience.		

Student Objectives	Activities	Organisation and Method
To develop a firmer understanding of the uniqueness of the individual and show respect for the individuality of others.	*I am* . . . . Introducing partner to others. If you are a 1/6th introducing your 2/6th partner: *Agenda* a) I am Susan and I came into the sixth-form because . . . . } difficult. / enjoyable. / different. b) I found . . . . c) I think I coped by . . . . *or* d) I am not sure whether I am coping because . . . e) Next year I think . . . . The tutor asks: 'Were you interpreted correctly?' *Clarification time* – *'I didn't say that'* or *'What I meant was . . . .'*	Each pair turns to another pair nearby, making a group of four. Having stressed the need for discretion (concern for the other person) each person in the group of four now introduces his/her partner as if he/she was speaking about him/herself. The tutor should give an example by choosing a student and demonstrating the use of the agenda opposite. Some of the statements about the partner will have demanded interpretation by the person who was listening. After each student has introduced someone, the person in question is given an opportunity to qualify or enlarge on their partner's interpretation.
To examine the role of the students in the institution.	*Questions about the process* – How well did you listen when your partner was speaking? – How much information did you absorb? – How well did you interpret what your partner was *not* saying? – How well do people in your group organise themselves?	Each student in each group has a turn at representing their partner. Some groups may finish more quickly than others. Tutors need to be circulating, asking additional questions to encourage continuing conversation until all the groups have finished, perhaps using some of the questions opposite about the group process.

Student Objectives	Activities	Organisation and Method
	Final discussion for everyone	A full discussion may follow, with an attempt to draw out what has been learned
	1 Are people enjoying life in the sixth-form generally, or finding it difficult?	a) about another student
	2 What practical considerations have we learned?	b) about themselves
	3 Is there anything to be done? As a group? As an individual?	c) about life in the sixth-form.
	4 Who needs help of some kind?	
	5 Can we provide it?	

Student Objectives	Activities	Organisation and Method

To help students to interpret the meaning of words used at sixth-form level.	*WHAT'S IN A WORD?*
	
	An activity to familiarise students with the definition of words often used in questions at this level.
	
	Agenda for discussion
	
	a) Which of the words have you already met?
	
	b) How many of them had you fully understood?
	
	c) How many of the words or meanings were new to you?
	
	d) Where are you most likely to meet these words?
	
	e) Shades of meaning of words.
		You will need
		For each group
		
		    One Word Board, APPENDIX 2
		    One Definition Sheet with the definitions cut into strips, APPENDIX 3
		
		Divide the students into groups of two, three or four. Read out a selection of words from the Word Board, APPENDIX 2, and ask the students to write down their own definitions of these words.
		
		Then ask them to place the definition cards on to the Word Board opposite the relevant word. Compare their own definitions with those selected by the group from the Definition Sheet, APPENDIX 3.
		
		A possible follow-up to this activity is to ask the groups to prepare, with definitions, more words which they are likely to meet, or have already met.
		
		The groups can then exchange lists.
		
		Follow-up discussion using the agenda opposite.

NOTE: This unit may be used briefly as a closing activity for the last session *OR* developed into a longer session in its own right. It is important, however, to continue to mix 1/6th with 2/6th students.

Student Objectives	Activities	Organisation and Method
To show an awareness of syllabus content and examination structure.	*UNDERSTANDING THE QUESTION* The students should 1 underline the important word(s) in the chosen question, i.e. the word(s) which tell(s) them what is required by the question. They should do this independently first, then compare ideas 2 discuss in their groups how they would tackle this question.	**You will need** Examples of 'O' Level and 'A' Level Questions (or general exams) on cards from all the subjects represented in the group, APPENDIX 4
To recognise key facts and fundamental concepts within subject areas.	*It is important to stress that:* the factual matter is not so important in this discussion as how to approach the question	
	3 look at several questions (provided on cards). Together, make a list of all the process words, i.e. those which tell them what is required, e.g. describe, discuss, analyse, tabulate, etc. An important question for group consideration: Is it always obvious what is required?	In fours (the same groups as in the previous session) the students select two cards from different level examinations, e.g. an 'O' and an 'A' level French question, or two questions from internal examinations at first- or second-year sixth level. The subject of the question cards should be relevant to the group if at all possible. Students may wish to regroup in pairs if they feel they can work better.
To enjoy and deepen involvement in chosen subjects, by showing a willingness to impart knowledge to others.		
To select and use information.	Finally, what are important differences between 'O' level and 'A' level questions (first and second-level internal exam questions)?	A way of working together to understand the questions is suggested opposite.

A SIXTH-FORM MASTER PLAN

It should be stressed that whilst this work is to be started upon entry to the sixth-form, it should be returned to at various times throughout the year and will have to be repeated at the beginning of the second-year sixth.

Note that considerable preparation of APPENDIX 5 may be necessary and should be done well before the tutorial period in which chart construction (Item 4) is to be undertaken.

The findings for each individual's 'master plan' could form the basis for a useful communication between staff, pupils and parents, so that parents can also become aware of the 'burden' which falls on their young folks during this period. The group tutor might also have the opportunity to follow-up any individual who appears to be under strain.

Student Objectives	Activities	Organisation and Method
To anticipate how the sixth years are going to be different, by determining the different demands made by course work in various subjects, by continuous assessment, by end-of-course examinations, by looking at examination demands, by planning a time-table and strategies to meet the demands.	*THE TWO-YEAR MASTER PLAN* 1 *The four tasks* a) Collection and compilation of information concerning subjects (see APPENDIX 6, 'Master Plan Fact Finder Sheet'). b) Adding other demands to the list (APPENDIX 6). c) Chart construction (APPENDIX 5, Master Plan Chart). d) Completion of a Master Plan Check List (APPENDIX 7). 2 *Collection and compilation of information concerning subjects* a) Introduction to the task.	**You will need** Duplicated copies of APPENDICES 5 and 6, Master Plan Charts and Fact Finder Sheets for each student and a supply of rough paper 1 *Preamble to this work* The tutor should stress that the work to be done should be useful for the next two years, if it is put together carefully. It may be diplomatic to forewarn staff colleagues about the questions which they will be asked, adding that it would be appreciated if they would answer the questions as accurately as possible in the spirit in which they are asked. 2a) Give out APPENDIX 6. Re-emphasise the importance of accurate information and careful setting down of answers on APPENDIX 5.

15

Student Objectives	Activities	Organisation and Method
To anticipate how the sixth-form is going to be different by determining the different demands made by: course work in various subjects; continuous assessment; end-of-course examinations; looking at examination demands; planning a time-table and strategies to meet the demands.		Give out rough paper and allow students to make a rough copy of APPENDIX 6 to take round with them on their fact-finding enquiries.
		The nature and intent of this sheet can be discussed whilst the rough copies are being drawn. Then students can ask questions on points needing further clarification.
	b) Clarification – a blackboard example.	b) Work through a blackboard example of how to fill in the sheet (an obvious example would be the group tutor's own subject and perhaps another one with which he is familiar).
	c) General information from the form teacher.	c) There may be some general information, for example, on the times of external examinations, which may be available for the group tutor to give out at this time.
	d) Fact-finding: collecting and collating information about subject-demands.	d) The students should be allowed a period of time before the next session on this work to find out what form of tests there are for each subject and when they occur by asking various subject teachers when next they meet them.
		Ask the students to find out if and when there is a final decision to be made about taking an exam or not. Then find out the approximate date of the final exam.
	e) Making a fair copy.	e) Transfer the findings from the rough draft to APPENDIX 6.
	3 *A list of other demands* As with the previous activity, pupils list any other extra-curricular demands upon their time and enter these on the	3 The tutor will probably have some idea of the various extra-curricular activities available in the school/college and of his tutor-group's own individual interests. For some students involved in, e.g.

Student Objectives	Activities	Organisation and Method
	Master Plan Fact-Finder Sheet (APPENDIX 6).	learning a musical instrument, regular commitment to Church or some other group *outside* the school, it may be useful to include them on the sheet, if only for the student himself to become aware of the difficulties of taking on too many commitments at this stage in his sixth-form career.
To demonstrate his grasp of the demands made upon him by his new time-table, choice of course and organisational changes.	4 *Chart Construction* Transfer of information from the Fact-Finding Sheet to the Master Plan Chart (APPENDIX 5). Emphasise the need for clarity and neatness so that the chart will be easy to read.	**You will need** Duplicated copies of APPENDICES 5 and 7 for each student 4 APPENDIX 5 must be prepared well before the tutorial period in order to tailor it to the individual school's holiday time-table and any other special circumstances. Depending on the ability of the group, the tutor might indicate how to fill in the chart, e.g. shade in a week's field course opposite the subject concerned; mark assessment tests with an asterisk in the appropriate space; write in anything which is unusual, e.g. oral test in languages or music.
	5 *The Master Plan Check List* APPENDIX 7 can be used to write out answers which can be obtained from the completed chart. *Agenda for discussion* a) Which time of year is going to be a busy one? b) What things might you have to do to cope with the busy times?	5 Help and advise students as they fill in the Check List (APPENDIX 7). On completion of this task divide the class into small groups to discuss the answers they have written on the Check List Sheet. Feed in questions similar to those in the Agenda opposite and any others that seem pertinent.

Student Objectives	Activities	Organisation and Method
	c) Do you feel apprehensive or scared about what is facing you? Why?	Move around the groups, picking up interesting and relevant points which may arise and feeding them into the discussions of the other groups. (See introductory note on step-by-step discussions – pp. xviii and xix.)
	d) Who could you ask for help or advice? What do you think they might say?	
	e) What could you do during the next two years that would help you?	Allow a few minutes for the discussion of a question and then move on to the next question.

NOTE: This unit needs approximately fifty minutes and cannot be split into two sections.

Student Objectives	Activities	Organisation and Method
To develop a critical approach to news, information and opinion.	*NEWS LINE* Producing, as a group, in a limited time, a three-minute news bulletin from information provided, to be read by one of the group at the end of the session.	**You will need** Fifteen newspaper cuttings covering a variety of topics, e.g. politics, weather, human interest, etc., for each group One tape recorder To prepare a tape of extra news items using APPENDIX 8, News Line. This will be given to the students as a pre-recorded tape (see 3 below)
		1 Ask the students to form groups of six to eight.
		2 Give each group an envelope containing the fifteen newspaper cuttings.
		3 Start the tape which will run for the duration of the activity.
		4 At the end of the allotted time, the 'newscaster' from each group reads his/her group's bulletin in turn.
	Agenda for discussion	5 Discussion.
	a) How were the items selected, e.g. what was the criteria?	
	b) How was the group organised? Who led, wrote, chose the reader?	
	c) How did the group cope with the pressure of limited time?	
	d) What happened to your other news when the new news items were given?	

NOTE: The writers are aware that the subject of families is a sensitive area. This unit can be developed into the student's personal life if the 'climate' of the group is supportive, and if the tutor feels it to be appropriate. If not, discussion can remain at a more impersonal level. Students who have been in care or have family difficulties may find it helpful to be able to talk more freely in a supportive group atmosphere.

Student Objectives	Activities	Organisation and Method
To develop an awareness of the fact that many social forces influence personal life.	*WHAT IS A FAMILY?* 1 *Creating an imaginary family* *Agenda for discussion* In this country we commonly talk about the average family as being two parents and two – four children. Obviously, the community is made up of widely differing types of family. What types of family groups can you think of – large, small, one-parent, etc?	**You will need** A copy of APPENDIX 9, What is a Family? as a model, and slips of paper for the students. 1 Ask the students to form groups of three, four or five, preferably mixed girls and boys. It is helpful if the tutor first constructs an example of a character, using suggestions from the tutor group. APPENDIX 9 is given only as examples of different characters.
To take an active part in developing tutor-group identity by being aware of the importance of everyone's contribution.	Assume that you, as a group, are a family. The family must be viable as a family unit.	2 Each small group then builds its own family. Each student constructs his/her own character card to fit the family they are in. All members of the group discuss and agree each character. (Much assistance will be required about incomes, personality, etc.)

Student Objectives	Activities	Organisation and Method

	3 *Find a new family*
	The object is not necessarily to find the original family, but to find a family in which you feel your character fits.
	Note what happens to 'odd' characters who don't fit anywhere.
	
	Agenda for discussion
	How were the families brought together?
	Which details had priority?
	How did you explain items which did not seem to fit?
	Was anyone rejected because a family did not want them if their details did not fit? How did it feel to be rejected? Did someone take them in?
	
	To encourage further discussion:
	a) What is the main role of the husband/wife in your family?
	b) Would the children be a source of stress/worry/pride?
	c) What other issues might there be?
	d) What makes this 'family' happy/sad/proud?
		3 The students then fold the papers in half and move around the room, exchanging papers four or five times, until they have no idea where their own paper is.
		Each student now reads the details on his/her piece of paper, and proceeds to match up with others to make a family.
		When a 'family' is made, all sit down and discuss. See agenda opposite.
		
		Experience has shown that discussion could be taken in a number of different directions, according to the teacher's additional objectives for the activity,
		e.g. sex roles in families
		     stereotyping
		     the generation gap
		     class
		     mixed marriage (race, colour, creed)
		     compatibility
		     strains and stresses of family life.

Student Objectives	Activities	Organisation and Method
	4 *Try again* How do people fit together this time? Did you go about it differently?	4 If time allows, exchange papers three or four times again, and find another family. An alternative is to suggest that students return to their original groups after swapping papers, and then develop a rationale for their family group. Very unusual groups, i.e. no adults, may need help. This is a good way to thwart the attempt to form stereotype families and so promote discussion.
	5 *Extending the family* What would happen if someone came for an extended stay? *Discussion. How would we cope?*	5 One additional slip of paper is given to each family, and each group thinks of a surprise extension which could happen to a family. e.g. grandmother comes to live aunt and uncle arrive from Australia new baby lost job. These cards are collected, shuffled and given at random to the groups, which discuss how their family would deal with this new factor.
	6 *Family portrait* Creating a living portrait of the family group. Questions to be interjected from time to time, to help the students think things out, could be as follows:	6 Each group is asked to place themselves in what they imagine might be characteristic poses for members of their imaginary 'family',

22

Student Objectives	Activities	Organisation and Method
		e.g. mousey wife, domineering husband, sullen teenage boy
		or happy husband and wife with new baby on the way
		or husband has just lost his job and is worried how the rest of the family will be affected
		Choose a time of day, e.g. tea-time. Make a picture of the family with the members of the group taking up a pose for their character. Then freeze the 'picture' for a moment.
		The rest of the class comments on how close to reality this picture might be.
	Would the husband be standing or sitting?	
	How near would they be to each other?	
	Would they feel the need to touch each other?	
	Where do you want the son/daughter to be placed?	
	How are they feeling towards each other?	
	Can you show us their feelings?	
	7 *What would your family 'portrait' look like?*	7 The form tutor might demonstrate a 'portrait' of his/her own family, either now or when he/she was a teenager, by choosing students to place themselves in characteristic poses of members of his/her (the tutor's) family, with the tutor directing.
	Agenda for discussion	
	Why have you put yourself in that particular place in the portrait? (Or any other member of the family?)	In small groups, ask volunteers to make 'portraits' of their own families, using members of the group. If there is a sensitive climate, discussion could follow as suggested by the agenda opposite.
	Will it be different in a few years' time?	
	What would make it change?	
	Do you want it to change?	

NOTE: The writers feel that this unit should not be an academic exercise, but a real test of planning and responsibility; therefore the outing should take place, be it London, as suggested here, or somewhere else in the country appropriate to the particular sixth-form group.

Student Objectives	Activities	Organisation and Method
To be able to plan work schedules and demonstrate the self-discipline required to adhere to them.	*PLANNING A DAY'S OUTING TO LONDON* For the whole sixth-form, this will take place one month from now, and include some stated educational objectives. *Stage 1: First session* *Agenda for discussion* a) Why this place? What do we want to find out/see? What are the objectives of this outing? b) What should we include in the day's programme (e.g. museum, park, film, theatre, shops, restaurants)? c) How shall we travel there?	**You will need** Copies of Master Plan Time-table for one month, APPENDIX 10 Copies of checklist Actions Required, APPENDIX 11 Copies of specimen Homework Time-table and explanatory notes, APPENDIX 12 and APPENDIX 13. One per person of each of the above Ask each student to find three or four others to work with. Encourage them to form mixed groups to ensure a useful range of opinion. Also suggest that working with people with whom they do not usually work may give different perspectives. *Stage 1:* i) Introduce the idea of a 'whole day' outing. Ask the students to discuss the day's programme, stressing the need for specific objectives. Elicit from the groups what needs to be done before the day, and ask them to appoint a secretary/recorder for each group. ii) Get contributions from each group about the general enquiries to be made before the next session (including travel costs, information) and suggestions for venue, and a statement of objectives.

Student Objectives	Activities	Organisation and Method
To select and use information.	d) What needs to be done before the day? (Collect information about transport methods and costs, theatres, films, museums. Put out information, collect money, etc.) e) Who is going to do all this? (Who is good at dealing with people, money? Appoint treasurer, secretary, etc.)	
To take an active part in developing tutor group identity by being aware of the importance of everyone's contribution.	*Stage 2: Second session* *Agenda for discussion* a) What have we found out (transport times, costs, theatres, street plans, etc.)? b) Planning the day: 　i) What will be the mode of travel? 　ii) Will there be alternative/optional activities? 　iii) Will the complete group come together at any time (e.g. for midday and early evening meal)?	*Stage 2* Ask the groups to discuss their findings, plan the day and write out a programme neatly, for comparison with the other groups later.
	Stage 3 *Agenda for discussion* a) Did any group fail to produce a programme for the day? Why? b) What are the main differences in content between the programmes? c) Were some programmes easier to understand than others? Why?	*Stage 3* Each small group submits its own programme for the day, which is read and examined by all the other groups. The group as a whole comes together and discusses differences in content and format between the various programmes.

25

Student Objectives	Activities	Organisation and Method
	Stage 4	*Stage 4*
	a) What now needs to be done to make the day a success (booking seats, collecting money, 'clearing' time-table changes, giving out information to staff and parents, etc.)?	Get the group to discuss what needs to be done before the day. Stress the need for careful planning.
		Give out checklist Action Required, APPENDIX 11, and ask the group to criticise, adding and amending where necessary, and to rearrange in the order of priorities on which they have agreed.
	b) Is the given checklist adequate? Are there any items omitted? Can we leave out any items? Are the actions in the correct order? Which must be done first?	Give out blank Master Plan Time-tables, APPENDIX 10. Get the group to complete, entering actions required and indicating deadlines.
	Stage 5	*Stage 5*
	a) Do the time-tables show good planning? Has everything been included?	Spread out the completed Master Plan Time-tables and look at them together.
	b) How are priorities indicated?	
	c) Can people see at a glance when their deadlines are?	
	d) Is this format in any way easier to understand than the day's programme we have looked at?	
	e) Why are such detailed time-tables essential? What might happen without them?	
	Stage 6: The outing	

Student Objectives	Activities	Organisation and Method
	Stage 7: After the outing *Agenda for discussion* Did we get it right? What was the best/worst thing? Did we achieve our objectives? Was this the best way of achieving them? Is there room for improvement? Has the planning taught us anything? What things were essential to do before the next things could be attempted?	*Stage 7* General discussion to help evaluate the whole exercise. Under the general headings opposite, small groups discuss and draw their own conclusions. Recap on the whole process – similar to critical path analysis.
To manage and organise his/her own time effectively, showing a healthy balance between work and leisure pursuits.	*Stage 8* Can we apply the same process to planning study time, leisure time, sports training, revision, homework, etc?	*Stage 8* Using specimen Homework Time-table and background notes, APPENDICES 12 and 13, students in pairs devise schedules, either for themselves or an imaginary person, e.g. a sportsman.

NOTE: The problems used as examples in this unit were drawn from 'A' level students in a trial school. Tutors in other situations will need to draw out different examples relevant to the circumstances of their own students.

The unit is intended for repeated use, to be 'dipped into' when appropriate.

Student Objectives	Activities	Organisation and Method
To be aware of the needs and problems of others in the group by showing a willingness to provide and receive support as one is sharing experiences. For the student eventually to have the confidence to seek help.	*TAKE A CARD* Looking at the kinds of problems people encounter in sixth-form life; suggesting solutions and ways and means of achieving them; imagining what it is like to be a person facing that particular problem.	**You will need** Six sets of cards covering a variety of issues and concerns, each set appropriate to a sixth-form term, APPENDIX 14 Also, see the note at the top of this page 1 Group sits round the table informally. 2 Piles of cards which are appropriate to the sixth-form stage are placed on the table. 3 The first student takes a card and reads it out. This person says how he/she would tackle the problem. 4 The rest of the group debate the issue freely, suggesting alternative solutions where possible. 5 Continue, preferably until those members of the group who feel that they have had experiences of this problem have had an opportunity to speak. Students may well draw out an issue card which may not be relevant to them, but this does not render the activity useless, since the group may be helping one student, who happens to be facing that problem, without realising it.

Student Objectives	Activities	Organisation and Method
To become a more efficient learner by learning to take effective control of his/her own approach to stressful situations.	*STUDY SKILLS: COPING WITH ANXIETY* (See Notes for the Tutor page xxii) Introductory activity using upper-sixth form experience. 'I coped by . . .'	The second-year sixth (2/6th) are invited to join the first-year (1/6th) for discussions on overcoming anxiety. Arrange pairs of 2/6th and 1/6th students into groups of four. Ask the 2/6th to reflect upon their time in the fifth- and sixth-forms and talk about the things which gave them anxiety or put pressure on them. Then ask them to tell their partners which of these they have combated most successfully and how they coped with them. En-courage the 1/6th to ask questions.
	Agenda for further discussion Ask the groups to discuss the following statements: 'My friends want me to go out with them; I want to join them, but I also know that I need to stay in and study . . .' 'Is it worth trying . . . It's all a matter of luck, anyway . . .' 'I look at the paper and I go blank; I can't remember anything . . .' 'I feel like a kid. I'm eighteen, but I don't feel my life's my own. I feel I'm watched and questioned at school and college and at home – timekeeping, study, priorities, where I'm going (short and long term) . . .' 'I don't know where I am. I'm told that the important thing is to be happy, enjoy life . . . but there are such expectations . . . I can feel them . . .'	The further discussion opposite may be carried out subsequently by 1/6th only, or by keeping 2/6th and 1/6th together. Groups of four to six. Feed in the statements one at a time. Move around during the discussion, picking up points from small groups which are worth bringing to the attention of the whole tutor-group, and feed them in for whole group discussion. The discussion should lead to an awareness that in-dividuals share some difficulties and concerns with others, and that they are not insurmountable. Experience and strategies should be examined in follow-up whole group discussion.

Student Objectives	Activities	Organisation and Method
To become a more efficient learner by learning to take effective control of his/her own approach to stressful situations.	'It's not always spoken . . . but it's there. My Dad got a good honours degree . . . my sister got three A's . . .' 'I've got to take . . . and I'm hopeless at it.' 'I can't get started . . . my intentions are good – I'm going to revise/prepare, but when the moment comes I just can't get down to it . . .' *I want to be able to* Draw two boxes on the board as a guide to this activity:	Lead towards a conclusion that perhaps the greatest anxiety is about the unknown; that many anxieties begin to recede once they are faced, seen for what they are, and ways of tackling them are discussed with other people. The 1/6th, now on their own, should be arranged in friendship pairs, and asked to think about two or three situations which they wish to improve. They should draw two boxes (see opposite) and write these objectives in the right-hand box. The role of the friend is to help his fellow-student with practical suggestions about how these objectives might be achieved. When both have completed their left-hand boxes, they should make a contract between them to carry through these strategies as thoroughly as possible for, say, a week, when they will report back.

I want to be able to

I want to be able to:	I want to be able to:
To achieve this I should: 1 2 3	....

In pairs, the students devise strategies for achieving their short-term objectives.

Student Objectives	Activities	Organisation and Method
To become a more efficient learner by learning to take effective control of his/her own approach to stressful situations.	*Report back – future session* Reinforcement. How did we do? Do we need more practice? Other areas of concern. Setting new targets. *Problem solving* 1 Sandra takes her 'A' levels in ten weeks' time. She enjoys folk-singing and is a member of a group which is just beginning to gain local popularity – and bookings. Performance also means practice. Her parents, her teachers, her own head tells her 'Exams come first – get the work done, get the results,' but she can't get the music out of her head – or out of her soul. 2 It's getting nearer and nearer to exams, and Terry can't settle down to revision at week-ends. He has a quiet, well-furnished room of his own, but when he closes the door he can't get started; he'll fiddle with his record player, his guitar, a magazine or his bike. Even when he does sit at his table he'll find himself sucking his pen, chin cupped in his hands and his mind 'far away'.	Students will report back on their successes and their difficulties at a future session. The tutor should circulate, picking up points of success or strategies which are worth sharing with the whole group. Discussion can then proceed to identifying new areas of concern, with a partner, and the setting of new targets in the same way as the original ones were set. The tutor intervenes as little as possible in these activities, leaving the students able to feel that they are in charge of their own situations and able to direct and improve their own learning. Further problem solving experience may now be afforded by arranging the students in small groups and asking them to discuss a problem – either 1 or 2 opposite, or a similar one of your own device. Ask the students to offer suggestions. Ask what can Sandra and Terry do about their situations? They can't change the date of the exams, or their need for good results if certain careers are to be pursued. Pose the questions: What can be changed in these situations – their habits? – their behaviour? Ask the small groups to devise strategies for tackling these situations.

Student Objectives	Activities	Organisation and Method
To become a more efficient learner by learning to take effective control of his/her own approach to stressful situations.	At the conclusion of this 'suggestion' period, the tutor might suggest that what is being learnt from these activities is that the students themselves can take hold of situations and reshape them through positive thought and action, instead of allowing events and situations to control them. Ask the students to note for themselves how anxiety decreases when they begin to feel themselves in control. *Making a prediction come true* Tom is seventeen. Says he's 'no good with girls'; he avoids them if possible, goes into corners at social events, is tongue-tied when they do try to talk to him and, although normally polite, can become boorish and aggressive if a girl tries to 'rescue' him. Do I predict failure for myself? Do I do anything to make my predictions come true? *Final question* 'Is responsibility for success/failure in your own hands rather than a result of outside forces?'	After ten minutes, ask each group for its ideas and write them on the board. Allow a further ten minutes in which each small group is to draw up its own new list of suggestions from those on the board, arranging them in their order of priority. They should also suggest what they see as the probable outcome of their suggested courses of action. After each group has reported, allow a further ten minutes for a concluding discussion with the whole tutor group. Before closing this session, it might be useful to link what has just been done to the concept of self-fulfilling prophesies (see example opposite). Break the whole group into pairs and ask them to discuss any situation in which they predict they will fail. Ask them to discuss these situations to try to identify whether there is anything which they do, perhaps unconsciously, to make their prediction come true.

32

Student Objectives	Activities	Organisation and Method
	From this base it is possible to go on to examine the students' approach to study and homework, and the decision-making involved therein. The way in which the student learns to make decisions may well influence his personal development and the kind of person he becomes. There will be a need to provide conditions/situations in which the student can become aware of his facility for both recognising and evading a task simultaneously, to evaluate how the accompanying attitudes help or hinder him, and also to experience and evaluate different ways of tackling study, through the programme activities and experiences provided in units such as: Learning From Others, p.7 What's in a Word, p.13 Planning Revision, p.34 Key Facts From 'Active Reading', p.36 Life of a Robin, p.48 Information Exchange, p.53 Time in Your Hands, p.57	

Student Objectives	Activities	Organisation and Method

To anticipate the demands of revision and to plan a time-table and strategies to meet these demands.	*STUDY SKILLS: PLANNING FOR REVISION*
	
	Things to do
	
	Obtain a complete examination time-table for your end-of-first-year-sixth examinations.
	
	Make a list for each examination subject of the main topics in each subject to be revised.
	
	Find out how much time you have available for revision (in days). Give each examination subject an equal amount of time (leaving some spare days).
	
	For each subject, plan out topic revision.
	
	How much revision time can you spare each day? An extra half hour a day may well be sufficient, if your plan starts four weeks in advance.
	
	An hour spent planning your revision programme will stop you worrying about what you still have to revise.
		You will need
		APPENDIX 15, Revision Plan
		
		1 Since we cannot assume that students are aware of effective techniques or concentration spans, it might be necessary to explain to them the necessity of planning a revision programme with reference to the examinations to be taken. (Link this work with the Master Plan, APPENDIX 5). Emphasis should be placed on the importance of a plan of action, however basic.
		
		2 To help them to use time efficiently, the following points might be worth emphasising:
		
		    For each topic, scan notes and select key facts and write them down.
		
		    Spend fifteen minutes doing this, and with any spare time reread your fact list, learning as you do so. If your topic seems too big for this, divide it up.
		
		    Do not spend more than fifteen minutes or so on a revision topic. Your concentration will flag. Repeat after a break for another topic or another subject.
		
		    After each learning bout or key fact search, give yourself a break or reward.
		
		    Do not be tempted to spend long periods of time on one subject. You will lose concentration and only waste your time.

Student Objectives	Activities	Organisation and Method
To anticipate the demands of revision and to plan a time-table and strategies to meet these demands.	Exams after the 1/6th will be as much an opportunity for you to test yourself and practice your revision programme as they are a test of the subjects you are taking. If you follow a planned programme diligently, next year's external exams should not present themselves as daunting obstacles, but as goals which you will have a technique to help you aim for.	This is a revision technique. Do not confuse it with homework, where you might have to write notes or an essay – this could take you an hour or more. Revision technique is short, sharp bursts of concentrated reading, writing and learning effort. The last, but nevertheless important, consideration is whether these examinations are important to you. If they are, then stick to your time-table and remember that revision isn't a social activity. You will need will-power to turn away from friends and get down to your own allotted portion of work each day.

Student Objectives	Activities	Organisation and Method

To develop good study habits and skills.
 	
To recognise key facts and fundamental concepts within subject areas.
	STUDY SKILLS: KEY FACTS/ACTIVE READING
	
	A sample exercise designed to stimulate active rather than passive reading. It gives activity in picking out key points, memory and recall, and rapid summarising.
	
	This is one sample only. It is suggested that similar passages are obtained from various departments to give further practice, and to emphasise the application of the same skills to all areas of the curriculum.
		The approach to this exercise is essentially positive and vigorous, rather than passive. This will be communicated by the tutor's approach, quite as much as by the activity itself. It is intended to communicate that learning means effort, means taking positive action—in reading
		
		    – picking out key points
		      (ringing and underlining)
		    – note-taking
		    – active recall
		    – summarising
		
		This is an individual (not group) activity.
		
		You will need
		APPENDIX 16, Brother Oliver's Wings, one copy for each student, and other passages of tutor's choice for summarising. The two sheets of the appendix should be duplicated back to back with the central dotted lines in alignment.
		
		Give out APPENDIX 16, Brother Oliver's Wings, folded with the story and questions inside.
		
		Allow 3 minutes for page 1 : Instructions
		          12 minutes for page 2 : The story
		          12 minutes for page 3 : Answers
		            8 minutes for page 4 : Summarising
		           (35 minutes altogether)
		
		as indicated. Give instructions when to turn over.
		
		Checking: Each student can now check his own answer on page 4 against the original summary on page 1, (e.g. This story is about . . .). There are certain to be points arising from this exercise which the tutor will wish to take up and re-emphasise again at the beginning of the next activity of this kind.
		
		Repeat with material provided by other teachers.

Student Objectives	Activities	Organisation and Method
To increase his/her range of study skills through practising alternative/divergent approaches to problem-solving.	*STUDY SKILLS: RIGIDITY AND FLEXIBILITY* (See Notes about Study Skills, p.xxii.) In this activity groups of students are asked to consider statements such as those below, in order to identify and discuss: 1 General tone 2 Intention/motive 3 Over-simplification 4 What is missing? 5 What is unstated but suggested? 6 Ambiguity. *Statements for discussion* 1 The winner of the Round Britain Cycle Race regularly drinks a pint of milk a day. Every winner of this trophy has also been a regular 'pinta' man. Why don't you try it? It'll make a man of you! 2 There were fewer murders in Britain in the 1930's and 40's. Then, in the 1950's the death penalty for murder was abolished … and what's happened? Thanks to the 'liberals', naughty children can't be punished, prison sentences are suspended and crime increases. We're too soft; there are no deterrents!	Organise the tutor group into smaller groups of four or five. Introduce the topic, perhaps by taking up points from the exercise on pages xxii and xxiii. Next, give each group at least one copy of one of the statements, or write one on the board. Ask them to discuss the statement in general terms for a few moments, and then feed in the points opposite, one at a time, listing them on the blackboard as you do so. Move around the groups listening, prodding and taking up interesting ideas from any one group to feed into whole group discussion, e.g. 'Now here's an interesting thought in this group – tell them what you were saying, Tom. Perhaps the rest of you may care to consider this point in your own discussion.' After, say, twenty minutes, halt the discussions and get each group to report briefly on its discussions. Allow questions from other groups. Throughout this discussion, emphasise constantly the six points listed in the Activities column above.

Student Objectives	Activities	Organisation and Method
To increase his/her range of study skills through practising alternative/ divergent approaches to problem-solving.	3 I firmly believe you can't take too many vitamins. I take vitamins A, C and E regularly, and B and D from time to time. At seventy-two I ride every day and swim regularly. I write a chapter a day and this means that I've never had time for household chores. I travel a good deal, spending January to Easter on the Mediterranean. I put my good health and long life down to vitamins and recommend them to everyone. Obtain more statements of your own, or ask the students to make some up, for future sessions. Advertising is the simplest source; others could be: religion politics race newspapers and examples reflecting exam questions in various academic disciplines should be included.	With these six points now listed on the blackboard, introduce another of the suggested topics and allow the groups to discuss them as before, whilst you circulate picking up points, and feeding them into whole group discussion, asking questions, etc. Then again groups report back and whole group discusses. Before the end of the session, the students should write down the six points from the board for future reference. Repeat this exercise with other topics until it becomes an instructive part of their intellecutal armoury.

Student Objectives	Activities	Organisation and Method
To develop an efficient system for recording and retrieving information.	*STUDY SKILLS: USING DIAGRAMS* Some people can think better visually than orally/verbally. This section introduces them to the practice of jotting down their ideas in diagrammatic form. The tutor could go further on his/her own initiative, and introduce box diagrams. The tutor may wish either to use duplicates of APPENDIX 17, or to build up the summary in stages on the blackboard or over-head projector.	**You will need** APPENDIX 17, Jesus, and APPENDIX 18, The Romans, or similar item on paper or on overhead transparency. Postcards Take either APPENDIX 17, Jesus, or better still a topic of your own choosing and develop in the same way. Using either the blackboard or overhead projector, write the topic in the centre and ring it. Then say to the class: 'What do we want to know about Jesus?' In this case, four simple questions suggest themselves: Who was he? Where did he live? What did he do? What did people think of him? These are spaced around the ring. Take each question in turn, asking for any ideas which suggest themselves, and link the question by a line, as shown in APPENDIX 17. Make the approach lively and 'punchy'. Move to and fro between the questions, adding and linking more information as it is given. The finished article can be used as a basis for essay writing, or as a revision note/technique.
	This is a useful revision technique. Key facts on a particular topic can be easily assembled diagrammatically on a postcard. In this way, key facts cards can be built up for revision.	Also try out APPENDIX 18, The Romans, or similar topic, in the same way, as a variation of lay out. Give out postcards and allow students to choose a topic which they can develop in the same way, using one side of a postcard. Try out some other topics, in groups or individually, from time to time.

Moving deeper into Study Skills generally, and Reading Skills in particular, we cannot do better than refer you to Douglas Hamblin's book, *The Teacher and Pastoral Care*, (Basil Blackwell, 1978) pp. 75–101. In emphasising the necessity for reading skills to be continuously boosted, increasing the speed of reading and applying intellectual discipline to reading and appraisal, he offers a comprehensive Study Skills questionnaire which he has developed as a self-diagnostic instrument for brighter fifth- and sixth-form students. It is in three parts.

1   Reading, which is subdivided into four parts:

    i)   a brief section on the mechanics of reading
    ii) a section on the development of recall
    iii) a section on the developing of new ideas
    iv) finally, some items on the use which can be made of reading.

2   Organisation and planning of study which is subdivided into four parts:

    i)   organising myself
    ii) efficient note-taking
    iii) answering questions efficiently
    iv) writing essays.

3   Homework and revision for exams which has two broad subdivisions:

    i) the general organisation of homework
    ii) effective revision techniques.

We commend these diagnostic instruments to you. The questionnaires would have to be typed and duplicated, but we would suggest that pages 76–77, 82–83, 87–88 and 93–94 are not duplicated and that, instead, the material on those pages is used by the tutor for purposes of introducing, linking and developing the topics. Douglas Hamblin gives a fuller treatment in his book, *Study Skills*.

It will be profitable to use the Active Tutorial Work processes of working in twos and fours with discussion, report-back and contract-making where appropriate, in order to secure greater involvement and commitment from the students.

This Study Skills section is concluded with activities on sequencing and making sense in writing, which may be helpful to students who demonstrate weakness in planning and logical sequencing in essay-writing.

Student Objectives	Activities	Organisation and Method

To develop skills in communicating ideas, orally and in writing, through practice in logical sequencing.	STUDY SKILLS: LOGICAL SEQUENCING – MAKING SENSE IN WRITING
	
	1 *Henry's first car*
	
	A sequencing activity which involves a time-scale (1896–1903) and a cause-and-effect scale (e.g. Had little money, therefore first car made of bits and pieces).
	
	The students are given a passage from which sentences have been extracted and printed at random. They have to reassemble the passage in a logical sequence.
		You will need
		APPENDIX 19, Henry's First Car – one copy per group and one per student
		APPENDIX 20, My First Holiday Abroad – one per student
		Scissors
		
		Give out one copy of the jumbled passage, Henry's First Car – one per student (APPENDIX 19).
		
		Allow a period of time for students to read through it and attempt individual solutions. (They might find it helpful to number the extracts.)
		
		Then form groups of four and give each group an extra copy to cut into strips.
		
		The next part could be made into a game in which the first group to reassemble the strips into what the tutor deems to be an acceptable (logical) order is the winner.
		
		Other groups may challenge the solution with rational argument.
		
		The objective is not to produce a rewritten account of Henry Ford's story, but to argue a route through a body of information:
		
		    introduction
		    development
		    conclusion
		    historical sequence
		    cause and effect.

Student Objectives	Activities	Organisation and Method
To develop skills in communicating ideas, orally and in writing, through practice in logical sequencing.	2 *My first holiday abroad* An exercise to emphasise that a narrative is built on what has gone before. Students sometimes have an ability to pull rabbits out of hats in the sense of introducing items out of context and out of sequence.	Give out APPENDIX 20, My First Holiday Abroad – one per person. Students work alone. Carry out a step-by-step discussion with the whole group as work progresses. Ask which extracts they think will be first and which will be last and why, etc. Take Extract 10, beginning *The hooter sounded and the strip of water between* . . . and ask: 'What else would I have to know for this passage to make sense?' (E.g. 'We'd have reached the quayside and boarded the boat.') From this, ask for suggestions about the sequences which might preceed it, leading back to find the introduction to the passage. If it does not arise in discussion, take Extract 1, *Weren't we glad when the coach slowed down* . . ., and treat as above (E.g. 'Before it slowed down, it must have started.') Now see if the group can sequence the events from the introduction to the boat's departure. Then ask what might have happened next, and why. Then look at Extract 2, *They were sometimes too high,* and treat as above. Carry on in a similar vein to the end of the passage, always emphasising that you cannot discuss or expand upon an item which has not yet been introduced into the account. *Reiterate:* They are looking for an introduction, development, conclusion, historical sequence, cause and effect.

This unit introduces the students to the brainstorming technique as a means of producing related, but random ideas, and then goes on to show how to sequence the ideas.

Two activities, a) and b), are provided as an introduction to c). It is suggested that the whole section is read through first, so that the best method of using the material can be selected. Either

    i)   go through a), and b) and c)

    ii) omit a) and b) and go directly to c)

    iii) use only the alternative suggestion marked c)* Alternative.

Appendices have been kept simple so that the emphasis can be on the process at this stage; alternatives at c)* could be at a more demanding level. For exercises at c)*, use can be made of topics suggested by other subject teachers, to help to reinforce learning in those subjects.

Student Objectives	Activities	Organisation and Method
To encourage the foundation of good habits and study skills by: i) helping students to understand and practice logical sequencing ii) giving practice in a method of identifying groups of ideas which 'stick' together, and utilise methods of marking, i.e. under-lining, bracketing, etc.	*STUDY SKILLS: PLANNING AND SEQUENCING* a) *Fire* Listening to a short passage and then rearranging random ideas on the same theme into a logical sequence.	You will need APPENDIX 21, Fire – a descriptive passage APPENDIX 22, Fire – a sheet of random ideas to be rearranged by students (one copy per student) APPENDIX 23, Fire – for the teacher APPENDIX 24, Journey of a River to the Sea (one per student) *Alternative material of your own choice Read APPENDIX 21, Fire, to the whole group, perhaps reading a second time to emphasise the paragraph breaks. Explain that they are now to be given a series of random words and phrases which are to be rearranged into a similar passage. Give out APPENDIX 22, Random Ideas, and go through the instructions with them. Work through the random ideas with the group, looking for ideas which could be linked together in paragraphs. APPENDIX 23 is provided as a guide for the tutor.

43.

Student Objectives	Activities	Organisation and Method
To encourage the foundation of good habits and study skills by: i) helping students to understand and practice logical sequencing ii) giving practice in a method of identifying groups of ideas which 'stick' together, and utilise methods of marking, i.e. under-lining, bracketing, etc.	b) *The journey of a river to the sea* A similar activity to Fire consisting of only three paragraphs and omitting the teacher's reading. c) *Using materials from other subjects* Other teachers who teach your tutor-group might be persuaded to suggest relevant 'subject' topics which can be used for further exercises in sequencing. c)* *Alternative* Simply ask the group 'What did you do yesterday in . . .', e.g. History, Politics, etc., and continue: 'Right let's imagine you were asked to write about (e.g. Churchill) . . . and let's see how we could go about it' . . . and lead the class step-by-step into produc-ing a list of 'ideas' as for Fire.	Give out APPENDIX 24. Arrange the tutor-group in pairs and let them work through this exercise in the same way that you tackled Fire. Arrange the tutor-group into small groups and, with the topic now chosen (see opposite), go on to discuss the general theme of the topic (a form of general introduction). Then give each small group about three minutes to jot down any ideas on the topic which comes into their heads. One person records for the group. You might wish to tell the pupils that this is known as 'brainstorming' – a method used to produce a lot of random ideas in a short time. It is used for 'high powered' sessions in the business world. (See Introductory Note.) Explain how one idea, jotted down, may, however flimsy or 'daff', lead on to another idea, and another, and another. This is how the random ideas about Fire came to be jotted down. Stress the need to jot down ideas quickly in the barest detail and fewest words possible. Next, ask someone from each group to read out the resulting (random) list, allowing other groups to pick up the points (good ideas) which they have missed. Finally, ask each group to arrange these ideas into a sequence of paragraph groupings, so that they will form the basis of a good story, as in previous activities.

Student Objectives	Activities	Organisation and Method

To encourage the foundation of good habits and study skills by:
 	
 i) helping students to understand and practice logical sequencing
 	
 ii) giving practice in a method of identifying groups of ideas which 'stick' together, and utilise methods of marking, i.e. underlining, bracketing, etc.
	Repetitions of this kind of activity, over succeeding weeks, can lead from:
	
	 i) group work in early sessions to individual work in later sessions
	
	 ii) using 'given' ideas to using their own ideas
	
	 iii) a 'given' topic to one which is a live issue for the pupil(s) concerned.
	
	 It will be useful to emphasise brainstorming as a means of:
	   Getting the mind working quickly and imaginatively.
	   Providing ample 'raw material' for writing.
	   Leaving sufficient material for middle and end sections.
	   Leaving material to round off work with style, instead of 'stopping dead'.
	   Avoiding the loss of ideas and drying up.
	   Helping recall.
	   Making written work more sensible, interesting and informative to others.
		You will need
		 Topics provided by other teachers/departments
		
		 This process needs to be repeated continually, at intervals, until it becomes a natural method of approach.
		
		 On future occasions, move from working in groups to pairs, to individual work, and then to giving the individual a piece of homework which he has been set for that evening to plan, using the techniques of planning and sequencing which he has been practising.

Student Objectives	Activities	Organisation and Method
To encourage the foundation of good habits and study skills by: i) helping students to understand and practice logical sequencing ii) giving practice in a method of identifying groups of ideas which 'stick' together, and utilise methods of marking, i.e. underlining, bracketing, etc.	d) *'Knife and Fork'* Planning through free association games. A refinement of brainstorming, introduced here in game form with i) the whole tutor-group ii) teams. Key facts: A development of free association. Pupils use postcards with a topic written on one side and the key facts listed on the other, or shown as a flow chart.	Brainstorming produces ideas almost completely at random, whereas free association tries to link the next word/idea to the last. Arrange the class in rows, or in a circle. Say to the first student something like 'Knife! Now you say what that makes you think of.' (E.g. fork, butter, etc.) This word is given to the next person for a response, and so on, round the group, speeding up as they get the idea. Next, break the whole group into teams of, say, eight or ten. 'Snap out' one word/idea, and the teams can do a 'free association' race to see which team can pass the idea from one to another first, through associated ideas. Repeat as often as is appropriate, and then link to the work done previously in c), brainstorming.

STUDY SKILLS: FOR YOUR FURTHER CONSIDERATION

Would it be profitable to mount shortcourses for your students on:

Scanning and speed reading?

Typing (and shorthand)?

Using libraries and other sources of reference – compiling bibliographies?

Methods of ascribing references, sources, credits, in a piece of written work?

The basics of computers – their operation as sources of reference?

Using modern aids – copiers   for effective presentation of
                      binders   dissertations, etc.?
                      Letraset

NOTE: The title for this unit came from a discussion about listening to boring lectures. The subject matter was one person's experience and in no way implies that this subject is of necessity boring. Students will often have to tackle subject matter which is not particularly interesting, and sometimes it is even less so due to the way in which it is put across. The authors recognise the delicate nature of this unit, but feel it to be important in helping students to deal with academic demands.

Student Objectives	Activities	Organisation and Method
To demonstrate the development of the self-discipline required to adhere to work schedules.	STUDY SKILLS: THE LIFE OF A ROBIN (See NOTE) What do you do if you have to listen to something which is boring?	You will need A pre-recorded tape of a talk which could be made from the script Life of a Robin, APPENDIX 25, or any subject matter which the students are likely to find boring. It must be read in a boring manner. It should last up to ten minutes
To recognise difficulties and take steps to overcome them.	Listen to the tape. What you hear will be very important. Agenda for discussion What did you do first? What happened as the tape proceeded? What things went through your mind? What have you learned/remembered as a result of listening to the tape? Were two heads better than one?	The tape is played without any preamble or introduction, apart from an instruction to listen to the tape (see opposite). The tutor should monitor the students' reactions. When it is finished, ask for immediate reactions, which can be summarised on the board. Individually, the students make a list on paper of all the facts they can remember from the tape. Then, in pairs, combine their lists.
To help students to use the facilities and organisation of the establishment effectively and efficiently.	Which teaching/learning techniques suit me? The tutor may introduce this section by pointing out that a variety of different teaching techniques are used by their lecturers.	In groups of three, prepare a list of all the different methods which are used by teachers/lecturers for imparting information or involving students in learning. A master list from all the groups may be compiled on the board.

48

NOTE: Whilst acknowledging that this unit may appear delicate in terms of professional loyalty, the writing team feel that its is important to help students to tackle *all* their learning difficulties, not just those of their own making. This unit has been carefully constructed to avoid discussion of colleagues.

Student Objectives	Activities	Organisation and Method
	Criteria for choices: I learn most this way. I learn better this way. I enjoy it. I want to find out more. Does everyone learn in the same way?	Each individual rewrites the list in his order of preference, according to the criteria opposite, on a slip of paper. The students then compare their lists with as many others as possible, to see where agreements or differences occur.
To recognise the influence exerted by individuals and groups.	*Helping yourself to learn* a) The best lecturer I ever had used to . . . and what I learned was . . . b) The worst lecturer I ever had used to . . . and what I did about it was . . . and as a result . . . c) I cannot finish these statements because . . .	The tutor may now write up the open-ended statements opposite, on the board. It is strongly suggested that the tutor completes them him/herself to indicate the style of the statements. Emphasis is on approach and teaching method which might have helped or hindered learning (see *NOTE*). There should be no discussion of personality and names are completely unnecessary. Still in groups of three, the students then take it in turns to complete all the statements or to choose one on which they wish to place special emphasis.
	Agenda for further discussion When these lectures took place what kinds of feelings were involved for you? for the lecturer? How difficult was it to take action? Do you still learn despite everything? How prepared are you to 'grit' your teeth and carry on?	This is followed by discussions of their answers. The tutor again circulates, taking comments from the groups which will lead through the agenda opposite. This is a very necessary part of the unit, to help the students to achieve the stated objectives.

Student Objectives	Activities	Organisation and Method
	Are there any ways in which changes in approach/teaching style could be brought about?	
	Are there any changes of approach or attitude which you could make?	
	What would be your first step . . . and the next . . .	
	Is/Are there special help you would special skills like to acquire?	
	What are the main differences between individual action and those which a group might take?	
	Big brother	Groups make a light-hearted scenario showing what might happen if a teaching machine broke down.
	What would it be like to be taught by a machine?	The tutor may wish to extend this section by continuing some work on teaching machines, perhaps with examples.

Student Objectives	Activities	Organisation and Method
To demonstrate the ability to take action and make decisions, both as an individual and corporately as a group.	*Getting the most from your lectures* What would you do, or what do you do, in a lecture if . . . . . . there is noise and distraction outside? . . . you arrived late and missed a third of the lecture? . . . the lecturer arrived late and tried to cram all the lecture into less time? . . . you understand very little? . . . you cannot hear properly? . . . you find the subject matter boring? . . . you have heard it all before? . . . you have just been playing sport and don't feel in the mood.	In fours, ask the students to consider a number of circumstances which might prevent them from getting the most from their lectures, giving items from the suggested list of situations opposite. The tutor should circulate and stop the groups from time to time, to allow the whole group to consider different solutions. *See* Step-By-Step Discussion in the preliminary notes on Working in Groups, p. xviii.
To develop awareness of barriers to learning.		Compare different people's solutions to the same problem. How many solutions would require an individual to pluck up courage to do or say something? How many solutions are for individuals and how many could a group get involved in?

51

Student Objectives	Activities	Organisation and Method
To recognise weakness or problems, and take steps to rectify them.	*Help* An activity to help students to get the most out of their lectures, by considering possible solutions to problems which may have arisen or are likely to arise. *Agenda for discussion* a) How swayed were you by the presenter of the solution, rather than by the solution itself? b) How varied were the solutions? c) Is it possible to have more than one solution to a problem? Can you have too many? d) Were the problems chosen actual or possible ones? e) Are any of these problems real problems for any of us? f) Can we discuss this? g) Can we discuss some of the steps which will help to cope with the problem? h) Can we help each other?	**You will need** One Lecture Board, APPENDIX 26, per group One set of Problem Cards, APPENDIX 27, per group Five sets of Solution Cards, APPENDIX 27, per group 1 Ask the students to form groups of five. 2 A lecture-board is placed in the centre of each group, and the problem cards are spread out, facing upwards. Students leave their 'hand' of solution cards face down on the table. 3 One member of each group chooses a problem card which he/she feels is relevant to him/her. 4 In turn, each student places a problem card in the centre of the board. The group then discuss possible solutions to each person's problem in turn, asking if these solutions seem helpful to the person concerned. Then they choose, from their sets of solution cards, the one which they feel is the most appropriate answer to the first problem, then to the second problem, and so on. 5 The group then discuss the merits and demerits of the 'prescribed' solution(s). It may be a good idea to have a few blank cards so that students can write down a problem or a solution which they feel is more relevant than the suggested ones. 6 Follow-up discussion with the whole class using the agenda opposite.

Student Objectives	Activities	Organisation and Method
To recognise the expertise and knowledge which already exists in the group. To develop skills in seeking information and to use the expertise of the people within the situations which surround them. To recognise the information and knowledge he/she already possesses.	*STUDY SKILLS: INFORMATION EXCHANGE I* A starting activity to encourage students to seek information and to demonstrate that it is often possible for them to help each other in this task, i.e. to recognise that any group of people are, in themselves, the source of a good deal of intrinsic knowledge and knowledge about sources of information. *Important note:* It is important to give several examples to show the range of possible questions. Students often go 'blank' at first and should be encouraged to think of the many things they know something about, e.g. cookery, music, sport, travel, TV, general knowledge, local knowledge, electronics, cars, astronomy, etc. Examples should also be given of what *not* to ask, e.g. 'What is my dog's name?' The questions must be about factual and not personal information. *Agenda for discussion* 1 How did you go about finding the answers? 2 What kind of response did you get? 3 What were your reactions? 4 Have you found out something which you didn't know before?	**You will need** One small piece of paper for each person 1 Each person in the tutor-group is asked to write down a question to which only they are likely to know the answer, e.g. someone interested in coin collecting may write down the question: 'What is the market value of a 1953 penny?' *See Important Note* opposite. 2 The question papers are now folded and the members of the group exchange papers (about five or six times). 3 Make sure that no one has got their own question. Then tell the students to circulate amongst those assembled, asking questions until they find the answer to the question on their paper. 4 When they find the answer they sit down. 5 Follow-up with a whole group discussion along the lines suggested by the agenda opposite. If the group is large, many people may not have had time to find the answer. They should now be given an opportunity to ask their question and receive an answer from the writer of the question. While this is happening, the tutor can use the opportunity to illustrate the point of the exercise by interjecting when appropriate: 'I didn't know you knew about that' or 'How did you get to know about that?'

Student Objectives	Activities	Organisation and Method

To recognise the expertise and knowledge which already exists in the group.
 	
To develop skills in seeking information and to use the expertise of the people within the situations which surround them.
 	
To recognise the information and knowledge he/she already possesses.
	STUDY SKILLS: INFORMATION EXCHANGE II
	
	Agenda for discussion by group as a whole
	
	1 *Lower sixth*
	   Was it easy to identify your own question? Did you know the answer?
	
	2 *Upper sixth*
	   Did you know the question that matched your answer, or did you just guess?
	
	3 Do you already know the person with whom you are now sitting? If you do, did you know what he/she was studying?
		You will need
		Students from both the lower- and upper-sixth-forms
		
		Short 'A' level standard questions on a variety of specialist subjects, written on separate cards
		
		A separate answer card for each of the above questions
		
		(Colleagues from each department in the school could be persuaded to supply the necessary questions and answers)
		
		1 Distribute the question cards to the lower-sixth-form students, one card per student.
		
		2 Distribute the answer cards to the upper-sixth-form students in the same way.
		
		3 Students are asked to exchange cards until they find the one which relates to a subject they are studying. It should be made clear that lower-sixth students only exchange cards with other lower-sixth students, and upper-sixth students only with other upper-sixth students. (It may be advisable to have some spare pairs of cards in case one or two students are left without a card appropriate to one of their subjects.)

Student Objectives	Activities	Organisation and Method
	4 What opportunities have you already had to meet the other year on an in-formal basis?	4 When each student has either a question or an answer card relating to one of the subjects he/she is studying, the group is told to 'pair them up', i.e. each lower-sixth student finds the answer to the question on his/her card.
	5 Discussion with partners – areas of common ground.	5 Students are now asked to sit down with their partners and discuss the subject area which they have in common.

Student Objectives	Activities	Organisation and Method
To enjoy and deepen his involvement in learning tasks and show a willingness to impart his knowledge to others.	*STUDY SKILLS: A TEACHING-LEARNING EXERCISE* This is a small-group task in which two members attempt to teach ten words to the rest of the group. The words to be taught should be in the form of a packet of cards, one word per card. The words should be appropriate to the group (see suggested examples).	The students form groups of five or six. Each group appoints two 'teachers'; the rest of the group will be 'learners'. Your task is to work with your teaching partner to teach ten words to your learners. The 'teachers' will be told that they should work together to teach ten words to the 'learners'; they are given an instruction card. Each pair of 'teachers' is given a few minutes to discuss and plan their teaching strategy.
To select and use information.	*'Learners' instruction* Think about how the task is introduced – Is it clear what you are being asked to do? Is the method/approach helpful? How are 'aids' used? Did you learn something? *Examples of words* achievement defensive judgement ambivalent encounter hierarchy conflict experience ownership consciousness expert process culture influence self-awareness This list of words can be altered to increase or decrease difficulty according to the level of the group. It might be possible to examine the influence of highly emotional or politically controversial words on their teaching style.	Explain what is about to happen to the rest of the group, asking these 'learners' to monitor their reactions whilst they are being taught. Closing discussion with the whole class embodying the questions opposite, along with others which flow naturally from the discussion. A sentence giving a suggested definition may be needed with each card, to help the 'teachers' to plan how they are going to put the word and its meaning across to their 'learners'. During the teaching process, approximately thirty minutes, notice: – How much time is allowed for 'learner' participation? – How flexible are the teachers? – How do they work together? – How much of the task do they manage to work through? (How many of the words do they manage to teach?) – How does the time constraint affect their style?

Student Objectives	Activities	Organisation and Method
To develop the ability to use free time effectively for private study and relaxation. To recognise and use the facilities and organisation of the establishment effectively.	*STUDY SKILLS: TIME IN YOUR HANDS* An examination of the use of 'free' time at school/college/home, and the value of planning for its use. *Introducing the task* Group pressure can be important. Some of the students who would gain most from the exercise in organising their time might have to be quite brave to stand out against a peer consensus in the group which started by insisting that they are 'OK', 'don't need help of this kind', etc. Thus, individual attempts, initially, might help to bring out and examine real individual problems, which might be lost by going straight into the group exercise.	You will need One Partially Completed Time-Table, APPENDIX 28 Three packs of Activity Cards giving: a) suggested activities for 'free' periods b) lunch-time activities c) suggested activities for time out of school made up from APPENDIX 29 Introduce the task. Explain it to the students and ask for suggestions for extending the range of activities to include in pack 'C' (e.g. voluntary activities, clubs, societies, etc.). Give out the materials APPENDICES 28 and 29 and allow students to work through the exercises on their own before joining together in the group task. Ask the students to find three others to work with. The task for each group is to place the required number of cards from each pack on the spaces on the timetable. There should be group agreement about the final programme. An alternative procedure is to print plenty of spare time-tables (APPENDIX 28) so that they may be consumable. Then, instead of making cards from APPENDIX 29, students make their choices and write them onto partially completed time-tables in pencil at first, and in ink when finalised. This saves the tutor some work in preparing cards. The groups then move around looking at and criticising other groups' programmes.

Student Objectives	Activities	Organisation and Method
	Agenda for discussion	Use the agenda opposite for a final follow-up discussion.
	a) How should free time in school be used?	
	b) How much time should be spent on homework?	
	c) How should we spend our weekends?	
	d) Is it important to give up some time to running societies, carrying out pre-fectorial duties, etc.?	
	e) Part-time jobs:	
	Are there any advantages in having one?	
	When should they be given up?	
	f) Can the allocation of leisure time be constant throughout the year? E.g. should there be a reduction in some leisure pursuits as exam time draws near?	Even when the need for organisation and planning in the allocation of time is appreciated, students do not react spontaneously or effectively to these findings (e.g. even when enough time is allowed for 'reading around' a subject, students still tend to leave the task until the last minute).
		Thus, there is need for reinforcement and stressing again and again the need to plan time, not only to survive in education, but also in order to make the best of life generally.

Student Objectives	Activities	Organisation and Method
		Two suggestions for tackling this are given below:
		a) Duplicate a large number of the partially completed time-tables and get the groups to enter their decisions on their individual copies as a reference for discussion and follow-up in both group and individual tutorials.
		b) Give each student two copies of blank time-tables, one to be completed with Actual Present Activities and the other showing improvements.
		Whatever approach is adopted, it would seem highly appropriate for the tutor to return to the topic after a short while asking 'Have you done anything about it, or are you still content to go muddling along?'

Student Objectives	Activities	Organisation and Method

To examine the nature of leadership and some of the different ways in which it is exercised.	*LEADERSHIP*
	
	1 *What is it? How is it exercised?*
	
	Those in positions of authority are usually also in a position of 'leading' groups of people.
	
	It is important to note that 'styles' of leadership exist only in the perceptions of others, either those being led, or those leading, or those observing the leading.
	
	2 *Who are leaders?*
	
	Brainstorm, quickly, the names of as many 'leaders', as the group can think of in one minute. Have two or three scribes to write up the names.
	
	3 *Three popular 'styles'*
	
	An authoritarian leader is . . .
	
	A democratic leader is . . .
	
	A *laissez-faire* leader is . . . .
		You will need
		To have briefed three students or three pairs of students to give a five-minute lesson – see 3 below
		
		1 Whole tutor-group consider generally when and how leadership is exercised:
		
		   in society
		   at home
		   at school.
		
		2 Brainstorming – see opposite – whole tutor-group. Encourage a broader interpretation than political leaders.
		
		Attempt to classify the names into categories of leadership, e.g. political, spiritual, moral, etc. Some names may need to be challenged and some defended.
		
		3 Ask the students to finish the sentences opposite to discover what perceptions they have about the terms.
		
		Use the three students or three pairs who previously have been briefed to prepare a five-minute lesson each demonstrating one of these styles.
		
		The object of the lesson could be to get the group to do a previously agreed task. The approaches should be practised and taken seriously – with follow-up discussion with those who were on the receiving end.

Student Objectives	Activities	Organisation and Method

To experience and then analyse the impact of differing styles of leadership, both on that task and on the interaction between 'leaders' and 'led'.	*NOTE*: This activity may be better carried out by one tutor-group working together, and using another unsuspecting tutor-group to 'experiment' with. Some help will be needed to develop the style, particularly *laissez faire*.
	
	Brief for the 'victim' group:
	
	'We would like you to help us with an experiment on styles of presentation. Please monitor how *you* are feeling whilst the experiment is in progress, but please respond as normally as possible, i.e. don't 'act' a response.'
	
	4 *Agenda for discussion*
	    Which style got things done?
	    Which style is most prevalent?
	    How did you feel?
	
	One of the purposes of a group leader may be to lead the group towards self-determination (autonomy).
	
	This model suggests that, as the leader exercises authority, he decreases the group's autonomy and vice versa.
		4 Follow-up discussion with the whole class.
		
		If the group of pupils is particularly interested in the concept of leadership, it may be valuable to continue the discussion in relation to the group's own experience of leading and being led, using the model opposite, asking whether their experience validates this model.

Student Objectives	Activities	Organisation and Method
To examine the nature of leadership and some of the different ways in which it is exercised. To experience and discuss the interchange of leadership and the interaction between 'leader' and 'led', in a simple task.	5 *Where do you fit?* There are many ways of showing leadership, and sometimes we need to 'follow' rather than lead, and vice versa. *Four hands on clay* An exercise in taking or following initiative and encouraging co-operation. *Agenda for discussion* If the activity has been carried out sensibly, and in a spirit of learning, discussion will flow naturally as soon as the silence is broken. What did it feel like? Did it tell you anything about yourself? Did you know who your partner was? What did you learn?	This activity needs some time and organisation, but is an interesting and worthwhile experience. It may be accomplished with the help of the art department. **You will need** Clean boards, overalls, scarves for blindfolds, and a lump of clay between two students With a large group, half could be observers and do the activity at a later date. All students taking part are blindfolded and led to a table with a partner – *unseen.* Some students should help to organise the activity, blindfolding and leading to seats, etc. Each pair has a lump of clay in front of them, and they are asked to make something together – *without speaking.* They have ten minutes in which to do it. Enforce the silence rule, and later make observations about how the pairs set about the task. Follow-up with class discussion.

Student Objectives	Activities	Organisation and Method
	Further activities Additional leadership activities could be provided by: a) Producing duplicated sheets of some famous speeches or situations and examining these in small groups to try to determine whether any kind of leadership is implicit and the way(s) in which it is made effective. b) Simulate situations in which different members of the group(s) can develop leadership, or ways of doing things, e.g. youth club, sixth-form committee, action group, etc.	

NOTE: Some tutors have found it better to tackle item 4, 'Who Has Authority?' before item 3, 'What is Authority?'. A few have found it useful to combine these two sections and tackle them together.

Student Objectives	Activities	Organisation and Method
To begin to think about authority; to examine its meaning and the ways in which it is both achieved and used.	*AN EXPLORATION OF AUTHORITY* 1 *'Mastermind'* What does it mean to be an 'authority'? The question and answer game as seen on TV. 2 *'Call my bluff'* Can you convince someone that you are an authority? How plausible, confident, inventive, can you be? Items 1 and 2 are intended as an introduction to the subject of authority and should not take too long. They should be concluded by a brief consideration of the difference in meaning between i) being *an* authority and ii) being *in* authority.	**You will need** To ask for volunteers to answer questions on a subject of their choice which must be submitted beforehand so that questions can be prepared. To recruit a chairman if necessary 1 It is suggested that this is done fairly spontaneously and not too seriously. Students need not be involved in 'swotting' up a subject, or researching obscure questions (i.e. simply a chair each for the chairman and contestant, surrounded by the class). 2 Invite students to choose a partner and try to convince him/her that they know all there is to know about an obscure subject which they have made up, or found in the Oxford Dictionary. The tutor may demonstrate first, either using the dictionary definition or one made up. Students may 'vote' true or false.

Student Objectives	Activities	Organisation and Method
To consider alternative points of view, defer judgement in argument and discussion, and build on other people's contributions.	3 *What is authority?*	3 Groups of four

Activities

3 *What is authority?*

What is it?	How do we react to it?	How do we recognise it?

What is it?	How do we react to it?	How do we recognise it?
power	respect it	through leadership
knowledge	resent it	someone's position
status	use it	being on the receiving end of it
responsibility	abuse it	having to exercise it
	accept it	
	reject it	

Student Objectives

To examine the nature of authority and individual reactions to it.

Organisation and Method

3 Groups of four

Introduce the topic by drawing three columns on the blackboard, using the columns opposite.

The session could then be conducted as a vigorous brainstorming session using the framework

or

The responses shown, which have been given by sixth-form groups (below), could be used as starters for discussion

or

Individual pupils could be asked to complete their own framework first, and then compare their own responses with those of others in the group.

Student Objectives	Activities	Organisation and Method
To develop insight into the viewpoint of people in authority, and the ways in which they exercise their authority.	4 *Who has authority?* Situations where authority is exercised: a) In society generally, e.g. police, media reports. b) In the family, e.g. parents – discipline – expectations brothers/sisters c) At school, e.g. headteacher/teachers examiners friends d) At work, e.g. boss/superior union mates machines *Agenda for discussion* How important is authority? Is it possible for a group, work force, society, to exist without authority, or will it always emerge in some form? How useful is it to explore a concept like authority?	Four groups. Each chooses one of the categories opposite to consider, and then enact a simple scene showing how authority is exercised. Encourage each group to show an obvious situation, and then a more subtle one. The demonstrations may be followed by a general summary of points which have been made or learned in follow-up discussion (see agenda opposite).

Student Objectives	Activities	Organisation and Method
To evaluate his responsibility to home (parents), community, school and self, and consider the relationship between responsibility and authority.	5 *Me and authority* This 'model' may help us to examine our own positions: **At school** **At home** .... **ME** ———————— **ME** .... **At school** **Under me** **Over me** Lower-school pupils — Headteacher (ME) — Form tutor Some of my friends — Subject teachers ?- Friend -? *Agenda for discussion* Why do we place some people 'above' or 'below' ourselves? Is it possible to coexist without authority? Is it always bestowed or can it emerge? How do we gain authority? How have others gained authority? Is authority sometimes confused with influence or responsibility?	a) Either in pairs or individually, the pupils use the model opposite, taking each situation in turn and writing names of those whom they think are in authority over them, or over whom they feel they have authority. b) Taking either of the lists, the pupils could then explore their feelings towards the people whom they have identified. The question is posed – How warm or cool do you feel to the persons on your list? The feelings could be shown diagrammatically as opposite (the length of the line or distance from *ME* indicating warmth or coolness).

67

Student Objectives	Activities	Organisation and Method
To show a willingness to make a positive contribution to the activities of the group, at the same time ensuring equal opportunity for everyone to take part.	*RULES AND RIGHTS: RULES I* Bits and Pieces (APPENDIX 30) – the need for rules. What happens when there are no rules?	You will need APPENDIX 30, Bits and Pieces equipment and task sheet The students form groups of five. With larger groups it is easy for students to 'opt out'. Each group is given an envelope with equipment and task sheet. All the groups should open the envelope and start the task at the same time. The activity finishes when either one group finishes, or when sufficient time has elapsed for the problem which is built into the activity to have become clear.
	Agenda for discussion What happened? Why did it happen? What made you decide to get up and go and ask someone? How did you set about the task? What feelings were aroused? What rules could be imposed which would help? Is the activity as much fun when abiding by the rules?	It is helpful if the tutor circulates, making notes on points which can be brought up in the following discussion. Follow-up with whole class discussion (see agenda opposite). *NOTE*: It can be interesting to try Bits and Pieces with and without the 'first to finish out to me' motivation, in order to examine whether or not behaviour changes under pressure/motivation. The questions may then be asked: Is this excusable? forgivable? acceptable? In the same groups, the students suggest a set of rules which could be applied to the activity so that the task could be completed in an orderly fashion.

Student Objectives	Activities	Organisation and Method
To re-evaluate responsibility to home, community, school and self.	*RULES AND RIGHTS: RULES II – WRITTEN AND UNWRITTEN* 'Let us clear our thinking on what we mean by rules.' *Agenda for discussion* What is a rule? Do existing rules fit our agreed definition? a) School rules? b) Are there rules for familes? 　　What are they? 　　Do they fit our definition? c) Are there rules for the places you go to, e.g. football matches, the cinema, youth club, etc.? 　　Do the rules fit our agreed definition? d) Are there rules for social situations, e.g. meeting people, between men and women, etc.? e) What other situations have rules? Is it correct, according to our agreed definition, to refer to all the above situations as having rules – or are they something else?	Still in groups of five, the students consider the first question on the agenda, trying to agree on a general definition, which should be written up. After working through the agenda opposite, continue using the step-by-step process to help the students articulate what they perceive to be the differences between rules and laws; society mores; group norms.

Student Objectives	Activities	Organisation and Method
To gain knowledge about the processes of socialisation, particularly with reference to norms, mores, codes, etc.	f) Where do all these rules, written or otherwise, come from? g) Are some rules fundamental to society at large? What is the 'Declaration of Human Rights'?	Outcomes of this discussion could be summarised on a chart under headings, e.g. | Situation	Written Rules	Unwritten Rules	Society Codes
---	---	---	---
				  Ask the students to try and find out about the 'Declaration of Human Rights' before the next session.

NOTE: This discussion is intended to lead into a study of the students' own rights under the law at certain ages; those which they feel they ought to have; and those which often engender strong feelings. The extent to which this unit is taken is left to the teacher's discretion.

Student Objectives	Activities	Organisation and Method
To show interest in and concern for major philosophical and moral issues, and begin to formulate his own philosophy.	*RULES AND RIGHTS: RIGHTS*	**You will need** APPENDIX 31, United National Organisation Declaration of Human Rights – one each or one between two An examination of the Declaration of Human Rights, APPENDIX 31, could lead to a discussion about rights, and could lead on to a discussion about which rules and laws uphold the Declaration, and which of the declared Human Rights are open to debate, even through recourse to a court of law, e.g. the European Court of Human Rights (for example, the case of caning pupils taken to the European Court by two parents in 1982).

Student Objectives	Activities	Organisation and Method
To demonstrate a knowledge of his/her rights under the law and be able to judge the consequences of certain actions and know what to do in certain situations, e.g. unemployment, claiming tax.	1 *An age continuum* At what age must you, or can you . . . 12 years a) leave home without parents' consent b) be held fully responsible for a crime c) hold a licence to drive a car d) vote e) join a trade union f) make a will g) enter a betting shop h) buy fireworks i) pay adult contributions to National Insurance j) pay adult fares on buses k) own an air rifle l) serve on a jury 16 years m) become an MP You may n) be employed full-time and leave pay tax school o) take part-time employment p) take out hire purchase q) hold a motorcycle licence r) drink in a pub s) join the armed forces t) buy cigarettes u) marry without your parents' consent v) choose your own doctor w) own your own house x) have your own passport y) see an 18-certificate film on your own 21 years z) claim supplementary benefit	1 An example of a continuum is given in the Activities column opposite. Draw this on the blackboard and then ask the students to draw an age continuum of their own on a sheet of paper. Next, give out the list of statements opposite, and ask the students to place them on their continuum according to the age at which they know or think they apply. Code letters a, b, c . . . may be used. Give a limit of, say, four to five minutes for this part of the activity.

Student Objectives	Activities	Organisation and Method
	Agenda for discussion	When the students have completed the placements a to z, they can then join up into twos or threes and compare their own continuum, discussing any discrepancies. It is important for the students to identify gaps in their own knowledge, and try to find out the answers before the next session.
	What has surprised you?	
	Was there anything that most of the group did not know?	
	Was there anything about which we all made the same mistake? If so, why was this?	
	How do we get to know this kind of information?	The agenda for discussion opposite may carry over two sessions before and after the correct answers are known.
	What consequences would there be in not knowing any of this information?	
To experience the sense of 'personal investment' which comes from advocating a point of view strongly, and the difficulty that can be involved in accepting other arguments and/or changing one's stand-point when one has already invested time, effort and emotion in the original stand-point/belief.	2 *Stand-point taking*	2 The previous discussion could be followed by this activity, particularly if the students feel strongly about any of the issues raised, e.g. differences of opinion about drinking laws.
	What happens when we feel strongly about something?	
	This is a ring-game activity; it is about taking a particular stand-point and arguing a case from that point of view.	Form two circles, an inner circle sits facing outwards, with the outer circle facing inwards; thus, each student has a partner.
	After arguing 'their' case twice to two different people, the participants reverse their stand-points and argue the opposite case with a third person.	a) The topic for the debate is given, and all the people in the inner circle must argue from one stand-point, and all the people in the outside circle argue from the opposite point of view. They have five minutes to marshall their arguments and try to convince their partner.
	Example: 'The licensing laws of this country are out of date. If young people can be married at sixteen, they should be allowed to drink in a pub.'	
	All the inside circle agree with this statement. Those on the outside disagree.	

73

Student Objectives	Activities	Organisation and Method
	Observation Whilst this activity is proceeding, observe what is going on, or select two or three students to do this, noting the following: Do some people find it difficult to get going? Who dominates and how? What strategies are used, gesticulations, etc.? What happens the second time when the time is cut? Is there evidence of people 'warming' to their own argument? What happens if someone cannot 'get a word in edgewise'? The activity can be stopped before three minutes have elapsed, to discuss the process. *Agenda for discussion* What happened? What did you find difficult/easy? How easy is it to listen when you have your own point of view which you want to put? Did you listen? How did you feel? Were you convinced by anyone else? Do you think you were successful? Did intimidation occur? How? After arguing one way, were you too committed to your argument to be able to change sides easily?	b) After five minutes, stop the debate. Suggest that now that everyone has had an opportunity to marshall their thoughts and hear the counter-arguments, they should be able to put their point of view clearly and succinctly. All the people on the outside move two paces clockwise around the circle, thus finding a new partner with whom to debate. Take the *same* stand-point as before, but this time allow only three minutes. c) After three minutes, stop. Now suggest that everyone must be really very good. The outer circle moves round two places clockwise again. They make ready to argue again from the same stand-point. At the *last moment* tell them that they have changed their minds. This time, all the people on the inside disagree strongly with the statement, and all those on the outside agree with it. They have three minutes to argue from this opposite stand-point. The time limits are important in helping to realise this particular objective which is about investment, involvement, commitment and stand-point taking. Deeper discussion should come in the follow-up discussion, using the agenda opposite. This process can be used to examine a number of issues, even though the impact of suddenly having to change sides is not there. Knowing this is coming adds a different dimension to the way in which the students use their arguments, e.g. anticipating counter-arguments.
To consider alternative points of view, defer judgement in argument and discussion and build on other people's contributions.		

74

NOTE: Everyone belongs to some group or other; the human group, the family, the work-force, boys, girls, wives . . . . For the purposes of this discussion, a smaller, more immediate group is intended. Even if any student feels he/she does not belong to any particular group, benefit will still be gained from the discussion.

Student Objectives	Activities	Organisation and Method

To develop an understanding of human relationships and what is involved in dealing with people.	*LOOKING AT GROUPS*
	
	One idea of how groups, other than purely social ones, function is that they usually have a task, and a 'climate'. It will be difficult to complete the task unless the 'climate' is satisfactory for the group members.
	
	Sometimes members have ascribed functions, e.g. chairperson, secretary, and sometimes they are 'roles' which are assumed by group members, perhaps better known as leader and recorder. Group members may perform different functions at different times.
	
	1 *Functions*
	   A brief group activity enabling students to experience the functions of:
	   i) chairperson
	   ii) secretary
	   during brief discussion of a given topic.
		The brief notes opposite may be used to lead into a general discussion on the role of chairperson. As most students have not had experience of 'chairing' meetings and taking minutes, it will be well worth providing some experience of this first.
		
		You will need
		To have selected a number of topics for discussion
		
		1 Divide the class into groups of six or eight, with a discussion taking place simultaneously in each group for approximately ten minutes. Ask one person to take the chair and another to act as secretary, taking minutes. An observer in each group will report on how the 'chairperson' performed, after the 'secretary' has read out the minutes.

To demonstrate listening and communication skills by being willing to develop arguments whilst respecting the opinions of others.	*Agenda for brief discussion* How did it feel to be chairperson? How did it feel to be secretary? What *feelings* were shown during your discussion? What feelings were *not* shown? How much control did the person in the chair have?	*Follow-up class discussion:* We know what took place, but how did it 'feel' to be a participant in this experience? Do the minutes necessarily tell us what the 'climate' of the 'meeting' was like? What do we mean by 'climate'?

Student Objectives	Activities	Organisation and Method
		You will need APPENDIX 32, Group Membership Functions
	2 *Other group membership functions* APPENDIX 32 gives a list of other suggested group functions: a) for getting the task done b) for maintaining the 'climate'.	2 General discussion with the students describing some of the behaviour which can be seen in groups and trying to identify it with the kind of functions a) and b) suggested opposite. Using APPENDIX 32, Group Membership Functions the tutor provides a label for the kind of behaviours described and writes them on the board or large sheet of paper, under the broader labels of 'task' or 'maintenance function'.
To demonstrate listening skills and a degree of self-confidence. To be aware of the needs and problems of others in the group, by showing a willingness to provide and receive support and share experiences.	**3** *Groups to which I belong* Agenda for step-by-step discussion. a) Tell the others to which groups you belong (e.g. family group, tutor group, friendship group, subject group, etc.). b) How long has it been a group? c) How did it form? d) How long have you been a member? e) What are the goals of the group? Are they obvious, stated ones, or hidden? f) How often does the group meet? g) Who holds the group together? h) Have your feelings towards the group changed? Finally, can you tell another person something about him or her and their group?	3 Form-groups of three. Lead the groups into a step-by-step discussion (see Introductory Note, Step-By-Step Discussion, page xviii). Use the agenda opposite for a consideration of what groups do. After a) they should go on to consider one particular group, other than the family group, each student choosing his own group for this deeper study. Point out that: • Some of the questions may not apply to all groups. • Each person should answer as it applies to the group which he has identified for himself. • Encourage the pupils to think more deeply about some of the questions, e.g. e) and h). The teacher will need to join each group briefly at this point, contributing the kind of lead or 'prompt' which will lead to this deeper, more thoughtful discussion.

Student Objectives	Activities	Organisation and Method
To take an active part in developing tutor-group identity, and becoming aware of the importance of every-one's contribution, including his/her own. To become aware of a tutor-group identity by showing interest in and concern for its members.	4 *Our group* 'Line Up' – this activity is used to emphasise positive contributions to the group by looking at what tasks the tutor-group has to undertake, and how the members perform them together, e.g. initiating – proposing things to do, defining group problems, suggesting procedures. The 'line up' shows who does this type of thing most often, and who only seldom. Most Seldom Often-/\-/\-/\-/\-/\-/\-Sometimes Where one person organises the line, the 'line up' is how the person doing the arranging sees things. Ask people if they are happy with their places. Ask if they would like to change this 'image'. Ask how they might set about changing it. Encourage discussion and disagree-ment. Encourage positive feedback for those who continually place themselves at one end. *Final discussion* Draw attention to the roles which people took in the activity, i.e. moving people them-selves or being pushed around, dissidents. Did we learn anything from this exercise?	4 Introduce the activity with whole tutor group discus-sion on the 'tasks' or 'purposes' of the tutor group. Write these on the board. If the tutor group is large, split it into two and deal with the two halves, either one at a time or simultaneously. Refer to the earlier lists of group-membership func-tions. Ask the group(s) to arrange group members in a line according to how often each member performs in that role, i.e. a concrete continuum of behaviour (see opposite). The groups may either organise themselves or, if they cannot agree, one person may arrange the line as he/she sees it. Have a different person organising each function. Students will often disagree with the places which other pupils allot to themselves, and will join in rearranging the line. Encourage full and free discus-sion as the movement and rearrangement proceeds. It is suggested that the objectives for this activity are shared with the group, to see if they have any meaning for the pupils.

77

Student Objectives	Activities	Organisation and Method
To understand the organisation and administration of an institution.	*UNDERSTANDING THE SYSTEM: SCHOOL CAREER* This activity enables students to re-examine their school career to date, objectively, and discuss some of the factors which might have influenced it.	Ask the students to find a partner who they believe to be most unlike themselves (see examples opposite). The students should have a short conversation with their partner to find out what other differences there are between them.
To take an active part in developing tutor-group identity, by being aware of the importance of eveyone's contribution.	Differences which would be used to determine choice of partner: • Someone taking different subjects. • Someone from a large or small family. • Someone who lives in a different neighbourhood. • Someone who was born in a different part of the country.	
Show a willingness to make a positive contribution to the activities of the group, at the same time ensuring equal opportunity for everyone to take part.	*Agenda* Tell your partner: where your very first school was what you remember about it **School** ↑ etc. | 14	
13	
12	
11	Started at
10	secondary school
9	
8	Moved to England
7	Changed school
	Unhappy
6	
Years 5	Started school in Scotland Liked it.		Then ask them to concentrate on schooling (see agenda opposite). Still in pairs, the students go on to discuss their school 'career'. It might be helpful if the tutor outlined his/her own school career first, using a 'ladder' analogy as in the example opposite.

78

Student Objectives	Activities	Organisation and Method
To listen and interpret meaning accurately.	What were the main influences during your school career?	Another 'ladder' beside the school one could be labelled *Home*, so that students could plot parallel events which they feel influenced their schooling. The pairs should be encouraged to help each other through discussion about the events.
To demonstrate listening skills.	Try to understand why your partner thinks a particular event or person was significant.	The tutor should encourage the students to check that they have understood correctly what their partner has said.
	Example:	There is often more than one interpretation (see example opposite).
	'When I was ten my mother was in hospital for a long time.'	
	'Were you worried about her?'	
	'Yes, and I couldn't talk to anyone about going to secondary school'	
	or	
To develop an awareness of others as individuals.	'No, but I had to do the housework and shopping and couldn't do school work properly.'	

Student Objectives	Activities	Organisation and Method
	UNDERSTANDING THE SYSTEM: WHO DOES WHAT IN SCHOOL/COLLEGE	
To develop an awareness of the influence exerted on education by individuals and groups.	This unit could follow the one on school career, or be treated separately.	In small groups, the students discuss their ideas of who decides what in their school or college, first listing all the decisions which they think have to be made (see agenda opposite).
	Agenda for discussion	
	1) What are the decisions which have to be made? Who makes them?	
	2) How many people share in making joint decisions?	
	3) Does one decision depend on what other decisions are made first?	The conclusions from the above discussion need to be verified. To do this some students might interview the people in school who, it is believed, make certain decisions, before the next session.
	4) What are the consequences or implications of these decisions?	
To select and use information.	*How do we know?*	All the group devise an agenda for the students to use in the interviews and practise the approach. (*See How do we know* opposite.)
	When approaching members of staff to verify conclusions —	
	What will you ask? Who will you ask? How will you ask?	
Develop critical awareness through an examination of the organisation of the establishment.	*NOTE:* Decisions need to be made about how to answer the question 'Why are you asking me these questions?'	
To take a leadership role in the group by making contributions to the activities of the group.	*Were we right?* About the kinds of decisions which have to be made. Are there any others?	You will need Copies of Education Acts
Demonstrate listening skills and a degree of self-confidence in challenging situations.	About who makes decisions — at what level, etc.?	The students, who have conducted interviews on the group's behalf into school decision-making, report back to the group.

Student Objectives	Activities	Organisation and Method
Develop an awareness of the social forces which influence personal life.	*UNDERSTANDING THE SYSTEM; SCHOOL LEGISLATION* *Agenda for discussion* What are the rules? How and why are they made? Are all rules written down? What are the 'hidden' rules? How are they made known? What influence do the students themselves have on a) the institution? b) one another? Are rules different in the sixth-form?	Each small group suggests a school rule which they feel is just and necessary, and one which they feel is not. A spokesman from each group must justify their choice to the rest of the tutor-group. The groups are asked to consider 'hidden' rules and expectations. This is followed by more general discussion along the lines suggested opposite.
To select and use information, developing skills in drawing conclusions from more general information which are relevant to personal life.	*Legislation in education* What is the extent of the students' knowledge of the 1944 and 1980 Education Acts? (Ref. synopsis from ACE). Consideration of a brief outline and summary of education before and since the 1944 Education Act. How are the terms of the Act enforced? Are the terms open to interpretation?	Teacher-led step-by-step discussion in small groups. The agenda for the various steps will need to be carefully prepared (see Introductory Note on Step-By-Step Discussion page xviii).

Student Objectives	Activities	Organisation and Method
To understand the administration of the establishment.

To entertain people in positions of authority with sincerity and without self-consciousness. | *Functions of Public Authorities, School Governors and the Inspectorate, Administrators, etc.*

Preparing for and receiving visitors.

Learning from the visitors. | This section lends itself particuarly to inviting LEA officials and HM Inspectorate to be visitors to the group, which prepares the questions and the social side of the visit carefully beforehand, taking all responsibility for the occasion, i.e. meeting the visitor, introducing him/her.

There should be consideration of how to make the visitor welcome:

● Who will ask the first question?
● What will it be?
● What do we want to find out?
● What personal questions can we ask?
● Who will bring it to an end? etc.

Each group of six or eight could be responsible for a different visitor, providing a range of experience and opinion, including parent, governor and student representative, Chairman of PTA.

(See Introductory Note on The Visitor, page xx.) |

Student Objectives	Activities	Organisation and Method
To understand the organisation of the establishment.	*UNDERSTANDING THE SYSTEM: THE SCHOOL CURRICULUM* What does the time-table tell us about the institution? Is anything missing? Could anything be left out? How are time-tables made? What kind of considerations have to be taken into account, including personal feelings and preferences? E.g. What do you think a teacher feels about substituting?	**You will need** School time-tables. Time-table game A discussion about the usefulness or otherwise of various subjects. Comparison with time-table from other institutions (possible examples from France, Germany, etc. if available). In groups of four, complete an ideal time-table for a teacher in their school, taking classes lower down the school, i.e. not a teacher who takes mainly sixth-form. The students should decide what subject 'their teacher' takes, and construct a balanced weekly time-table for this fictitious teacher.
To understand what the sixth-form tutor can do for the students in his group, and how they can help him to function most effectively, and know the role and function of other members of staff.	*Visitors* Interview with the member of staff responsible for constructing the time-table.	The students could find out from the 'time-tabler' in the school what is involved in making a time-table, through a 'visit', and find out from their own tutor in a similar way what is involved in being a form tutor.
To be able to assess his/her own skills realistically, and compare it with the assessment of others.	*UNDERSTANDING THE SYSTEM; ASSESSMENT* Analysing forms of measurement and assessment used in the school.	1 An introductory activity might be to set up a light-hearted competition, e.g. Strength Beauty } to lead into the topic of General Knowledge assessment and difficulties of standardisation and judging, etc.

Student Objectives	Activities	Organisation and Method
	Agenda for discussion	2 In groups, the students discuss the main forms of assessment which they have experienced.
	– How are external exams set and marked?	Using the step-by-step agenda opposite, the tutor helps the group to explore their attitudes to assessment.
	– How much say is there as to which exams to take?	
	– What happens to you in an exam?	This could lead to a longer discussion about self-assessment and how they might go about it, drawing on published material ref. D Hamblin, *Study Skills*.
	– How do you prepare yourself?	
	– What do you think about preparing the questions beforehand?	
	– Should you be able to take books into the exam?	
	– Which do you prefer – continuous assessment or end-of-year exam?	
	– What are the merits and demerits of either?	
	– Where does self-assessment fit in?	
To develop the ability to marshall arguments, put forward views succinctly.	*UNDERSTANDING THE SYSTEM: STAND-POINT TAKING*	Make two circles, one person sits facing outwards, with his partner in the outer circle facing him.
	Exploring all aspects of the topic of assessment.	The tutor outlines the two opposing view points and assigns one view point to each circle of students (see opposite).
	How far does the existing assessment system further competition or co-operation between students?	
	How effective are exams, and how far do they influence the curriculum?	

Student Objectives	Activities	Organisation and Method
To be able to take a broad view of issues and listen to more than one point of view before making up one's mind.	1 All the people in the inner circle think that examinations are ineffective, an unnecessary evil and could be replaced by some other form of assessment. All those in the outer circle think that examinations are essential and are the best form of assessment.	1 The students must set out the view point assigned to them, regardless of whether they hold with it, and try to make their partner, in about five minutes, change their view point.
	2 The first time was a 'practice'. The students in the outer circle now move round clockwise, two places, and try again to convince the new partner from the *same* stand-point, that their arguments are more persuasive.	2 The students are told they will have only half the amount of time this time, so they must try to be as succinct as possible.
To take an enthusiastic part in debate, by being prepared to follow up discussions and take the trouble to become more informed.	3 The outer circle moves on two places again, but just before they start, tell them that they have changed their minds, i.e. all those in the inner circle take the view which has just been argued by those in the outside, and vice versa.	3 The tutor should watch for various points to use in the discussion after the activity is over, e.g. anyone finding it difficult to change anyone finding it difficult to argue from a point of view they don't hold anyone raising their voice or gesticulating in an effort to dominate their partner anyone who cannot get a word in 'edgeways', etc. These examples should be described by the students themselves, involving how they felt.

Student Objectives	Activities	Organisation and Method
To consider alternative points of view, defer judgement in argument and discussion, and build on other people's contributions.	*Agenda for discussion* Who found it difficult? What happened? How did you go about it? Who changed/gave up as a result of hearing their partner's argument? Where did your arguments come from? What could be learned from this exercise?	
	Moderating Marking each other's essays. Developing criteria for moderating or 'standardising' subjective assessment.	The students could be asked to write an essay on assessment (or another topic) and suggest a mark out of a set score for their own work. In three's, students then read each other's work in-dependently, and award one another marks, so that each student gets three separate marks for their own essay.
To assess his/her own progress and compare it with the assessment of others.	*Question for discussion* Do you feel able to assess your own work and monitor your own progress?	These are put side by side and compared. The teacher could also provide a mark for each student. All these results should be discussed in groups of three, to see if the marks should now be revised.

86

NOTE: The following activities – Pairs, I've Got a . . . , Famous People, I Believe . . . – form a unit which is meant to develop over several sessions. A line –·–·–·–·– denotes a suitable breaking point.

Student Objectives	Activities	Organisation and Method
To take small steps towards imaginative and creative, rather than rigid and repetitive approaches, and move from convergent to divergent thinking.	*PAIRS* A quick warm-up activity to demonstrate how lacking in originality we often are. *Agenda for discussion* – Why did so many people think of the same words? – If we did the same exercise again, say in two weeks' time, do you think you would give the same responses? – Has it to do with our 'pattern of life'?	**You will need** One piece of paper for each student 1 Give each student a blank piece of paper and ask him/her to write on it the first word that comes into his/her head when he hears certain words read aloud by the tutor. 2 The tutor reads about ten common words, *e.g. pen, house, tree*, etc., from a prepared list. The list should be read fairly quickly, so that the students only have time to write down the first word they think of. 3 When the list of ten is completed, go through it again, asking for a show of hands to indicate how many people in the group thought of the same words each time. –·

Student Objectives	Activities	Organisation and Method
To take small steps towards imaginative and creative, rather than rigid and repetitive approaches, and move from convergent to divergent thinking.	*I'VE GOT A . . .* An activity to stimulate original thought.	1 Tell the students that you would now like to move on from common words to one which you are sure they have not heard of before. This is a . . . (it should be your name spelt backwards, e.g. ALIEHS = SHEILA, but do not reveal this information at this stage).
		2 Describe the use or origin of this word, being as original and inventive as you can, e.g. an *aliehs* is a very unusual whistle which derives its name from the sound it makes, 'ali–ehs'. It is a means of communicating secretly with other *aliehs* owners in code. It is obviously cheaper than the phone and means that if I visit a strange town or country, I have only to use my *aliehs* to be connected with 'friends'.
		3 At this stage, hold up a piece of paper with the word written on it in capitals. It does not take long for some of the students to realise what it really is.
		4 Ask the students to practice saying their names backwards to each other. It is sometimes easier to write it down first.
		5 Divide the students into threes. Each one creates and then describes to the others some 'invented' object to which they give their name (backwards).

Student Objectives	Activities	Organisation and Method
	Agenda for discussion	6 Follow-up discussion (see agenda opposite).
	Have you ever been involved in creating anything original? Encourage the students to think of simple things, e.g. baking a cake, playing music in a group, painting, either a picture or a bedroom.	
	Can you think of anyone who became famous because they followed their original inspirations, even though they may have seemed silly to others at the time, e.g. Darwin, Florence Nightingale, Bell, Stephenson, Picasso, etc.? Which three people do you admire most? Think about it before next session.	

Student Objectives	Activities	Organisation and Method
To take small steps towards imaginative and creative, rather than rigid and repetitive approaches, and move from convergent to divergent thinking.	*FAMOUS PEOPLE*	**You will need** One piece of paper per student 1 Divide the students into groups of six – eight. 2 Give each one a piece of paper. 3 Ask them to write on it in 'unrecognisable' capitals the names of three famous people whom they admire because they followed their original inspirations. 4 Ask the students to fold their papers once only and then exchange them within their group about five times. 5 The students then open the fifth paper they receive (checking that it is not their own) and then try to decide who, in the group, is likely to have chosen the three people whose names are on the paper. 6 Give them a few moments to decide this and then the students, in turn, read out the names on their paper, adding the name of the student to whom they think the paper belongs. 7 The paper is returned to its owner. 8 When all the papers are back with the owners, the students now say, in turn, why they chose those particular people. 9 Follow-up discussion – see agenda opposite.
	Agenda for discussion – How surprised were you at . . .? – Do these people have any qualities in common? – How easy/difficult was it for them to follow their inclinations? – Did they work alone or with others? Which is the easiest? – If you have an interest, how could you meet other people with similar interests (e.g. join a society)? – Before the next session, think of a society (existing locally or not) which you might like to join.	

Student Objectives	Activities	Organisation and Method
To be aware of the philosophies/ beliefs of other people.	**I BELIEVE** A group activity to encourage students to think about their beliefs and to listen to and comment on the beliefs of others.	**You will need** One piece of paper per student 1 Ask the students to sit in a circle. 2 Give each student a blank piece of paper and ask him/her to write his name on one side and, on the other, a statement beginning with: *I believe . . .*, e.g. *I believe that capital punishment should be reinstated.* Make clear that statements such as 'I believe I have a chemistry exam tomorrow' are not statements of belief and, therefore, are not acceptable for this exercise. 3 One student (A) is asked to read out his statement and then place his paper, name downwards, on the floor in the centre of the circle. 4 The other students are then asked to place their paper, names upwards, on the floor somewhere between where they are sitting and where the statement has been placed in the centre of the circle, depending on how much they agree with it. 5 Student (A) now chooses one of the names on the floor and asks its owner to comment on why he has placed his paper in that particular place. 6 The papers are then picked up and the process is repeated, either by taking turns around the group, or by the student who has just been asked to comment putting his statement into the centre.

Student Objectives	Activities	Organisation and Method
To be aware of the philosophies/ beliefs of other people.	*Agenda for discussion* a) What did you think of that (develop other questions from the answers given). b) How extreme are most of your views? c) How easy do you find it to tolerate the strongly-held beliefs of others? d) Did you, or did you not, want to hear the views of those who held the opposite of yours (from the way they positioned their papers)? Why? e) How frustrated were you if you were not chosen to comment about strongly held views? f) Did the person saying 'I believe . . .' have any other significant influence (pressure, friendship, extreme views, etc.)? Did knowing whose belief it was colour whether you agreed or disagreed? g) How and why do you feel you chose that particular belief? h) Is it easier to follow the crowd than feel 'out of it'? i) Did you discover someone who had the same/different beliefs? j) How do you think your views, as a group, agree or disagree? k) What did you think of the method?	7 General discussion (see opposite). It is unlikely that the objective will be achieved in one session, but this is an activity to which the group can return easily and profitably at intervals.

NOTE: Tutors may wish to revise the dialogue which is provided. The essential principle is simplicity and directness to allow for an ensuing discussion about the complexities of varying conflict situations.

Student Objectives	Activities	Organisation and Method
To begin to develop and be aware of a personal philosophy of life. To develop a sense of tolerance and understanding and sympathy for other people's views.	*ALL YOU NEED IS UNDERSTANDING 1: CONFLICT AND CONFRONTATION* A simple role-play enacting a conflict/confrontation situation.	You will need APPENDIX 33, Dialogue of Role-Play *Introductory activity* Tutor to introduce the scenario for a simple role-play of a confrontation situation. The whole tutor-group may be divided amongst those groups indicated in APPENDIX 33, in order that they are involved from a particular standpoint. See Introductory Note on Role-Play, p. xxvii. The actors are chosen and the simple role-play enacted with the minimum of preparation and fuss.

To develop an awareness that many social forces influence personal life.
 	
To recognise the influence exerted by individuals and groups.
	Agenda for discussion
	
	What do we understand by the terms 'conflict' and 'confrontation'?
	
	Are they all as simple as the first activity might suggest?
	
	How does conflict arise?
	
	Suggest other situations which contain potential for conflict, and in which confrontation might arise, nearer to the students' experience, e.g.
	    home and family
	    between friends
	    at school/college.
		It is followed by the whole tutor-group engaging in discussion along the lines suggested opposite.
		
		The discussion is the key activity for which the role-play is simply the stimulus.

Student Objectives	Activities	Organisation and Method
To develop a sense of tolerance and understanding for other people's views.	*ALL YOU NEED IS UNDERSTANDING II: AN INDUSTRIAL DISPUTE or 'NOTHING IS EVER THAT SIMPLE'*	You will need APPENDIX 34, suggested Scenario and Characters for 'An Industrial Dispute' APPENDIX 35, Loaded Statements, one copy of each per person
	Preparation for group standpoint taking in a stereotyped scenario which might be taken from a news item on TV or from a daily paper.	In groups of four, students are asked to adopt the stand-point of one of the groups represented in the scenario, using APPENDIX 34, An Industrial Dispute. One volunteer from each group acts the main character, helped by the group during discussion. Each group has some time to rehearse attitudes and dialogue.
	'Line Up' – Where do your sympathies lie? Line up in sympathy groups, and alter the sympathies/line up as the scenario develops.	One member of each group stands in a line to represent each point of view, and is given a card which summarises the viewpoint, which he may read out or enact (role-play) if he wishes. The tutor asks everyone to line up behind the representative group with which they have the greatest sympathy. APPENDIX 35, Loaded Statements – information to supply on cards to each group representative. The representatives now read the information on their card in turn. Stress the need to listen carefully. Be aware of how an emotional appeal may influence.
	Agenda for discussion Was it difficult to decide where your sympathies lay? How much movement was there as each stand-point was put forward? Is it possible to see everyone's point of view?	After each statement in turn, students are invited to change groups if their sympathies towards a group change. A short discussion following each realignment of sympathies may be needed, with a final discussion of the whole process (see agenda opposite).

Student Objectives	Activities	Organisation and Method
To show an interest in and concern for philosophical and moral issues, and begin to formulate a personal philosophy. To develop the power to argue a case, and yet see other points of view.	*TAKING IT ALL ON BOARD* Personal philosophies. How are they formed? What influences them? This topic is approached here through discussions of topical issues. If the objectives are to be achieved, work of this kind will have to be undertaken more than once. There is enough material on the issue cards to allow this unit to be returned to several times.	**You will need** One sheet of Issue Cards, APPENDIX 36, per student 1 Distribute sheets of issue cards to students, instructing them to choose one card which they feel is *most* in tune with their personal philosophies. Point out to the students that there may not be a card with which they can totally agree, and therefore compromises may have to be made. With some groups it may be necessary to go through the issues in APPENDIX 36 explaining the meanings of words and phrases where necessary (e.g. 'head of state', 'forfeit their own lives'). It may be necessary to amend the cards with some groups in order to make them appropriate to their level. 2 After giving the students a specified time in which to have chosen their card (e.g. five minutes), ask them to sit with a partner. 3 Students should then be given about ten minutes to formulate their ideas through discussion with their partners. 4 If it becomes apparent that a student has chosen a card which he did not fully understand, he could be allowed to change it at this stage. 5 The students should now be regrouped into threes or fours. Each student is allowed about five minutes to 'defend' his card.

Student Objectives	Activities	Organisation and Method
To show an interest in and concern for philosophical and moral issues, and begin to formulate a personal philosophy. To develop the power to argue a case, and yet see other points of view.	*Agenda for discussion* a) How easy was it to choose a card in the first place? b) How many students realised later that they had not fully understood the meaning of all the points on their card at first reading? c) How difficult was it to defend the points which they had to decide to compromise on? d) Which points did students in general feel most/least strongly about? e) How are our philosophies formed? (Influence of parents, teachers, friends, personal reading, media, advertisements, personal experience, etc.) f) How do we, as communities, reach decisions on contentious issues (see Organising Opinion p. 122 and Community Concerns p. 116). With groups who have done this kind of topic before, or who consider themselves very 'aware', the emphasis can be changed by adopting the approach given opposite.	6 The whole group is now brought together for further discussion (see agenda opposite). In place of 3 above, the emphasis should be on *supportive* questioning in order to explain and clarify the other's viewpoint. No 'attacking' questions should be allowed at this stage. Rearrange the group into pairs of twos (fours). In turn, each partner advocates their partner's viewpoint and supports their partner as the other pair 'attack' with challenging questions.

Student Objectives	Activities	Organisation and Method
To show an interest in and concern for philosophical and moral issues, and begin to formulate a personal philosophy. To develop the power to argue a case, and yet see other points of view.		These sessions can produce intense frustration, but the lessons of tolerance and support are well learned. A further exercise may be to allow the groups of four to choose items from their issue cards and together form them into the 'backbone' of a manifesto which, if time permits, or on some other occasion, can be placed before the rest of the group in a form of mini-election campaign. This links well with Community Concerns p. 116.

Student Objectives	Activities	Organisation and Method
To encourage personal assessment and identify limitations. To promote a happy climate within the immediate peer group (the tutor-group).	*DREAMING* A light-hearted activity to introduce or break up a more serious session on preparation for the future. The students indulge in dreaming over the sort of future they would like to see for themselves, given no constraints or limitations. Examples of 'dreams': swim the Channel both ways sail round the world become a chess grandmaster be a dancer form a pop group. (Add others which may be more relevant to the particular group.) Example of indirect questions: Why do you enjoy solo sailing? (Round-the-world yachtsman) *Agenda for discussion* Were you surprised by anyone's dream? How did you find out or why did you guess a particular person? What would stop you realising the dream? Do you think you will ever try to achieve it?	In twos, the students talk to each other about what they would like to do or become in their lives, if there were no limitations. Encourage imagination and flights of fancy! The tutor might begin by talking about what he or she would have liked to have done, instead of teaching. On separate pieces of paper, each student writes his/her 'dream' as briefly as possible. The papers are folded and all the students exchange their papers with each other until they are sure they have not got their own paper back. Back in the original pairs, the students try to work out whose 'dream' is on their piece of paper. They are then encouraged to see if they guessed correctly, or find out whose 'dream' it is by moving around and asking *indirect* questions, giving the paper back to its owner when they find him. They sit down when they have been given their own paper back and have found the owner of the paper which they have received in the exchange. Encourage discussion in small groups about the 'dreams'.

Student Objectives	Activities	Organisation and Method
To encourage personal assessment and identify limitations. To promote a happy climate within the immediate peer group (the tutor-group).	*Epitaph!* An alternative approach to the 'Dreaming' activity. *Agenda for discussion* Similar to 'Dreaming', plus: — Was it more difficult to identify people by what they would least like to be remembered for, than for what they would like to be remembered? — If so, why? — Do we know less about people's fears, feelings of guilt, etc.?	*Alternative or supplementary activity* Ask students what they would most like to be remembered for in years to come. Ask them to write this down on a slip of paper and collect the slips, folded. Read out the statements on the slips of paper, one at a time, and ask the group to guess the identity of the writers. After they have all been read out and identities guessed, the true identities may be revealed. The group can then be invited to question the writers. The process can now be repeated, posing the question 'What would you least like to be remembered for?' The last question would need sensitive handling, but could prove moving and helpful in the hands of a skilful and sensitive tutor.

Student Objectives	Activities	Organisation and Method
To identify personal strengths and weaknesses and come, through discussion, to a higher degree of self-acceptance and a positive acceptance of another person's view of him/her.	*THIS IS ME* A card game for four people in which each person tries to collect a 'hand' of seven cards bearing both positive and negative personal attributes which he considers to be appropriate to himself.	**You will need** One set of 'This is Me' Playing Cards, APPENDIX 37, per group 1 Divide the main group into groups of four. 2 Each group sits around a table and is given a 'pack' of cards. 3 One of the students in each group deals seven cards to each of the four players, placing the remaining cards in a pile face down on the table. 4 The students study their seven cards and decide which they will keep and which they would like to discard. 5 The object of the activity is to choose seven attributes which they consider apply to them. Four of the attributes should be ones which the person concerned sees as positive ones and three of them which he perceives as negative. *NOTE:* Students sometimes wrongly understand this as collecting four attributes which apply to them and three which do not. 6 The first player picks up the top card on the pack, looks at it and decides whether to keep it or not. If he keeps it then he places one of the cards in his hand which he does not want, in the centre of the table face-upwards. The next player can pick up this card or the next one from the face-down pile. The play continues until all four have collected seven suitable cards.

Student Objectives	Activities	Organisation and Method
To identify personal strengths and weaknesses and come, through discussion, to a higher degree of self-acceptance and a positive acceptance of another person's view of him/her.	*Discussion* The follow-up discussion will probably vary from group to group. With some the emphasis may turn on group acceptance of individuals, with others it may be self-acceptance; another group may move on to discuss what they might wish to change in themselves and yet another group may see the exercise as the development of a vocabulary for extending self-awareness. Some of the following points might lead to profitable discussion. *Agenda* Did you agree that all the cards which your partners ascribed to themselves as negative were negative in your eyes? Why did you consider 'X' as being a negative quality? Are there any surprises in anyone's personal choice of cards? Which card do you think most accurately describes you? Which of the cards do you like to 'own' most/least? Which of the negative cards do you find most difficult to bear? Why? What would you most like to change? How easy/difficult is it to accept criticism? How can it be used/given constructively?	7 They then lay their 'hands' on the table and discuss each other's choice.

Student Objectives	Activities	Organisation and Method
To identify personal strengths and weaknesses and come, through discussion, to a higher degree of self-acceptance and a positive acceptance of another person's view of him/her.	*A Personal Profile* An extension of the first activity; the qualities from the personal attributes cards are used as the basis for a personal profile chart. Personal Profile – This is me! Am I forceful, gentle . . . etc. This is you . . . as I see you! *Agenda for discussion* Do we agree? What do we see differently? Who's right? Is there something in our personal standpoint/perspective which affects the way in which others see us? Is it difficult to see ourselves as others see us? What gets in the way? Am I satisfied with myself? What would you like to change? How can one change? Does one need help from friends/colleagues to change oneself or one's role?	**You will need** Five copies of APPENDIX 38, A Personal Profile, per student 8 Arrange the students in groups of five and give out five Personal Profile sheets per person. 9 Give students about five minutes to complete a profile of themselves using APPENDIX 38. Ask them to put a tick in the appropriate column to indicate to what degree they are more self-reliant than retiring, or vice versa . . . and so on. Urge them to be decisive and avoid the 'safe' neutral, middle ground wherever possible. 10 When this is done ask the students to put the names of the other four students in the group on to one each of the other profile sheets. Then, give them no more than ten minutes to complete profiles for each of their companions in the groups. We are concerned only with recording general impressions rather than an in-depth study, so keep the activity moving at this stage. 11 One student in the group is now asked to show his profile sheet to the rest of the group. They use their profiles of him as a basis for comparison and discussion of how they see him (see agenda opposite). This is repeated until each student has discussed and demonstrated his own profile.

NOTE: This unit could last over several sessions depending on the depth of discussion at each stage. The tutor would have to decide where to make a break in order to be able to carry on next time. The tutor could choose to work in random groups if the tutor-group were still at a stage of getting to know one another better and not used to this way of working.

Student Objectives	Activities	Organisation and Method
To evaluate potential with regard to skills, abilities and the use of creative powers. To develop a desire to exploit his or her own skills in a creative way. To embrace life and accept its challenges by examining issues and concerns objectively and develop flexible responses to changing and challenging situations. To develop a degree of self-confidence in challenging situations through involvement in discussion and action research.	*STARTING FROM SCRATCH* An activity in which a small group considers the talents and personal attributes contained within the group, and thinks of ways in which they could best be combined. 1 *How others see us* An introductory activity to create random groups in which the students exchange cards until they have acquired two or three cards which they feel bear attributes typical of themselves. *Agenda for discussion* Have you got the cards you wanted? How many times were you given the same card before you would keep it? Did you have to be persuaded to take a card or did you accept it readily? Are there any cards you would have preferred to receive?	The activity can be carried out in random groups or in groups of friends. This would depend on how well the whole group know each other and on whether everyone would be incorporated into friendship groups (see note above). **You will need** Two or three sets of Attribute Cards, APPENDIX 39 The cards are given out randomly, two or three to each student. The members of each group are then asked to decide for which member of that group these attributes are most fitting, e.g. who is particularly gentle, capable, talkative etc. Next students give their cards to the chosen person but must receive one in return. At all times the students must hold two or three cards. When he is satisfied with the cards a student may stand aside from the group or sit down with other students as they finish, making small groups of four or five. The last four or five students may hold cards with which they are dissatisfied. They can also form a group and take part in the general discussion (see agenda opposite).

Student Objectives	Activities	Organisation and Method
To evaluate potential with regard to skills, abilities and the use of creative powers.	2 *Identifying personal qualities* Use Check List, APPENDIX 39, to discuss a variety of qualities as they apply to each small group.	You will need Check List, APPENDIX 39, Identifying Personal Qualities
To develop a desire to exploit his or her own skills in a creative way.		This stage may continue from stage 1, with the students in the same small groups or the whole unit may start at stage 2 with the students in pairs (friends) looking at the check list together, then moving into fours to compare.
To embrace life and accept its challenges by examining issues and concerns objectively and develop flexible responses to changing and challenging situations.	*Agenda for discussion* Was it easy to identify your own position or did your partner/group have to help? Are there any qualities/attributes missing from the list?	A final discussion within the groups using the agenda opposite to help to identify the skills and interests within each group and so help to prepare the ground for the next stage.
To develop a degree of self-confidence in challenging situations through involvement in discussion and action research.	See if you can answer the following questions in your group: If you could arrange a sponsored event to suit *your* capabilities what would it be? What hobbies/interests have you which you might like to develop?	
	3 *Getting together with others* Think of a 'project' which this group could tackle together. *Examples* a) Non-profit-making ventures – building a boat and planning a trip together, creating a street-theatre group, raising money for charity, writing a community newspaper or magazine.	As a group of friends or acquaintances, having identified some of the personal qualities, skills and attributes which each person could provide, each small group now thinks of a project which the group could tackle, which might provide some fulfilment for them all and would be an alternative to being on the dole (see examples opposite). If needed, starting capital could be available in the form of a small grant.

Student Objectives	Activities	Organisation and Method
To evaluate potential with regard to skills, abilities and the use of creative powers. To develop a desire to exploit his or her own skills in a creative way. To embrace life and accept its challenges by examining issues and concerns objectively and develop flexible respsonses to changing and challenging situations. To develop a degree of self-confidence in challenging situations through involvement in discussion and action research.	b) Ventures which might incur running costs – giving a service, e.g. window-cleaning, house-painting etc., catering for parties, running a crèche. c) Small business or profit-making enterprise on a small scale (e.g. gardening). d) i) What could your group do together? ii) What would each member of the group bring to the project? iii) What kind of skills/talents/personal qualities would be required? iv) What would be each person's primary contribution to the project and why? v) What would be each person's secondary contribution?	The groups are then given fifteen – twenty minutes to consider items d) (i–v) opposite. *NOTE*: The tutor should make sure that at the end of the period every member of each group has a slip of paper with his/her own primary and secondary contributions written on it and how or why they have such a contribution to make, e.g.: *Jane Project* – Market garden. I would display and sell the produce because I have an artistic eye and I am patient. Secondly, I would help to grow the produce but someone else would have to tell me what to do.

Student Objectives	Activities	Organisation and Method
To evaluate potential with regard to skills, abilities and the use of creative powers. To develop a desire to exploit his or her own skills in a creative way. To embrace life and accept its challenges by examining issues and concerns objectively and develop flexible responses to changing and challenging situations. To develop a degree of self-confidence in challenging situations through involvement in discussion and action research.	*Agenda for discussion* Would any new skills have to be learned or any qualities need to be developed or subdued? Would you need to rely on anybody or anything outside the group for making a 'go' of it, e.g. distribution, extra workers? What are the strong points of your project? What are its weak points? 4 *Starting again* Without wanting to emphasise failure, this phase is added to encourage flexibility. *Agenda for discussion* Who had to change their primary/secondary contributions around? Who had to set out to learn something completely new? Who decided who should do what in the group? Who do you think would have the most influence on how your project would proceed? Who or what would keep the people in the group happy? Who might prove to be the most flexible in making the project work?	After fifteen – twenty minutes, each group is asked to present its project to the others explaining what each person in the group would bring to it. The points opposite could then be used to lead into a follow-up discussion. Having identified weak points in the project which might or might not lead to failure or breakdown of the project, the students are asked to leave their original groups and try to find another group of people with whom to start a new project. The basis for forming the new groups will be what they have written about themselves and their qualities. These personal statements will be the basis for devising a new project. In this second round the emphasis should not be on what the project needs and what I could do for it, but rather on how can we channel our personal resources into something we could all find rewarding. When the groups have settled and suggested a new 'project', general discussion may follow as suggested opposite.

Student Objectives	Activities	Organisation and Method
To evaluate potential with regard to skills, abilities and the use of creative powers.	*What is flexibility?* Is it adaptability, being easily led, changeable, or what else?	
To develop a desire to exploit his or her own skills in a creative way.	Are you flexible under our agreed definition?	
To embrace life and accept its challenges by examining issues and concerns objectively and develop flexible respsonses to changing and challenging situations.		
To develop a degree of self-confidence in challenging situations through involvement in discussion and action research.		

Student Objectives	Activities	Organisation and Method
To examine his/her reactions to, and demonstrate an awareness of, the ease with which people are typecast and then dismissed, for example, people who are known and 'labelled' within the community.	*LABELLING, STEREOTYPING, PREJUDICE* 1 *An introductory activity to encourage recognition of the kind of labels which are easily attached.* *For Doctor:* Q. Do I have a dark skin? A. No. Q. Do I have a white skin? A. Yes Q. Am I well qualified? A. Yes. *NOTE:* Most of the answers will be ambiguous, according to the views/feelings of the person providing the answers. There may be more than one person with the same card on their back. *Agenda for discussion* What happened? What other 'characters' could we have used? Where do the labels we use for characters come from? When we know a 'character' personally, e.g. a doctor, would these labels cease to apply? When is a label a label, and when is it a description of someone?	**You will need** APPENDIX 40, Stereotyping 1 List of character cards: doctor, labourer, model, teenage rock fan, nurse, politician, teacher, policeman. A character card is pinned on the back of each student (e.g. doctor). The students circulate with the statement sheet in hand, trying to guess which character they are from the responses they receive to the questions which they have posed, (see examples opposite). Answers must be given as 'yes' or 'no'. The activity need not be prolonged until everyone has guessed. When several people have guessed, or it is too difficult to make a correct guess from the conflicting information being received, a discussion about what happened may ensue.

Student Objectives	Activities	Organisation and Method
	2 *Personality inventory of Mr X* Each student is asked to see himself as a student newly arrived at college/ university, awaiting the arrival of an unknown room-mate. He is given certain limited information, from which he and his group try to form a picture of the expected new arrival. Unknown to them, each group is told that the new room-mate attended a different kind of school, and the object is to see if this prejudices the picture which is drawn by the different groups.	2 The tutor-group must be divided into four groups for this activity. **You will need** APPENDIX 41, You Have Just Arrived at College, one per person APPENDIX 42, Your New Room Mate, one per person APPENDIX 43, Analysis of Results, one per group Have APPENDIX 41 and APPENDIX 42 stapled together before they are distributed. Each group will be given a different APPENDIX 41, but it is essential that all groups believe that they have the same information. Each of the four versions of APPENDIX 41 is identical, except for the last line. Each individual completes APPENDIX 42 as instructed using the information given on APPENDIX 41. Then one person is appointed 'scribe' in each group and he collects the individual assessments made on APPENDIX 42, and collates them on the analysis sheet, APPENDIX 43. When this is done, the group use this information to draw up a collective pen picture of the awaited room-mate.

Student Objectives	Activities	Organisation and Method
	The pen pictures are read out and compared.

Agenda
What happened?

On what criteria did you base your judgements?

What happened when there was disagreement in your group?

The main question is: Did the information about the 'A' level results make a difference to the judgements about character?

3   *Who said it?*
An activity to discover whether *who* said something influences us, or whether we are able to judge the statement on its own merits.

NOTE: Of course, the reason for disagreement about the statements between the groups may be for other reasons entirely than just 'who said it', and these reasons also need to be discussed, particularly if the group is going along with one person's view. | After about twenty minutes each scribe is asked to read out his group's collective assessment to the whole tutor group.

As each 'pen picture' is read out, major differences should be noted and questioned in the general discussion.

The groups may be wondering why each group's pen picture is different (which is what usually happens). Can they guess why this is so, and which piece of information might have been different for each group?

You will need
A fairly provocative statement printed on a card, for each group, but each one attributed to a different famous personality. APPENDIX 44 provides some examples

This activity may follow on the last involving the same groups, although the students may be alerted to any 'tricks' this time, and guess that they have the same statement to discuss, but with some slight difference.

The groups are asked to discuss the statement and come to some group agreement as to how they feel about it, stating finally whether they would support it or oppose it and why. |

Student Objectives	Activities	Organisation and Method
	Agenda Why have you come to this particular agreement? Have all the group reached the same conclusion? Does who said it influence us at all? Have we been influenced in the past more by the person than by what they said? Does it happen often in daily life – in politics, religion, etc.? Can we all think of a time when we have been close-minded about something? Is it difficult to be objective about it? Can we come up with a definition of close-mindedness? Might there be a link between close-mindedness, prejudice, lack of information, narrow outlook?	The groups could list quickly all the times when close-mindedness has occurred or is most likely to occur for them.

111

Student Objectives	Activities	Organisation and Method
To recognise his/her own areas of prejudice and examine whether or not there are logical reasons why he/she should feel as they do about certain issues or particular people.	*PREJUDICE* An activity designed to help students to think about prejudice in general and their own prejudices in particular. Each group of four is to receive the four students A, B, C and D, and each of the four students within the group chooses the one who is to stay with him/her.	**You will need** One piece of A4 paper per student One copy of APPENDIX 45, Prejudice, for the tutor 1 Divide the whole group into groups of four. 2 Give out one sheet of paper per student and ask them to divide their papers into four equal squares labelled A, B, C, D, and number each one from 1 to 10 down the left-hand side. (Set out as in APPENDIX 45.) 3 Ask students to imagine that they are going to be involved in an exchange which will involve someone of their own age staying with them and followed by a return visit to their visitors' homes. Each visit will last for about two weeks. APPENDIX 45 describes the four young people who are coming on the visit, A, B, C and D, and lists ten descriptive points concerning each of them. 4 The four people to be described are being allotted to each group of four. Each person within each group has to accept one of the visitors. The tutor now reads out description A point by point, followed by description B, and so on, after explaining that the only way to ensure that a student can get the visitor he wants is to put a tick on his paper as soon as his decision has been made, i.e. if you have decided after hearing five things about visitor B that he/she is the one you want then place a tick in square B against No. 5.

112

Student Objectives	Activities	Organisation and Method
To recognise his/her own areas of prejudice and examine whether or not there are logical reasons why he/she should feel as they do about certain issues or particular people.		5 When all four descriptions have been read out the students compare decisions. If, for example, two people want visitor B, and one made the decision at point 5 and the other at point 8, then the first person would get that visitor and the other student must choose another one. Because of this it may be useful for the students to jot down the information as it is read out.
	Suggested agenda i) Why did you choose . . .? ii) Are there particular reasons, items in the descriptions which caused you to reject any of the four? Why? iii) Did particular things attract you? iv) Why do you feel as you do about . . .? v) What is prejudice? vi) How does this vary from one person to another? vii) How many of our prejudices have we inherited from our family?	6 Group discussion followed by general discussion on prejudice. *Possible follow-up* The students could then be asked to write down similar statements to those in APPENDIX 45 which they think would describe them.

Student Objectives	Activities	Organisation and Method
To help the students to become aware of the feelings of others, and how these emotions can affect their actions or decisions.	*WHAT NEXT?* An activity which will enable students to become involved in a situation in which emotions play a large part.	**You will need** A large piece of paper or blackboard divided into six or eight squares 1 The tutor should prepare a situation which is fairly emotional and involves about four or five people. Divide the story into an equal number of parts, e.g. a) Parents go off to spend Saturday night away, leaving teenage son and daughter. b) Son, who has passed his test, decides to 'borrow' mother's car. Sister and brother fall out about it. c) He goes out in the car. d) Returns home very late, the worse for drink and without car. Sister, who has been very worried, is now angry. e) Parents return home the following day, full of the joys of an enjoyable weekend. f) A party at home while the parents are out. g) ……… 2 As there are four main characters in this story, divide the tutor-group into fours. 3 Tell the story to the students, at the same time drawing simple 'stick' pictures in the squares to denote each stage of the story. The last square is left blank. 4 At the end of the story, each student is given a role, e.g. one student in each group is mother, one is father, and so on.

114

Student Objectives	Activities	Organisation and Method
		5 In their new roles, the groups are now asked to decide what the outcome of the story should be, and how each person would re-act emotionally.
		6 Allow time at the end for each group to present its solution and for individual comments on the actions and/or emotional responses of the characters involved.
		7 This could be repeated at a later session when a student may like to present a situation.

'A most profitable and *adaptable* unit.' (A trial school)

'*Versatile* and capable of a number of *different uses*.' (Another trial school)

Student Objectives	Activities	Organisation and Method
To appreciate the concerns of others in the community and to develop an insight into the responsibilities and decision-making of those in charge of community problems.	*COMMUNITY CONCERNS* An activity to encourage students to look at community problems and decide on priority areas of concern. *Agenda for discussion* *Stage 1* a) Were there solutions which would solve more than one problem? b) What are the main areas of concern? c) Were any of the problems specific to an age group?	This unit links well with Organising Opinion, p. 122. **You will need** One set per group of APPENDIX 46, Community Concerns Problem Cards One set per group of APPENDIX 47, Solution Cards Ask the students to find three or four others to work with. Encourage them to form mixed groups, to ensure a useful range of opinion. Also, suggest that working with people with whom they usually do not work may give different perspectives. Provide each group with a set of Community Concerns cards and a set of solution cards, made from different coloured cards. *Stage 1* The students are asked to place the appropriate solution card over the problems displayed on the Community Concerns cards until all the problems are covered. If the students feel that it is necessary, allow them to make duplicate copies of particular solution cards. Follow-up with discussion (see opposite).

Student Objectives	Activities	Organisation and Method
To appreciate the concerns of others in the community and to develop an insight into the responsibilities and decision-making of those in charge of community problems.	*Stage 2* a) On what basis did you decide your priority areas? b) How would you feel if you had to make these decisions 'for real'? c) What *pressure* is put on the officials who have to make the decisions? d) What voluntary and government agencies could be involved? *Stage 3* How did your group come to an agreement? a) What happened first? b) What *feelings* were shown? c) What feelings were not shown? *Alternative* a) Nothing happened until . . . . b) I thought . . . c) The others seemed to . . . . d) In the end we	*Stage 2* Introduce the idea that the group have not enough resources to solve all the problems. They *must* remove solution cards to the value of 80 points. (It may be necessary for the teacher to impose a time-limit on both stages.) Whole class discussion, taking up contributions from each group – see agenda opposite. *Stage 3* Ask the group to focus on the *process* of removing solution cards and remember the details of their decision-making. Suggest each member writes his own version of what happened, either in response to the agenda opposite, or responding to the unfinished sentences, as quickly as possible.

Student Objectives	Activities	Organisation and Method
To appreciate the concerns of others in the community and to develop an insight into the responsibilities and decision-making of those in charge of community problems.	*Stage 4 – Conclusion* a) Can we learn about something as complex as community issues from a distance? b) How much *do* we know about our own community and how decisions about it are made? c) Where does our knowledge come from? Newspapers, hearsay, knowing someone 'in the know'? d) How indifferent are people to the issue we were 'playing' with? e) What do we mean by 'process' rather than 'content'. The adaptability of this unit can best be demonstrated by some of the suggestions offered by trial schools, (see opposite).	*Stage 4* General discussion of what this activity was about, using the agenda opposite for step-by-step discussion (see Introductory Note on step-by-step discussion). *Adaptability* Instead of the negative 'cuts' exercise (removing 80 points), the opposite approach could be used, i.e. giving 'x' million pounds to spend on various projects, giving each card a monetary value and then choosing what to *include* in the programme. One group used a more complex scoring structure, involving combining solutions as problems to encourage lateral thinking. This provoked more and deeper discussions. Another group developed the manifesto idea from Taking It All On Board, p. 95, i.e. various 'political' groups used the manifesto which they had drawn up and made their 'cuts' based on the policy which they had advocated.

Student Objectives	Activities	Organisation and Method
To appreciate the concerns of others in the community and demonstrate a desire to make an unselfish contribution to the community.	*COMMUNITY RESPONSIBILITY*	**You will need**
	An approach to the problems of litter and vandalism in the local community.	One Village Plan and one set of cards, using three different colours of card in each set for each group of four, as shown APPENDIX 48
To consider alternative points of view and build on the contributions of others.	Students are involved in coping with these problems by designing a game activity on this topic. To do this successfully they will have to	The students should be told that this unit is about vandalism and litter just to see what initial response the statement arouses.
	view the problem from many angles, have some involvement with younger pupils in the 'testing stage', either in their own school or a nearby school.	These reactions can then be reflected back to them and queried.
		Next ask the students to work in pairs, starting by closing their eyes and thinking of a special place.
	Somewhere special	The students describe 'their place' to each other, in pairs, explaining why it was so special.
	A warm-up activity to introduce the above topic.	Now say: 'You visit it again and it has been vandalised.'
	Think of a special place – somewhere you have been before and remember as somewhere special.	
	Try to remember all the details – sounds, colours, smells, etc.	
	What would spoil 'your place'? How would you feel if it was spoiled in some way.	

Student Objectives	Activities	Organisation and Method
To appreciate the concerns of others in the community and demonstrate a desire to make an unselfish contribution to the community. To consider alternative points of view and build on the contributions of others.	*Litter*[1] First, a simple 'game' in order to get the groups more involved before tackling the major task of game construction. *Agenda for discussion* Q. How might a visitor to the village at the end of a Saturday in summer know what had been going on in the village that day? A. From the litter lying around. Q. What would the litter tell him? E.g. There was a wedding at the church etc. Q. What could be provided to improve the environment? A. Waste-paper bins. Q. What about the litter which will not go into a waste-paper bin, e.g. rusty bike, mattress?	Pairs move into fours, and each group is given a set of village cards and a Village Plan constructed from APPENDIX 48. Do not issue the Litter Cards yet. The groups arrange the cards around 'their village' discussing as they do this, how their 'ideal village' would be laid out. After posing the questions opposite, the 'litter' cards are then 'dumped' or emptied in the middle of each village and the group are asked to place them in appropriate places, around the village. The groups then deploy their six waste paper bins in the best place in the village, and discuss the best method of dealing with 'dumping'.

[1]This activity was devised by Val Sibley and colleagues at Northampton School for Boys.

Student Objectives	Activities	Organisation and Method
To appreciate the concerns of others in the community and demonstrate a desire to make an unselfish contribution to the community. To consider alternative points of view and build on the contributions of others.	*Construction of an activity designed for younger pupils, e.g. first year/eleven-year-olds which will help to promote more responsibility towards keeping the place tidy.* a) The 'game' should be suitable for eleven-year-olds. b) It should contain an element of shock, e.g. 'dumping' litter so that those involved in the activity will be taken aback. c) It should lead to more sustained activity, e.g. surveys, action research into the cost of anti-litter campaigns, providing litter bins, etc. d) It should be easy to organise. e) It should have obvious learning built in. *Final discussion* Constructing 'games' is a complex business. It is the process of constructing the game which is important, not so much the end product, although we hope that, too, will prove to be useful. Therefore, it is concluded by asking 'What have we learned?'	This forms the basis for the main task as outlined opposite. The groups should now set about refining the activity so that it meets certain requirements (opposite). The students should state what limited objectives (purposes) their 'game' will have and suggest what questions might be asked of a group of eleven-year-olds after 'playing' it. The students should be encouraged to carry out their own consumer 'tests' on their game, and be given every assistance in terms of materials which they might require.

121

Student Objectives	Activities	Organisation and Method
To become better informed upon how individual citizens organise themselves through groups or political parties in order to achieve what they see as an improvement in the quality of life, and also to voice their objections to those facets of public endeavour which meet with their disapproval.	*ORGANISING OPINION – PARTIES, PROTEST AND PRESSURE* 1 *Protest and Pressure* This is an activity in which different 'interest' groups work out their attitudes to a local issue and decide how best to organise pressure and protest in support of their point of view. Explanation: A new firm is coming. What kind of firm – discuss. What will it be like? The 'game' (Part 1, Stages 1 and 2) is simply the introduction and initial stimulus for the general discussion which follows, and for Parts 2 and 3. Part 1 without 2 and 3 reduces the unit to 'entertainment'. Do try to find time for the 'visitor' section. If organised as detailed in the notes (and using the Introductory Note on Visitors) it can prove invaluable.	**You will need** To make a copy of APPENDIX 49, A Local Issue, and cut it into seven pieces (e.g. residents, town council, etc.). Make arrangements for and brief visitors (MP and member of local press) for a later session You will need a large group of about thirty-six students – perhaps two tutor-groups combined. Start off with all the students standing around a table. Place the 'A Firm' piece of APPENDIX 49 on the table and explain that a large company is going to develop a new industry in your locality. There will be heavy traffic during and after the building stage; there may also be some noise and unpleasant smells. Many new jobs will be created. Ask the whole group to discuss and decide there and then what type of firm and product(s) may be involved. Continue to unfold the scenario by placing Residents A, Residents B etc., on the table in roughly the positions shown in APPENDIX 49, making whatever introductory comments seem necessary or appropriate.

Student Objectives	Activities	Organisation and Method

To become better informed upon how individual citizens organise themselves through groups or political parties in order to achieve what they see as an improvement in the quality of life, and also to voice their objections to those facets of public endeavour which meet with their disapproval.	Form six groups:
	
	    Group 1: 8 councillors
	    Group 2: 8 residents A
	    Group 3: 8 residents B
	    Group 4: 4 the firm
	    Group 5: 4 the trade unions
	    Group 6: 4 the environmentalists
	
	Representatives of the press prepare a 'rumour' of the new development and its implications.
	
	This must be done quickly – if this leads to a slightly garbled report, so much the better.
	
	They report that 'rumour' to the 'locality'.
		Stage 1
		
		Next, divide the students into six groups as suggested opposite. If the total number is more or less than thirty-six, alter the size of these groups proportionately.
		
		Give the groups time apart from each other to discuss the implications of this issue and what their stand-points and responses are likely to be. The tutor moves around the groups to ensure that their tasks are clear and that profitable discussion is proceeding.
		
		Before proceeding to Stage 2, ask each group to second one of its number to become a member of the press group which is observing the development of this 'local issue'.
		
		Tell the press group that they have just three minutes in which to prepare a brief 'rumoured report' of the development and its implications from the information which they have to hand.
		
		Stage 2
		
		Bring all the groups back together and arrange them in a similar layout to that shown in APPENDIX 49.
		
		A representative of the press group now reports the 'rumour' which they have heard about the new industrial development.

123

Student Objectives	Activities	Organisation and Method
To become better informed upon how individual citizens organise themselves through groups or political parties in order to achieve what they see as an improvement in the quality of life, and also to voice their objections to those facets of public endeavour which meet with their disapproval.	*What do you think of it so far?* Ask the residents and the environmentalists to respond to this rumour. Have they any questions to put to the council or the firm? Allow the firm and the council to respond and the trade unions to make their feeling known. *Agenda for discussion* How do you feel about the discussion? Were you able to get your point across? Is it always as easy as this, in real life, to meet the decision-makers face to face? How can you 'reach' them? What other means of persuasion could the firm, the council, the trade unions use? How could the ordinary people influence the council and the unions? How can people organise to put a jointly held point of view? to protest, when necessary, about things which they feel are wrong or against their interest? *Examples:* public meetings · letters to press · join parties · advertisements · rallies · marches · posters · vote · letters to individuals · letters to MPs · question candidates · form/join pressure groups	Begin the discussion of the issue by obtaining contributions from selected groups as indicated opposite, and withdraw gradually as the exchanges begin to flow naturally. Allow about fifteen minutes. Halt discussion of the issue and ask for a press report, following up with a general discussion of the activity using the agenda opposite. Although the discussion starts with protest and seeking redress of grievance, it should lead to the more positive consideration of how people/groups organise to get things done, including looking at the part which political parties play in our national scene.

Student Objectives	Activities	Organisation and Method
To become better informed upon how individual citizens organise themselves through groups or political parties in order to achieve what they see as an improvement in the quality of life, and also to voice their objections to those facets of public endeavour which meet with their disapproval.	2 *Opinion, Pressure and Parties: Research* Gathering information for use at the next session.	**You will need** Duplicated copies of APPENDIX 50, Assignment Cards At this stage the students should be directed towards personal or group research, to be undertaken before the next session. Make up assignment cards from APPENDIX 50, and distribute them amongst the groups. Alter them or add to them as you deem appropriate
	Report back (next session) Preparation of a wall display from the findings of the students' personal research.	**You will need** Felt-tip pens and drawing pins; large sheets of paper or card for wall display Arrange students in groups so that all those with Assignment Card 1 are in the same group, and so on. The students then discuss their findings/information received. After some minutes' discussion in their groups, ask them to present their findings clearly and concisely, for wall display, on one of the large sheets of card.
	Wall display of discussion: 'What we have found out about the conduct of local affairs.'	When the cards are complete, ask students to pin them to a wall board. They can then look at the work of others and ask questions during a short period of informal discussion. Ask students if they could rearrange the boards and add linking captions, etc., which would unify the display and make it meaningful to others.

Student Objectives	Activities	Organisation and Method
To become better informed upon how individual citizens organise themselves through groups or political parties in order to achieve what they see as an improvement in the quality of life, and also to voice their objections to those facets of public endeavour which meet with their disapproval.	3 *Parties, Power and Popular Opinion* *Inviting visitors* A further session, inviting visitors to the group(s) who could give further insights into politics, protest and pressure in a local and national context. The session should be prepared thoroughly, following the guidance given in the Introductory Notes. In preparing the students' questions, it is essential that they get 'into the person' first before going on to wider issues, so that the students feel that they are dealing with real people rather than quizzing stereotyped images of what an MP or reporter is supposed to be. In addition to briefing the visitors on what to expect and how to conduct the session; the MP might be asked to clarify the party system, parties in government, parliamentary committees the pressman might be asked to deal with the role of parties in local government as the observer sees it; trying to achieve a balance between power, public good and popular opinion through the local press.	A good way of rounding off this unit might be to invite a couple of visitors to a future session. The large group could be split in half with each group entertaining both visitors in turn, so that everyone can be more easily involved in discussion. The suggestion here is that your MP and a member of the local press should be invited. Your group might suggest someone different, e.g. a CND campaigner. *Important:* If you have already undertaken another unit involving the use of visitors you will be familiar with all the preparatory steps. If not, it is essential that the Introductory Note on Using Visitors is read before undertaking this section. Briefly, the steps are: Who shall we invite? Who does it and how? How do we greet him, make him feel welcome? What do we want to know? Who asks what? How do we begin? How do we finish?

NOTE: The end product will not be concrete conclusions but a growing awareness of adult view-points and some of the factors which shape them. Hopefully, students will also enjoy a degree of mental stimulation.

Student Objectives	Activities	Organisation and Method
To appreciate the needs and concerns of others in the community. To develop a firmer understanding of the uniqueness of the individual and a respect for the individuality of others. To examine to what degree people are the product of their experiences, i.e. how experience shapes attitudes and beliefs.	*PARENTS AND ADULTS* *Why are they as they are?* *Why do they think as they do?* *Why do they hold their particular philosophies?* 1 *Agenda for discussion* Do you ever watch 'Question Time' on TV? If there are two politicians on the programme, how often do they agree or accept something of the other's point of view? Do you ever watch 'Party Political Broadcast' on TV? Have you ever heard a Tory have a good word for a Socialist, or vice versa? What makes people so intransigent, even bitter, about other beliefs, other points of view (e.g. in Ireland)? Is it their upbringing? Or something in their past experience?	You will need APPENDIX 51, Forming Attitudes APPENDIX 52, Probable Attitudes and Beliefs Three sheets of A4 paper per student 1 This topic, about what moulded and/or shaped our parents is approached indirectly at first, through a generalised introduction by the group tutor, along the lines suggested opposite. Whole tutor-group discussion. It would be invaluable to set aside a whole half day for this unit, at the end of a term, for example. If it has to spread over several sessions, it would be divided most profitably as follows: Sections 1 and 2 together over one or two sessions Sections 3 and 4, a session each or together over two sessions Section 5, with 4 or 6, but not on its own Sections 5 and 6, together over two sessions Section 7, in one or two sessions (where one session lasts approximately twenty minutes).

Student Objectives	Activities	Organisation and Method
To appreciate the needs and concerns of others in the community. To develop a firmer understanding of the uniqueness of the individual and a respect for the individuality of others. To examine to what degree people are the product of their experiences, i.e. how experience shapes attitudes and beliefs.	2 *How do people become what they are?* Here is an activity based on one person's family and one or two of their neighbours. Read through the statements on APPENDIX 51, and then make a broad assessment of those people's characteristics in APPENDIX 52. 3 *We all tend to judge people* Often we judge people on little evidence. Students now write down what they think is the evidence for their assessments. 4 Each pair of students now examines the work of another pair. As the students discuss and evaluate the assessments of the other pair, they are bound to compare them with their own findings. Hopefully, they will become increasingly conscious of how people and their actions may be seen differently from different stand-points (see diagram below).	2 At this point arrange the group in pairs and give the introduction opposite as you give out APPENDICES 51 and 52, which contain their instructions; ask the students to work through the exercise in pairs. They are given only the briefest pen-pictures and, consequently, students will be attempting to construct broad rather than detailed pictures of the people described. 3 On completion of APPENDIX 52, students then go on to use the A4 sheets as instructed. They should only complete the first column, *Why?*, at this stage (see instructions at the bottom of APPENDIX 51). 4 When this has been done, two pairs of students should join together in groups of four and exchange APPENDIX 52, Probable Attitudes and also their A4 *Why?* sheets. Each pair then reads through the attitudes and *Why?* sheet compiled by the other pair, and writes in the *Justification* column of the sheets they have just received whether or not they think what is written under *Why?* justifies the assessment of probable attitudes and beliefs ascribed to people on APPENDIX 52.

128

Student Objectives	Activities	Organisation and Method

Student Objectives

To appreciate the needs and concerns of others in the community.

To develop a firmer understanding of the uniqueness of the individual and a respect for the individuality of others.

To examine to what degree people are the product of their experiences, i.e. how experience shapes attitudes and beliefs.

Activities

a) Given

Forming Attitudes	Probable Attitudes
My Dad	Caring Socially conscious

Is what is written in c) sufficient justification for the conclusions arrived at in b)?

5 Agenda for discussion

a) What did *we* bring to the situation?

Why can different people see the same thing differently, or reach different conclusions from the same information?

Is it possible that people are not exactly as we label them? E.g. Is it possible that we sometimes distort others because we look at them through the 'spectacles' of our own experience, desires, prejudices etc.?

b) *Them*

Why are people as they are?

Do events/situations shape them?

Are there other reasons why people display certain characteristics?

Organisation and Method

b) First Pair Assessment

c) First Pair Reasons for Assessment

d) Done by Second Pair

Why?	Justification
Upbringing Religious conviction	I tend to agree, but. . .

5 Brief follow-up discussion before proceeding to the next stage (see opposite), involving the whole tutor-group.

Student Objectives	Activities	Organisation and Method
To appreciate the needs and concerns of others in the community. To develop a firmer understanding of the uniqueness of the individual and a respect for the individuality of others. To examine to what degree people are the product of their experiences, i.e. how experience shapes attitudes and beliefs.	6 *Significant adults in my life* Mum tutor Dad principal grandparent(s) teacher elder kin policeman friend JP vicar/pastor politician(s) hero neighbourhood/local/ national figures Suggest that actual names are not written on their sheets. *Agenda for discussion* Why are they as they are? Why do they think as they do? Why do they hold their particular philosophies, values, beliefs? What shaped them? Are they valid reasons? Does this help us to understand them? Does it help us to talk to them; make it possible to discuss ideas, issues, beliefs, differences? Can we learn anything about what is shaping ourselves? What will we be like ourselves? Are we helpless victims? Must we be 'shaped'? Are we just the product of our 'shaping', experiences, or is there something beyond our control?	6 Suggest that students repeat the first stages of the activity which they have just completed making up their own list of people to replace APPENDIX 51, Forming Attitudes. They won't need to provide pen pictures as they will be asked to choose, say, eight people who are significant in their own lives: see suggestions opposite. After making their lists, they ascribe characteristics, attitudes, beliefs, points of view, prejudices, etc., which they see in these significant 'others', particularly things which lead to dispute, misunderstandings and the souring of relationships. They then seek out a partner with whom they have some rapport or degree of trust. In turn, each student passes over his sheet to the other, who asks questions of his own choosing to make the writer work backwards from his conclusions to discern what might have been significant events, experiences, situations in the past which might have led to particular stand-points. Students can then be led step-by-step to consider the agenda opposite.

Student Objectives	Activities	Organisation and Method
To appreciate the needs and concerns of others in the community. To develop a firmer understanding of the uniqueness of the individual and a respect for the individuality of others. To examine to what degree people are the product of their experiences, i.e. how experience shapes attitudes and beliefs.	7 *A good way to round off* A visit by the educational psychologist. Brief the groups to follow-up the 'Nature v. Nurture' theme. Brief the psychologist to satisfy the students' prepared questions and then lead the discussion round to a more general discussion of behaviour. *NOTE*: The written sheets are not designed to be records of the exercise; they are merely prompts for deeper thought and discussion and it would probably be wise to collect and destroy them at the end of the session.	Here we are leading into the classical 'Nature v. Nurture' debate. A good way to round off this unit would be to invite one of your educational psychologists to be a visitor to the group using the 'visitor' technique, see Introductory Note on Visitors.

131

Student Objectives	Activities	Organisation and Method
To understand, through demonstration, how facts can become distorted when a story is told and retold.	*TRUTH – RUMOUR, DISTORTION AND CRITICAL FACULTIES* 1 *Whispered rumours*	1 Arrange the whole tutor-group in a circle. a) One person is selected to whisper a short statement, e.g. 'In principle, the Principal is the principal lecturer,' to the person on his left who in turn whispers what he has heard to the person on his left. Ask the students to do this quickly and without hesitation. This continues until the statement has been whispered round the circle. The last person then relates the statement which he has received to the rest of the group for comparison with the original statement. The statement given to the first person for circulation should be written on a card. b) Now try two longer statements. i) For fun, try something like: 'A ten-ton tipper from Tipton carries ten tons of toilet tissues to Timothy Whites in Tooting'. ii) Now try something of more complex meaning, of your own choice. c) Repeat this activity with two different statements being sent round the group simultaneously – one clockwise, the other anti-clockwise. In each case the statements are passed right round the group and the two last people repeat the statements which they have received for comparison with the originals. At some point one person will find himself being offered both of the statements at the same time.

Student Objectives	Activities	Organisation and Method
To understand, through demonstration, how facts can become distorted when a story is told and retold.	2 *Agenda for discussion* a) How much had the statement changed? b) When more than one statement is being passed at the same time, can the statements become confused? Do people mix up or confuse the 'stories' which they carry in this way?	2 At the end of a), b) and c) discussion follows.
	3 *Agenda for further discussion* a) How does a story become distorted, even with best of intentions, when it is shortened for retelling? b) I don't believe it! Have you found yourself saying this when someone insists that an unbelievable story about someone you know is *true*? c) How easy is it for apocryphal stories to be born, perhaps unintentionally, by the linking of separate incidents into one story? d) Do you think that some people pass on such stories, even though they don't believe them, because they make a good story? e) Gossip! What is gossip? Do you think that gossip can begin in the ways in which we have seen here? Is it harmful?	3 Experience has shown that even the shortest and simplest statements can be distorted when passed round a large circle. Interesting extensions of these activities are: a) To lengthen the statement to twelve and fifteen words or more, so that some paraphrasing becomes inevitable. b) To circulate two closely-related statements simultaneously (e.g. different yet similar incidents concerning different people). c) Before embarking on the further discussion opposite, you may wish to try this more complex example: Give a card containing a written statement to one person, and another containing a different statement to the person on his/her left. Tell this person to whisper the statement to the person to his left, and so on round the circle. When it reaches the sixth person, start the other story going in the other direction.

133

Student Objectives	Activities	Organisation and Method
		Let the stories 'cross' and then, at about the fourteenth person, quietly tell that person to reverse that (first) story and send it back to the right, to the beginning. When the second is about six from the end, quietly tell the recipient to reverse it and let it be passed left to its source of origin.
		Choose two similar stories. Don't reveal them, and make the changes of direction unobtrusive.
		d) Afterwards, make comparisons as before.
		4
		You will need Pencil or felt-tip pen, sketch pad, or paper
To demonstrate how different people interpret what they have seen.	4 *That's what I saw!*	Arrange the group in a circle. One person draws a stick picture illustrating a situation which he/she has experienced.
		This is shown to the person on his left and on his right.
		They make a silent interpretation of the picture and whisper their deduction to the person next to them. One interpretation goes clockwise and one goes anti-clockwise, half way round the circle.
		The last two pupils in the half circle repeat the stories which they have received. The group then compares them with each other and with the original interpretation which, in turn, is compared with what the 'artist' had really meant to illustrate.

Student Objectives	Activities	Organisation and Method
	Agenda for discussion	Follow-up with discussion – see agenda opposite.
	a) Apparently, we may all witness the same incident, yet 'see' different things.	
	b) Why do we 'see' different things?	
	Is it due to eyesight, concentration, or what we bring to the situation, e.g. the kind of people we are, our past experience, our beliefs, etc.?	
To continue to develop listening skills, and become aware of variation in ways of perceiving situations.	5 *Rumours*	**You will need**
	Perceptions:	Two or three attractive and brightly-coloured pictures, with some detail contained in them, e.g. reproduction of well-known paintings or, alternatively, pictures with strong social content
	Can we distinguish facts from our own interpretation?	
	Do we filter out things that are unimportant to us – aurally and visually, i.e. not always hear and see correctly?	5 Ask five students to volunteer to go out of the room. The remainder study a picture together and decide upon a clear and accurate description of it. Bring one student into the room and show him the picture for two minutes. Then bring in student number two and ask the first student to describe the picture to him. Number three is then brought in, and number two describes the picture, and so on.
	What does 'keeping an open mind' really mean?	The group should keep very quiet and listen intently, watching for embellishments and changes in ascribed meanings, etc. After the sixth description the picture is displayed. The group comments on the accuracy of the final description, and points out where and why mistakes were made.

Student Objectives	Activities	Organisation and Method
	Agenda for discussion Have there been times when we have been victims of rumours or misinterpretation? How did it arise? Was it malicious, or could it simply have been misunderstanding? What were the consequences? Do we listen enough?	Now split the tutor-group into smaller groups and pose the questions opposite.
To develop the ability to select issues of social/topical relevance from the media; to be able to discuss them critically with a small group of peers and to practise and develop communication skills by interpreting and summarising an argument in the report back to other groups.	6 *The truth, the whole truth and nothing but the truth?* Developing critical faculties towards reported events by using a local newspaper to compare the newspaper report with an eye-witness (what really happened) account of a recent local incident.	6 ┌─────────────────────────┐ **You will need** Copies of recent local newspapers Sheets of writing paper └─────────────────────────┘ a) Obtain copies of local newspapers which have reports of a local incident/event of which some members of the class have first-hand knowledge. b) Split the tutor-group into small groups and read out the account, asking for comments where necessary. c) Discussion in small groups using the comments made by students in the whole-group session, and their personal knowledge. d) Groups report their findings back to the whole tutor-group, and the tutor lists inaccuracies, exaggerations and omissions on the blackboard. e) Each group is now asked to draft its own 'revised' version of this incident from their collective ideas.

136

Student Objectives	Activities	Organisation and Method
		f) One person from each group will read out his group's account of the incident, and the class will choose one of these accounts, which might then be pasted alongside the original newspaper article on the class notice-board.
		g) In the ensuing discussion, ask the class to consider the difference between their version and the newspaper version of this incident.
	Discussion	
	How do these disparities occur?	
	i) Biased – because of differing viewpoints?	
	ii) Haziness and/or inaccurate reporting?	
	iii) A good headline – a good story which will capture interest being more important than absolute accuracy?	
	If we can find marked disparities in the reporting of comparatively minor local events, is it possible that we are misled by accounts of major things in national newspapers, on the radio, or TV newscasts?	

Student Objectives	Activities	Organisation and Method
To demonstrate the ability to carry out critical personal enquiry by: a) selecting and bringing to the tutor-groups items which they judge to be of national, international, or sectional interest in radio and TV news b) selecting a key issue for research, enquiry, critical assessment and presentation from time to time.	7 *Developing a critical approach to the news* Preparation of students will have been done at a previous session. *An introductory activity* Monitoring, reporting back on and evaluating TV and radio news broadcasts.	7 **You will need** To ask students to bring cuttings from newspapers and/or magazines for this session, which could then be divided under the headings current national interest current international interest You will also need to ask for volunteers to carry out three tasks, on a particular evening: i) some people to watch 'News at Ten' on ITV ii) some people to watch the BBC nine o'clock news iii) some people to listen to the news on Radio 2 and jot down in rough the main news items in the order in which they are reported Draw two columns on the blackboard with the headings *National* and *International*. The monitors report back on which items featured in the news bulletins; the tutor-group indicates in which column the item should be entered. Briefly discuss which items are common to all three bulletins as well as asking the group to comment on the order of priorities which the different bulletins gave to the same items. Make the observation that the same thing can be done with newspapers.

138

Student Objectives	Activities	Organisation and Method
To demonstrate the ability to carry out critical personal enquiry by: a) selecting and bringing to the tutor-groups items which they judge to be of national, international, or sectional interest in radio and TV news b) selecting a key issue for research, enquiry, critical assessment and presentation from time to time.	8 *What the papers say* Collecting and displaying news cuttings under three headings and evaluating the accuracy of their placement in these columns. *Agenda for discussion* Are there differences between various reports of the same news item? Why might this occur? Are they accidental? Are they due to a particular stand-point, bias? So-called news – are some items too trivial? Can an item of news have more than one view-point, e.g. politics? Is there any doubt about the accuracy of any item? (Local events may illustrate any discrepancy most clearly.) Add items of your own to this agenda.	8 You will need To have prepared a frieze on the notice-board with the headings: *local, national and international,* over three columns A supply of drawing pins and card Ask the students to pin the cuttings which they have brought under the heading which they think is appropriate. Break the class up into groups of five or six and begin to feed in items from the agenda opposite for step-by-step discussion (see Introductory Note, p. xviii) in which items of interest which are raised by one or other of the small groups are also fed into the discussion for consideration by the other groups. The depth of the discussion will depend upon the quality of the response and the time available. Groups may want to investigate one item or discuss one topic in greater depth. It may be, too, that some groups may wish to continue with this news-gathering process as a regular event, or that they may wish to follow up the development of a news item as it unfolds, monitoring the different approaches which are followed by: different newspapers different media the same media at different times.

139

NOTE: This activity is perhaps best used as an introduction to the exercise on Verbal and Non-Verbal Communication.

Student Objectives	Activities	Organisation and Method

To develop the students' awareness of feelings and emotions expressed non-verbally.	*GIVE US A CLUE*
	
	A starting activity to help students become involved in the non-verbal communication of emotions.
	
	Agenda for discussion
	
	1 How easy is it to communicate emotions non-verbally?
	
	2 What misunderstanding can result in the misinterpretation of facial expressions?
	
	3 Can we cover up how we really feel inside?
	
	4 How much do our feelings affect our work and relationships with others?
		You will need
		Four cards per group, with a different emotion written on each one, e.g. frustration, delight, contentment, anger
		
		1 Arrange the students into groups of four.
		
		2 Give each student an emotion card and ask them not to show it to the other members of the group.
		
		3 Ask the students to think of a situation which would bring about the emotion on the card.
		
		4 One member of the group mimes a little of the situation, displaying the emotion to the rest of the group.
		
		5 The rest of the group have to guess:
		    a) the emotion
		    b) the events that caused that emotion.
		
		    They can ask questions to which the mimic can answer only yes or no. Additional mime may be called for if necessary.

140

NOTE: This unit has sometimes proved difficult for first-time users. Nevertheless, members of the project team have proved it to be both a successful and valuable exercise and would urge your perseverance. It is not unusual to have adverse reaction and comment from participants in the initial stages. Explain that the initial stages are not ends in themselves; they are essential stages in creating an awareness of, and sensitivity to the presence of non-verbal elements in our communications with each other. This awareness and sensitivity will then be put to use in the later stages of this unit. (*See Feedback from Schools* at the end of this unit.)

Student Objectives	Activities	Organisation and Method
To listen and interpret meaning accurately.	*VERBAL AND NON-VERBAL COMMUNICATION* 1 *The things we say and how we say them* What do we tell people, both in our speech and in our actions, about ourselves? *Agenda for discussion* Reactions to the exercise. Ask questions to find out if reactions were different to different words. Did the group find that different meanings could be taken from the way in which the words were spoken. Give examples. Can you say where the meaning came from, e.g. mannerism, tone of voice, facial expression? E.g. 'Yes' can convey: agreement surprise reluctance questioning submission enthusiasm sarcasm understanding	1 As an introductory activity, the students are asked to choose one word from the following three: *Yes, No* and *I* They circulate around the room saying the word which they have chosen to the people whom they meet, putting any emphasis or meaning into the word which they choose (e.g. they may say 'No' abruptly, gently, with a laugh or a raised hand . . . etc.); they may also alter the emphasis from one person to the next, if they wish. Stop the activity after a minute and, whilst everyone is still standing around, ask for comments about the activity (see agenda opposite). Ask the students to move round again, concentrating on the word 'Yes'; ask them to say it in as many ways as they can think of (see examples opposite).

Student Objectives	Activities	Organisation and Method
	2 Meaning comes from not just the words spoken, but also from the expression and intonation with which they are said.	2 In pairs, guide the students to identify all these different interpretations of the word 'Yes'. Next, ask the students to say the word 'No' to their partners, giving it as many different meanings as they can think of, taking turns until they run out of ideas. This activity could be developed by asking the student whose turn it is to listen to think of a phrase or sentence which would convey his/her interpretation of the way in which his/her partner said 'No'.
	Examples You said 'No' in a matter-of-fact way, suggesting 'I don't know', probably given in answer to a question. You said 'No' defiantly, angrily; I think you meant 'I won't/will not'.	
To explore verbal skills in a creative way. To demonstrate and practise listening skills.	3 Practising skill in conveying meaning through tone of voice and expression.	3 The pairs join up into fours. Each person selects a single common word, e.g. 'you', 'me', 'well', 'now', 'what', 'never', and thinks of a situation in which their word might be used. Each person in turn says their word, trying to convey the atmosphere or circumstance of the situation which they have envisaged, e.g. worry, excitement, etc. The others write down the meaning. After everyone has had a turn at saying their word and writing down meanings, the members of the group compare their perceptions (see agenda opposite).
	Agenda for discussion How well did you get your message across through the way you said your words? Were some words easier than others? Did you use any other cue, e.g. gesticulating?	

Student Objectives	Activities	Organisation and Method
		Still in groups of four, but working in pairs, the students visualise several other circumstances in which their particular words might be used. Words which go together appropriately can be used together in some circumstances, e.g. 'well now', etc.
		Each pair picks out three or four words and rehearses them together in order to refine emphasis, facial expression, gesticulation, etc., and then repeat them to the other pair in order to convey certain messages or impressions.
		The other pair write down their perception of how the word is being used and what is going on. It is possible that they may also receive information about the relationship between the two people involved in the example situation.
		Follow-up with a brief discussion, using the agenda opposite.
	Agenda for discussion What gave you clues as to the message? What did the word, tone and expression tell you about the situation and/or relationship between the two people?	
To listen and interpret meaning accurately.		

Student Objectives	Activities	Organisation and Method
To take an enthusiastic part in debate, by being prepared to follow-up discussions and take the trouble to become more informed.	4 *Observation* *Observer's task* Watch the people in your group. Watch what happens and what they do. Try not to hear *what* is said, but listen to *how* things are said. Try to be factual. Some examples of what to watch for: facial expression sudden intakes of breath hand movements bodily position } indicating: depth of feeling, pleasure, agreement, support, anger, hostility, disagreement, wish to say something, withdrawal, disenchantment, etc. *Group task* Try to forget the observers. Discuss the topic for ten minutes. (The topic should be controversial enough to rouse the group members into active participation through comment, statement of opinion, declared stand-point, belief, etc.)	4 Form larger groups (e.g. fours join to make eights). Appoint two observers who withdraw from the group slightly. The observers and the groups are each given tasks as opposite. **You will need** A prepared list of topical/controversial issues for discussion The discussions may be stilted at first, but given time the group members will warm to the subject and want to have their 'say'. The observers may need to make a few notes and should try not to be drawn into the discussion. At the end of ten minutes, each pair of observers should withdraw to combine what they observed into a composite report; one report for each group. While they are doing that, a brief general discussion may be held on what the group members think will have been observed.

144

Student Objectives	Activities	Organisation and Method
To select and interpret information about other people correctly.	*Reporting back* This is a skill, but it can be boring if too much detail and repetition are permitted. Limit the time and push it along at a brisk pace. a) Encourage the students to be succinct, selecting material which is to do precisely with the task, e.g. 'Then Mary said she thought that Bob was wrong in what he had said about . . .' is not useful, *but* 'Mary interrupted Bob by leaning forward and using her hand to cut in,' is useful and good observation.	The observers then report back. During the reports, the teacher should listen for comments which are interpretations, e.g. 'John was obviously feeling angry . . .' Statements like this should be challenged: 'How do you know that?' 'What evidence have you for saying that?'
To demonstrate awareness of the feelings, skills and abilities of other members of the tutor-group.	b) The first 'reporter' has a wide open field. How do the succeeding reports build on the previous ones and how does the last person feel when everything else seems to have been said?	After each report, ask the group concerned if they agree or have anything to add. The Fifth Year Active Tutorial Work Book contains some work on observation (pp. 28, 29). It would be useful to repeat these units here, or introduce them at this point, if the work is new to the sixth-form.

145

Student Objectives	Activities	Organisation and Method
	5 *Further observation* How do people indicate: a) boredom? b) polite interest? c) concentration? d) gossip about a third party? e) jealousy? f) that they like someone else? g) that they dislike someone? Are there signs, mannerisms, which are common to everyone in a given situation, e.g. yawning when we are bored? Or are the signals so subtle as to be unique to every individual? Consider the craft of impersonation and mime. Observation is the key, but could anyone become an impersonator or mime artist if they practised observation? Impersonation can be cruel. What can we do if a friend/colleague has an irritating mannerism?	5 The students are asked to observe pupils in the school during the week (observing should not be made obvious!) and make notes about some of the ways in which non-verbal signals indicate the messages opposite. During the next session these notes can be discussed and compared in twos.

Student Objectives	Activities	Organisation and Method
	Feedback from schools *School 'X'* 'The whole exercise was worth while and everyone joined in with enthusiasm.' 'The report back and observations of the group leaders were interesting and helpful. They were frank and truthful about each individual's response. This made each member of the group think about his/her contribution (or lack of) to the outcome.' 'It was an interesting exercise and the group could show whether or not it had benefited by having a further similar exercise about six months later.'	*School 'Y'* 'As a leader, I found it murder!' 'A very difficult one.' 'It was difficult in the initial session to get a discussion of differences in 'yeses' and 'noes'.' 'Too bitty and repetitive.' 'Suggestion: We worked in a circle, one person said a word with a particular emphasis, and the next person used it in a sentence to demonstrate their interpretation of the meaning. They sent a word to the next person . . . and so on.'

147

Student Objectives	Activities	Organisation and Method
To be able to reconcile conflicting issues and to experience and develop some skills in negotiation.	*DEMOCRACY IN THE FACTORY* *Negotiating* What is involved in negotiation? When, how often and in what circumstances, do we have to negotiate? Are we aware that we are doing it?	The group will need to be large enough to split into six groups of three or more. **You need** APPENDIX 53: Six sets of Workers in Industry Cards and twelve sets of Job Priority Cards The tutor starts by asking the students to respond to the general questions opposite. Draw out as many kinds of negotiation as possible, leading to a recognition that life could be seen as a negotiated existence.
To take an enthusiastic part in debate by being prepared to follow-up discussions and take the trouble to become more informed.	*Viewpoints* Creating random groups. Can each group agree on a list of priorities of gains from a particular job perspective? *Example* 'If you were a maintenance worker in a factory, which of the priority cards would you put at the top of the list?'	Distribute the Workers in Industry Cards at random, and ask the students to find fellow workers of the same category and form a group. Each group has a set of Job Priority Cards and is asked to put them in rank order of importance (see example opposite). It may be necessary to hold a general discussion first, to clarify some of the items on the priority list. The groups are then given fifteen minutes to decide on their priority list from their own job stance. They should try to arrive at a consensus through discussion, rather than by taking votes on their final decision.
To modify personal opinions in the interests of a group decision.	*Agenda for discussion* Could you come to an agreement about the priorities? Are the priorities different for different types of workers? On what knowledge/evidence did the group base its final ranking? If you had more time, do you think the order might change?	After fifteen minutes, a brief general discussion could follow along the lines of the agenda opposite.

Student Objectives	Activities	Organisation and Method
To take a leadership role in the group by accepting responsibility for the actions of the group, making contributions to the direction the group takes.	*Example for negotiating:* A representative from the maintenance workers negotiates with: the foremen/engineers and vice versa the production workers and the managers the clerical workers and the directors. The objective in these negotiations is to produce three new agreed lists of job priorities.	Each group writes two lists of its own rank order of priorities and chooses a spokesperson to act on behalf of the group. Each 'representative' now moves to another group with one of his/her group's lists and the spare set of Job Priority Cards. The other list is retained by the group who, in turn, receive a representative from another group. The 'reps' must now proceed to negotiate with the new group in order to produce an agreed rank ordering of the job priorities, using the second set of cards alongside the original 'ordered' set. A suggested 'pairing' of groups is given opposite. At five minute intervals and at a given signal all the reps return to their own groups for a short period to: a) report progress b) seek advice c) explain what compromises they have had to make or may need to make d) receive instructions on what compromises may be made and which priority must stay in its position on the original list at all costs.

Student Objectives	Activities	Organisation and Method
To examine issues and concerns objectively and develop flexible responses to a variety of situations.	*Agenda for discussion* Negotiators: What was the most difficult aspect of the task? What was easy? How was the negotiating conducted? What happened? Groups: What was your reaction to the negotiator? What were the sticking points, if any? Do you think you gained/lost any 'ground'? What compromises were you prepared to make? General: Have you gained any insights into what is involved in negotiating? How much of oneself is invested in a particular stance? How carefully (or otherwise) did you listen to the negotiator? Etc. A final question: Would it be possible for all the groups of workers to arrive at an agreed list?	At another given signal the reps return to the 'negotiating table' to resume talks. After a suitable time, a full discussion about the whole process should be conducted (see suggested agenda opposite). A further stage, if time allows, could well involve the whole group, with perhaps three elected negotiators leading the discussion. An attempt should be made to reach a democratic decision which is acceptable to all the groups. This is probably a tall order and could lead to an examination of methods of reaching an agreement which exist in negotiating machinery, e.g. open vote, block votes, secret ballot.

NOTE: This unit is similar to one in the Fifth Year Book called Living Together, which could also be used to develop these objectives.

Student Objectives	Activities	Organisation and Method
To develop critical awareness through the examination of local and national issues. To demonstrate listening and communication skills by being willing to develop arguments whilst respecting the opinions of others. To appreciate the concerns of others in the community.	*TOWN DEVELOPMENT*[1] Looking at what is involved in decisions about redevelopment. site for redevelopment *Basic information about the town* It is an average-sized industrial town where the centre is being redeveloped because the nineteenth-century buildings are unsuitable and unsafe. There are standard facilities, but none is especially modern or outstanding, therefore there is plenty of scope for development. Possible uses for the site: 1 Police station with training facilities attached 2 Fire station and ambulance depot 3 Hospital and casualty facilities 4 Modern shopping precinct/car park/crèche facilities	**You will need** To draw, either on board or on a large sheet of card, a simple diagram of a piece of waste land in a town centre (see example opposite) It should be explained to the whole group that the diagram before them is an area of a town centre (waste ground) scheduled for redevelopment. Give the group the information opposite. Ask the students to make suggestions as to useful purposes for the land, which should include items such as those given in the list opposite.

[1]This activity was devised by Juliet Johnson of Kendrick School, Reading, Berks.

Student Objectives	Activities	Organisation and Method
To develop critical awareness through the examination of local and national issues.	5 Library/museum/arts centre/day centre facilities	Divide the students into groups of about six. Explain that each group is going to represent one of the projects, and put the case for its being accepted for planning development to a council meeting.
To demonstrate listening and communication skills by being willing to develop arguments whilst respecting the opinions of others.	6 Park with all facilities for all age groups (lake, adventure playground)	The projects may be allocated to each group with no choice in the matter, or each group may arrive at a choice approved by each person in the small groups.
To appreciate the concerns of others in the community.	7 Theatre/concert hall/cinema	
	8 Swimming pool/disco/skating rink	
	9 Brewery.	
	Agenda for the group to prepare the case for their project	
	1 Think of all the reasons why the town would benefit from your particular project.	The room may be arranged as for a council meeting, with someone in the chair.
	2 What might people say against it?	Draw lots for who puts forward a project first, and the whole group takes the floor to support the spokesperson.
	3 How will you answer them?	After three minutes, cross-questioning from the chair is allowed, and from the floor; any members of the presenting group may answer.
	4 How can you best put your case to the council meeting? How can you make an impact and persuade the councillors that yours is the best project?	After each group has put its case, take a vote. *NOTE:* No-one votes for his own project!
	You have only *three minutes.*	
	Agenda for discussion	
	Why do you think a particular project won?	
	Was it its usefulness for the town?	
	How important was the personality/persuasiveness of the spokesman?	
	Was the cross-questioning particularly weak?	

NOTE: This unit is an interpretation of one of the basic trust exercises referred to in Notes for the Teacher in Active Tutorial Work Books 1–5.

Student Objectives	Activities	Organisation and Method
To show sensitivity to other people's feelings, for example, by being able to take on their 'role' or to describe how it feels to be a person in a given situation.	*PUTTING YOURSELF IN SOMEONE ELSE'S SHOES*	1 Brief discussion of the question: Is it possible to put yourself in the place of someone else?
		'Let's take a particular example and see if we can do it.'
To accept responsibility for the welfare of another person.		Ask the students to form pairs and, with their partners, to find spaces round the edge of the room. Then ask one member of each pair to close his/her eyes and see if he/she can begin to experience what it is like to be blind, while the other acts as his/her guide. Suggest that each guide helps his partner to reach the other side of the room without colliding with furniture or with other people involved in the activity, and concentrating on the safety and comfort of his charge.
To create a caring atmosphere in the group.		
		The pairs should then reverse roles and return to their starting points.
	Agenda for discussion Were you safe? Did you feel safe? Did you feel confident?	This section of the activity may be kept short and be dealt with fairly crisply to allow the group to get over any initial embarrassment, and the students may then be asked questions like those set out in the agenda opposite.

Student Objectives	Activities	Organisation and Method
To show sensitivity to other people's feelings, for example, by being able to take on their 'role' or to describe how it feels to be a person in a given situation. To accept responsibility for the welfare of another person. To create a caring atmosphere in the group.	*Agenda for discussion* Was that as easy as the first time? Was that as pleasant as the first time? Was it a different experience? *Agenda for follow-up discussion* 1　Did you feel safe? 2　Did your guide make the walk interesting? How? (Ask the students to enlarge on any interesting situations starting, perhaps, with ones which you observed.) 3　Did you notice anything that surprised you, e.g. light and dark, the feeling of being in a big space or a restricted one, temperature changes, floor textures, etc. (Let the ideas come from members of the group.)	2　Now suggest that the students try the activity briefly in complete silence. To do so, the guide may need to change his way of helping his partner. 3　Ask the group if they now think that they could guide each other on a longer, more adventurous walk, negotiating real hazards like swing-doors or stairs. Guides should consider ways of making the walk interesting – describing, 'showing', answering questions. (It should be stressed that those who are being guided should not cheat, but should try to keep their eyes closed throughout the whole period.)

154

Student Objectives	Activities	Organisation and Method
To show sensitivity to other people's feelings, for example, by being able to take on their 'role' or to describe how it feels to be a person in a given situation.	4 Did any of you start to take initiatives of your own while being guided, or make requests to your guide?	
To accept responsibility for the welfare of another person.	5 Do you think that you actually experienced any of the feelings of a blind person?	
To create a caring atmosphere in the group.	6 Which did you like doing best – leading or being led? Why?	
	Now enlarge the discussion to:	
	1 What were we doing?	
	2 Was it pleasant to be able to put your faith in someone?	
	3 Are we always as trustworthy as that?	
	The theme can be developed in many ways, based on ideas which emerge from the group.	

NOTE: This unit should be introduced when trust and sensitivity have been built up within the tutor-group. It is not the intention to highlight the fact that someone may be isolated, nor to make everyone be a 'joiner' if they do not wish to do so. Rather, the unit is designed to allow students to explore their own position with regard to friends and friendship making, and decide for themselves whether they would like to change it or stay as they are. There is no right or wrong way to be.

Student Objectives	Activities	Organisation and Method
To join in discussions about the nature of friendship and suggest factors which influence friendship.	*FRIENDSHIP* *What is a friend?* An introductory activity might be useful to lead into the topic. Two suggestions are given opposite. 1 *Breaking Out* *Agenda for discussion* *Example:* 'Sue, I heard you say "Oh! I don't like it," when everyone got close. Can you describe how it felt?' 'Did other people feel the same?' 'No, John, you didn't. How did you feel?' Etc. Can you draw a parallel in real life with what we have just done – say, amongst a group of friends?	You will need To look up APPENDIX 54, Friendship Patterns 1 Breaking out: students stand in circles of five or six with one volunteer in the centre of each. The circles close tightly around the central person who must try to get out of the circle. Other volunteers could be encouraged to stand in the centre. Different reactions should be noted and a brief discussion, with everyone still standing, should follow, using the actual reactions of students as a lead into the discussion (see agenda opposite). It is not necessary to labour this discussion too much, and if the point of the exercise does not readily emerge, i.e. a parallel with the norms and pressures of a close-knit friendship group, it does not matter. The students should be asked to reflect on what they have just done, and its possible meaning, and the activity can be returned to at a later stage.

Student Objectives	Activities	Organisation and Method
To join in discussions about the nature of friendship and suggest factors which influence friendship.	2 *Things in common* A useful approach for creating groups, for discovering more about each other, and for considering whether having things in common is an important consideration in friendship-making. Groups may guess what people in other groups have in common, if time allows. 3 *What does friendship mean to you?* or *What is involved in making friends?* loyalty dependability time trust sense of humour accessibility different levels of friends *flexibility* interests What do you understand by that term? (Other terms could be focused on to deepen the discussion if time allows, or continued next session. The introductory exercise could be repeated, if there is a break.)	2 Things in common: this has been used as an introductory exercise in another unit, but it bears repeating as students will be paired up differently. Arranged in pairs or threes, they should identify as many things as they can which they have in common. Next, ask them to find two or three other people who have two or more things in common with themselves. They should sit down when they have formed a group, all of whom have two or more things in common ('nothing in common' may be accepted as one item!) 3 Now ask the groups to consider their opinions on the question(s) opposite. The tutor should circulate, making a mental note of useful points, qualities, characteristics of friendship making, etc. After a few minutes discussion, 'brainstorm' all the ideas which have been produced in the group discussions. Everyone's ideas should be noted on the board (see opposite). (See Introductory Notes on Brainstorming.) When all the ideas have been used up – the tutor adding some to complete the picture, perhaps, one or two ideas may be ringed and followed up in closer discussion in small groups (see example opposite).

Student Objectives	Activities	Organisation and Method
To join in discussions about the nature of friendship and suggest factors which influence friendship.	4 *Are there different levels of friendship?* What are the levels of friendship? Can friends be classified as: close friends other friends (others) brief acquaintances. (The students may use other words to suggest these differences.) *Agenda for discussion* What distinguishes these levels? *NOTE:* If any student has a tendency to generalise when making a statement, e.g. 'It's easy to make friends – you just get talking and find out what people are interested in,' point out that we can only speak for ourselves and not for everyone else: 'Are you speaking for yourself, for me or for all of us?' or 'Does everyone agree with what Gary has just said?'	4 This question/suggestion will almost certainly come up and could also be looked at in more depth, in order to help the students understand their own position and attitudes towards friends and friendship making. (See note at the beginning of this unit.) Still in groups, students discuss the question opposite to clarify their thoughts and come to some agreement about a broad definition of categories. Point out that we do not and cannot be expected to agree – friendship means different things to each person. The tutor should be alert to the need to get participants to understand that they should *only* speak for themselves (see note opposite). To draw the discussion to a close, show the students a visual way of describing friendship, e.g. as opposite. APPENDIX 54 is given as an example of diagrams showing differing friendship patterns.

Student Objectives	Activities	Organisation and Method
To join in discussions about the nature of friendship and suggest factors which influence friendship.	*NOTE*: Point out that it is not possible to give a hard and fast judgement, only speculation, unless we know more about the person concerned. *Points to remember* 1 There is no right or wrong way to be. 2 Everyone is different and we should not judge. 3 Some people may need help and support. 4 We are a tutor-group and everyone belongs to it and should feel that they do. 5 None of us need be fixed in our relationship patterns. We can change them if we wish. *NOTE*: If 'breaking-in' is done practically, it needs to be directed very carefully and we do not recommend it, without the tutor having had some experience of it him/herself. It is particularly important that students who may habitually be on the edge of groups generally are not inadvertently pushed out yet again.	In small groups, the students should discuss, with the limited information given, what these patterns reveal (one line within a ring means one friend, one acquaintance, etc.). Finally, at the tutor's discretion, the students may be encouraged to consider their own friendship patterns. They should be urged to remember the points opposite. This unit could be closed as it started, with trying to break out of a close-knit circle. The point of this activity may now become apparent, if students had missed it before. They may also consider the 'other side of the coin' – breaking in (see note opposite).

Student Objectives	Activities	Organisation and Method
To be able to prepare for the future after finishing full-time education. a) To be aware of and understand the processes which enable one to select a career. b) To modify personal job ambitions in a rapidly changing world. c) To be able to develop a coping philosophy.	**JOB FORUM** *Preliminary activity: Agenda for discussion* i) Do I work with people? ii) Do I work out of doors? iii) Did I have to train for a long time? iv) Was there an apprenticeship? v) Do I wear a uniform? *NOTE*: No direct questions of the type 'Am I a doctor?' should be allowed. *Yes* or *No* answers only should be given. *Profiles* 1 *Could this be you?* Students listen to profiles of ficticious individuals as they are described by the group of tutors.	**You will need** Several job cards, i.e. pieces of paper with names of jobs written on them Arrange students in groups of about six. Tutor issues a job card to each student, face down, but they must not look at the job card. One student passes his card, still face downwards, round the group. Other members of the group take note of the job. The student is now allowed to ask two questions to each member of the group to enable him to arrive at his job identity (see agenda opposite). The student attempts to identify his job and the process is repeated in turn with the remaining members of the group. **You will need** APPENDICES 55 and 56 Julie and Kenny Other members of staff who have been briefed on developing profiles The tutor will be joined by members of staff in this activity to form a panel of consultants/advisors.

Student Objectives	Activities	Organisation and Method
To be able to prepare for the future after finishing full-time education.	2 *Agenda for discussion*	Students are invited to listen to the profiles of ficticious individuals as they are developed by the tutors in a 'chain-description'.
a) To be aware of and understand the processes which enable one to select a career.	i) Are the profiles realistic?	Tutors then take it in turn to describe and develop the background of *ficticious* students to highlight their circumstances upon entering the sixth-form, and their likely prospects after the sixth-form. Each tutor could take one or two paragraphs of a profile in turn. This will also afford staff panel members the opportunity to suggest how a student might cope with a crisis point in his/her career. Sample profiles (APPENDICES 55 and 56) are given to provide introductory examples. Additional ones could be constructed by the staff panel. After each profile has been outlined by the staff there should be follow-up discussion in small groups along the lines suggested in the agenda opposite, to identify the pressures and processes which affected the future of the individual described.
	ii) Are there one or two significant events which seem to have been responsible for the situations the students find themselves in?	
b) To modify personal job ambitions in a rapidly changing world.	iii) How would you advise the students described in the profiles?	
c) To be able to develop a coping philosophy.	iv) What other information would you have liked to have about the ficticious students?	Arrange the whole group into pairs.
		Each student is now asked to write a personal profile for him/herself in the style of those which have been presented by the tutors. This should be followed by discussion in pairs in order to see if they can give help or advice to each other.
	This is me – my successes, my disappointments, my difficulties and doubts.	
	Helping a partner – giving hope, encouragement, devising helpful strategies.	Tutors should move around the pairs, listening, posing helpful questions, pointing out other directions of approach and picking up useful points for feeding into whole group discussion.

161

Student Objectives	Activities	Organisation and Method
	Book 5 dealt at some length with preparing for the world of work. Where students have not used this approach in their fifth-forms, it might be useful to refer to Book 5, pp. 71–88:	
	Why do we go to work?	
	Finding out from the world of work – what it is like	
	Filling in the picture (curriculum vitae)	
	Interview activity	
	Looking to workaday world (more about form filling)	
	Which job? Will I get it?	
	Money in your life	
	Joining the union	

NOTE: The principal objectives of this unit might well appear to be 'helping others' or 'working with or for others'. The main, underlying objective is oblique learning – i.e. because the students do not feel 'preached at' they take to heart, learn from, become interested in the 'lessons' which, ostensibly, they are seeking to make available to others.

'Used after reading Orwell "1984" – there had been remarkably smug lethargy about views initially. This unit stimulated discussion to dispel this, and led to more serious consideration.' (Trial school)

Student Objectives	Activities	Organisation and Method
To develop a greater ability to review situations, change places and develop a repertoire of strategies for coping with new situations.	*DR WHO* *A leap into the future – What kind of world will it be?* This activity is introduced by the tutor reminding students how difficult it was for them to decide: Which 'O' levels? Which 'A' levels? Which course? Which career? in recent times.	Whole tutor-group. Introductory session led by the tutor, leading to questions on foreseeing the future and anticipating the demands which it will make upon individuals. **You will need** Copies of APPENDIX 57, Fear extract from 'Daily Mail', one per student
To develop flexibility and adaptability in anticipating and planning for his/her own future, by helping younger pupils to do the same thing.	He continues by asking the students to consider: How much has changed in these two, three, four, five years? Did they have enough information about future trends with which to look forward and anticipate intelligently? Could they anticipate all the changes which have taken place, e.g. automation, computerisation, video, unemployment etc.? Would they make different decisions now? Which? Why?	The tutor continues his introductory talk using the questions opposite, rather like rhetorical questions, i.e. to provoke comment and stimulate thought, rather than to produce deep or prolonged discussion.

Student Objectives	Activities	Organisation and Method
	Is it getting even harder for youngsters to make the right decisions at fourteen – sixteen?	
	Consider for a moment, would it be possible for us to help pre- 'O' level students to see into the future more clearly, more vividly?	Switch now to a rapid, brainstorming activity.
	'Brainstorming'	Draw five columns on the blackboard (see opposite) and ask anyone in the class to suggest changes which may have taken place in two years, five years, etc.

2 years	5 years	10 years	20 years	50 years
End of sixth	End of university, college, poly-technic	Job change Marriage		

Jot the ideas down quickly, briefly, in the appropriate column.

What might have changed by the time you finish in the sixth-form? By the time you finish university, polytechnic or college of education?

The object is to stimulate the imaginative and inventive processes of the brain, so press on, making the activity lively and enjoyable. Encourage people to build on and develop the ideas of others.

In say five years, what kind of world will it be? Have you taken the right course?

In ten years? Will you be married? Have children? What kind of homes, schools, transport, kitchens, etc.?

In twenty years? Still in the same job? etc.

In fifty years?

By now the ideas should be flowing freely, so move onto *Who used to watch Dr Who?*

Student Objectives	Activities	Organisation and Method
	Who used to watch Dr Who on TV?	The tutor now begins to lead the discussion towards the construction of an activity for pre- 'O' level pupils.
	Could we use the format of the Dr Who programme for involving younger pupils in informed discussion of the future which awaits them?	After posing the questions given in the Activities column, the tutor-group is split into three smaller groups (with a large tutor-group split into six).
	Let's imagine that we're going to present our own Dr Who programme for them to watch and discuss.	Each group (or pair of groups) discusses and decides upon the scenario which it would provide for life in one of the three time bands, e.g. one group discusses what life will be like in five years, and so on.
	Dr Who comes out of the Tardis (old London police box):	
	in five years' time	
	in fifteen years' time	
	in twenty-five years' time.	
	What kind of world does he find?	
	Small group discussion – see opposite.	After discussion is nicely under way, halt it for a few minutes and hand out copies of APPENDIX 57 for individual reading as extra stimulus.
	Reading 'Daily Mail' article Fear, APPENDIX 57.	
	Report back to the whole tutor-group	After a period of discussion, each group now outlines its ideas for the era which it has been discussing to the whole tutor-group, and invites comments and further suggestions.
	What might be the effects of the kind of world portrayed on the personal future of individual pupils/students?	The 'listening' groups are then asked to suggest follow-up questions for the scenario presented which would help the pupils for whom it is intended to think about the situation more deeply and creatively (see examples in Activities column).
		These are written down by the 'presenting' group.

165

Student Objectives	Activities	Organisation and Method
	What implications are there for:	
	i) social/technological movements, mobility in employment, career change, family life?	
	ii) for subject/university/career choices?	
	iii) what skills will be { in demand? less in demand? redundant?	
	What are the total implications for the fifth- and sixth-former who is trying to plan ahead?	
	What do you think of it so far?	Whole tutor-group discussion (see agenda opposite).
	Agenda for discussion	
	Where are we getting to?	
	Can we present this to younger pupils?	
	If so, is it simply to be in dialogue form, or is it to be a dramatic work with 'props' etc.	If it is to become a 'drama project', defer further discussion until a future session, and perhaps involve a colleague from the drama department.
	Are the three sections to be presented separately or linked together? If linked, does this require additional material?	
	Which pupils? What age group are we preparing this for? Now that we know this, do the material or the questions need to be modified?	Whole tutor-group discussion continues with the review of other practicalities of the project (see opposite).

Student Objectives	Activities	Organisation and Method
	What are our objectives? What do we want the recipients to get out of this activity? What additional modifications, if any, might be needed to achieve this? *What have we learned?* Are there any lessons we have learned/any insights gained from this exercise?	Closing discussion. Whole tutor-group. This activity could be developed further, if necessary, by using excerpts from TV, in the style of Fiat automated workshop advertisement for further discussion, or by inviting visitors from science, industry, academia, the media etc. using the visitor technique (see Introductory Note on Visitors).

NOTE: This unit follows on quite naturally from the unit 'What Is a Family?' It depends, however, on the depth and quality of the discussion which the students have been able to undertake about their feelings concerning their own family life. The earlier unit may need to be tackled more than once for students to gain maximum benefit from this one.

Student Objectives	Activities	Organisation and Method
To prepare for independence by gaining insight into what is involved in living away from home. To develop skill and judgement in managing financial and personal affairs.	*LIVING AWAY FROM HOME* 1 *The good and bad of family life* What is a family (see p. 20)? What do we all enjoy about living in the group called the family? What irks us?	**You will need** APPENDIX 58, Life Styles Sets of cards cut up individually, in envelopes marked *Living at Home, Living in Digs,* etc. A discussion about a definition of a family may be profitable first. Individually, the students write their own lists in answer to the questions opposite. Alternatively, ideas may be 'brainstormed' into a composite list on the board. Ask the students to choose one or two main things from their lists of likes and dislikes about home life, and find a group of five or six others who share similar likes or dislikes. Five groups will be needed altogether.
To develop a firmer understanding of the uniqueness of the individual by showing respect for the individuality of others.	2 *'One man's meat . . .'* Looking at the pros and cons of some different life-styles which students may be able to choose for themselves when they leave or, perhaps, have no choice about.	Each group is given a set of cards with statements about a particular habitat or environment, e.g.: living at home living in digs from APPENDIX 58, Life Styles.

Student Objectives	Activities	Organisation and Method
To examine issues and concerns objectively and develop flexible responses to a variety of situations.	Instructions for each group: Look at your set of cards and sort them into 'advantages' and 'disadvantages' according to your group's view. Next, try to put the advantages and disadvantages into a hierarchical order of importance. *Agenda for discussion* Was this easy? Is one person's disadvantage another's advantage? Why is this?	The groups are asked to arrange the cards first into a 'pro' set and a 'con' set, (e.g. 'advantages' and 'disadvantages') and secondly, to arrange both groups of cards into an order of importance upon which all the group can agree. Follow-up discussion with the whole group (see agenda opposite). Each group nominates someone to speak for the group, after receiving some help with preparation, putting forward the pros and cons of their allotted 'habitat'. As an *aide-memoire* a prepared OHP or printed list could be displayed when all the groups have made their presentations.
To begin to assess his/her future life patterns.	3 *An auction*	Ask the groups to put the options for each of the five 'habitats' into an order of preference. From all of these each group then picks out what it considers to be the ten most important factors in choosing a way of living.

169

Student Objectives	Activities	Organisation and Method
	Agenda for discussion a) How would you really like to live when you leave school/college? b) Do you have a choice about where you live, or is living at home your only option?	Ask the groups to bear in mind and discuss the questions opposite as part of their process of selection.
Take an active part in developing tutor-group identity by being aware of the value of everyone's contribution.	c) If everyone in the group has chosen freedom from supervision as the most important factor, does this correlate with the 'habitat' which the group has chosen as the most desirable?	
	Instructions for the 'bidders' Discover from your group which characteristic of any 'life style' they would like to 'buy'. Decide how much you are prepared to 'pay'.	*Instructions for carrying out the auction* a) The tutor becomes the auctioneer. b) Each group elects a bidder, who is the only person who may make a bid. c) The bidder decides on a method of signalling a bid. d) The auctioneer decides on the steps in price for each item.
To modify personal opinion in the interests of a group decision.	Have secondary 'purchases' in mind in case you lose your first to another group.	e) Each group is given an imaginary £1,000 with which to bid. f) Someone keeps a check on how much each group 'spends' so that they do not over-bid. g) The groups may buy up to three 'lots'. h) The bidder operates on instruction from his/her group.

Student Objectives	Activities	Organisation and Method
		A composite list of fifteen items of the most important characteristics of the life-styles should be arrived at through general discussion, and these will be the 'lots' for the auction. The bidding commences and continues until all the 'lots' have been sold.
		Each group reads out what it has bought and how much it has spent.
To begin to gain insight into personal values and attitudes.	*Agenda for discussion* How much were you prepared to 'pay' for your top priority characteristic? In other words, how important is that particular feature in a life-style going to be to you? What collection of features/characteristics has your group now acquired? What 'habitat' would they fit? Is it the one which you as an individual would choose or did you go along with the group choice? Have we forgotten any important factor involved in any of the 'habitats', e.g. living away from home, would you be homesick?	General discussion should follow (see opposite).
In the long-term – to begin to develop a positive approach to life and accept its challenges.	From this discussion on living away from home, 'I realised that . . .' 'I have learned that . . .'	Finally, in pairs, the students say which option they would prefer and why. They are then asked to complete on a slip of paper, without revealing their name, the statements opposite. The slips can then be displayed so that everyone can read them and see what people have learned from this unit.

APPENDIX 1

THE LOWER SIXTH FORM

1   I shall be expected to organise my own time and homework schedules.

2   My work is much more meaningful to me.

3   The work I am doing will be much more difficult than the fifth-year courses.

4   Lessons are different because teaching groups are smaller.

5   Lessons are different because we have to take our own notes and cannot rely on dictated information.

6   We have more privileges and responsibilities than in the fifth year.

7   We have more authority over younger pupils.

8   The staff expect us to help in running clubs and societies.

9   We have more contact with the year above us than ever before.

10   We have a different relationship with staff.

11   Teachers will not mind if we give in homework late.

12   I shall need to read more around my work and make notes on what I read.

Are these the most appropriate statements to use? Could they be more open-ended?

e.g.   1   I shall be expected to ....

　　　　2   My work is ....

　　　　3   Lessons are ....

APPENDIX 2

WORD BOARD

Place the appropriate definition next to each word.

TRACE	
COMPARE	
CONTRAST	
CRITICISE	
DEFINE	
DISCUSS	
DESCRIBE	
DISTINGUISH BETWEEN *or* DIFFERENTIATE	
EVALUATE	
EXPLAIN	
ILLUSTRATE	
INTERPRET	
JUSTIFY	
OUTLINE	
RELATE	
STATE	
SUMMARISE	

APPENDIX 3

DEFINITION SHEET

	Follow the development of the history of a topic from some point of origin.
	Look for similarities and differences between; perhaps reach a conclusion about which is preferable.
	Set in opposition in order to bring out differences.
	Give your judgement about the merit of theories or opinions or about the truth of facts; back your judgement by a discussion of evidence or reasoning involved
	Set down the precise meaning of a word or phrase. In some cases it may be necessary or desirable to examine different, possible, or often-used definitions.
	Investigate or examine by argument; sift, debate; give reasons for and against. Also examine the implications.
	Give a detailed or graphic account of.
	Look for the differences between.
	Make an appraisal of the worth of something, in the light of its truth or usefulness.
	Make plain; interpret and account for; give reasons for.
	Make clear and explicit.
	Often means much the same as *illustrate*.
	Show adequate grounds for decisions or conclusions; answer the main objections likely to be made to them.
	Give the main features, or general principles of a subject, omitting minor details and emphasising structure and arrangement.
	a) Narrate – more usual in examinations. b) Show how things are connected to each other, and to what extent they are alike, or affect each other.
	Present in a brief, clear form.
	Give a concise account of the chief points of a matter, omitting details and examples.

APPENDIX 4

EXAMPLES OF 'O' LEVEL AND 'A' LEVEL QUESTIONS

Sheet 1

History 'O' level

Why were improvements needed in road, river and canal transport in the eighteenth century? What improvements had been made by about 1820?

History 'A' level

Compare the relative importance to the British economy of the improvement of inland transport by road and water before 1830.

Maths 'O' level

Three points on level ground, A, B, C, are such that A is 100m. west of B, and C is 70m. south of B. A man at A observes the top of a tower whose base is at B to have an angle of elevation of 40°. He then walks to C in a straight line.

i)   What is the height of the tower?
ii) What is the angle of elevation from C?
iii) What is the closest that the man approaches to the base of the tower?

Maths 'A' level

A man observes the top of a tower is at an elevation $\propto$ to the horizontal from a fixed point on the ground. He walks a distance x straight towards the tower and finds that the elevation is now θ. Express the height h of the tower in terms of a, x and θ.

Find $dx/d\theta$ and show that as θ increases by E, and x by z, then

$$h = \frac{Z}{E} \sin 2\theta$$

Woodwork 'O' level

Sketch and describe what is meant by the term 'gate-leg' table. When did such tables first become popular? Illustrate your answer by drawing a typical example of the period.

Woodwork 'A' level

The problem of extending the surface area of a dining table has been solved in a variety of ways in the past. Sketch FOUR examples of different solutions from different periods between 1550 and 1950. Add notes to show that you know the approximate date of each, and the kind of timber most likely to have been used.

176

Biology 'O' level

A normal winged Drosophila (fruitfly) is crossed with one having vestigial wings, and all the offspring have normal wings. When these were interbred there were approximately three times as many normal winged flies as vestigial winged flies in the offspring. Give a genetical explanation of these results.

Biology 'A' level

Describe how scientists have used a) population studies, and b) laboratory experiments to investigate whether smoking causes lung cancer. What are the advantages and limitations of each method, and how conclusive do you consider such data to be?

Chemistry 'O' level

Describe briefly how each one of the following substances is manufactured from the given starting material:

a) nitric acid from ammonia;
b) sodium from sodium chloride;
c) sulphuric acid from sulphur dioxide;
d) ethanol from ethene.

Chemistry 'A' level

'The study of chemistry is difficult to plan because one concept often arises out of another.'

Discuss whether any changes in the order you used to study 'A' Level chemistry would improve the logic of the course, and whether it would improve the course if some topics were taken further or others shortened.

Home Economics 'O' level

Give the composition of baking powder. State under what conditions it reacts and name the products formed.

Describe the changes that take place during the making and baking of scones and a loaf of bread.

Home Economics 'A' level

Explain fully the physical, chemical and biological actions of raising agents used in cookery.

Physics 'O' level

a) Sketch a velocity – time graph for a car moving with uniform acceleration from 5 m./s. to 25 m./s. in 15 seconds.

b) Use the sketch graph to find values for:
   i) the acceleration
   ii) the total distance travelled during acceleration.
   Show clearly at each stage how you used the graph.

Physics 'A' level

In this question you are asked to say how you would start an experimental investigation.

The paragraphs a) and b) below both describe a 'problem situation'; from each of them several possible problems might be selected for starting an investigation. You are asked to choose *one* of the situations a) or b) and to devise any *one definite problem* from the different possibilities.

Having stated clearly the problem you would investigate, you should then describe *two experiments* that you would propose. You should state:

– what measurements you would make
– how you would make them
– with what equipment
– how you would get information from these measurements
– how you would relate this information to the problem under investigation.

Where possible, make quantitative estimates, especially where these can guide the choice of methods to be used.

Credit will be given for choice of a *well-defined* and *worth-while* problem as well as for the choice of experiments proposed and the methods of tackling them.

Paragraphs on Problem Situations

a) Open-top freezers Food for sale in shops is sometimes kept for display and sale in open-top freezing or chilled cabinets. The temperature at which an item is kept, or the maximum temperature it could reach, may depend on many things: on the shape of the cabinet, the amount or arrangement of other items packed in the freezer, growth of frost on the inside of the freezer or on packets of food, the disturbace of cold air in the chest by people removing items. The behaviour of the freezer may be influenced by the air temperature in the shop. The freezer works by evaporating a fluid within tubes in the wall of the freezer, so taking heat from the side of the chest, and condensing it at a higher temperature (and pressure) in a radiator at the back of the freezer. An electric pump and, possibly, heater use electrical energy in this process. The freezer is rather like a heat engine working backwards. You may or may not want to investigate some aspect of its functioning instead of its performance.

b) Model racing cars Small model racing cars use electric motors of approximate size 2cm. × 1cm. × 1cm. A 12 V.d.c. supply is connected to a pair of rails on the track; the car has flexible wire brushes at the front which connect the rails through brushes and a commutator to a set of three coils wound around a rotor which turns in the field of a permanent magnet. In designing such a car, the efficient conversion of the electrical power from the d.c. supply is not as important as high accelerations and decelerations, stability of the car and reliability of the various electrical contacts. The motors at present used generally make up about 50% of the total weight of a car. In a race, each competitor varies the

178

speed of his car by varying the potential difference supplied to the track and, on track circuits which usually consist of alternating straight and curved sections, he has to accelerate and decelerate to attain the maximum speeds consistent with keeping on the track round the bends. (Credit will not be given for discussions of the technicalities of model car racing unless these are related to the problem and proposed experiments.)

Economics 'O' level

Explain the significance of the Bank of England as a central bank.

Economics 'A' level

How does the government influence the suply of money in the United Kingdom? Explain how monetary policy can be used to reduce the level of aggregate demand.

Religious Education 'O' level

Give an account of the events which took place on the road to Emmaus and at Emmaus itself. Include in your answer details of what was said.

Religious Education 'A' level

New Testament
a) What was the problem which led to the meeting of the Council of Jerusalem?
b) Comment on the significance of the Council of Jerusalem as a turning point in the history of the early Church.
c) To what extent did the decisions made at the Council prove effective?

Old Testament
a) Comment on the nature and function of myth in the Hebrew tradition.
b) Illustrate your answer by a critical study of the 'myth' in Genesis 1 and 2: 1–4.

Metalwork 'O' level

What is meant by the term 'case-hardening'?
When must this process be used instead of hardening and tempering?
Describe *one* method of case-hardening used in a school workshop.

Metalwork 'A' level

The thermal-equilibrium diagram for carbon steels may be assumed to have the following points:

% carbon	lower critical point	upper critical point
0	720°C	900°C
0.83	720°C	720°C
1.1	720°C	850°C

179

Assuming that all the heat-treatment ranges are bounded by straight lines, draw the diagram to a convenient scale.

On your diagram show
  a) the critical range
  b) where the material is austenite
  c) where the material is ferrite + pearlite.

With the aid of your diagram, explain how to
  i) harden 0.6% carbon steel
  ii) anneal 0.7% carbon steel.

Quote maximum temperatures as obtained from your diagram.

Explain briefly the different need for each of the following processes: tempering, normalising, annealing.

German 'O' level

Ihr deutscher Brieffreund (bzw. Brieffreundin) hat Sie eingeladen, im August eubuge Wochen bei ihm (ihr) zu verbringen, und Sie haben akzeptiest. Leider konnen Sie aber dieses Jahr nicht mehr fahren. Schreiben Sie an die Ettern Irhes Brieffreundes (Ihrer Brieffreundin) um ihren die Sache zu erklaren und sich bei ihren zu entschuldigen!

German 'A' level

Schreiben Sie einen Brief an Ihren Abgeordneten, in dem Sie ihm sagen, wie man am besten Englands wirtschaftliche Probleme losen konnte.

English Literature 'O' level

Give an account of the scene in *Julius Caesar* in which Antony addresses the crowd in the market place, from the beginning of his speech up to the point where the crowd leave. What methods does Antony use to gain the support of the crowd, and what do we learn of his character in this scene?

English Literature 'A' level

King Lear. And worse I may be yet. The worst is not
      So long as we can say 'this is the worst'.

Discuss the view that *King Lear* is a play of unrelenting and ever deepening pessimism.

Art 'O' level

Write a short essay on *either* the period of architecture known as Regency, *or* the Victorian Gothic Revival. Illustrate your answers with *one* representative example.

Art 'A' level

The fronts and fascia boards of most shops in our towns and cities have undergone radical redesigning over the last decade or so. Analyse, compare and contrast *two* such current designs with *two* designs of a more traditional nature, and give your assessment of their relative merits and any reasons for the changes noted. Illustrate your answer.

APPENDIX 5

SHEET 1　　*Master Plan Chart*　　SIXTH FORM / FIRST YEAR　　1983–1984

				Wk	1	2	3	4	5	6	7	8	9	10	11	12	13	14	15	16	17	18	19	20	21	22	23	24	25	26	27	28	29	30	31	32	33	34	35	36	37	38	39	40	41	42	43	44	45	46	47	48	49	50	51	52
Subject	Level	Syllabus	Nature of Exam		15	22	29	5	12	19	26	3	10	12	24	31	7	14	21	28	5	12	19	26	2	9	16	23	30	6	13	20	27	5	12	19	26	2	9	16	23	30	7	14	21	28	4	11	18	25	2	9	16	23	30	6
					Aug			Sep.				Oct.				Nov.					Dec.				Jan.					Feb.				Mar.				Apr.				May				June				July					Aug.

Example holiday markings spell the following down the grid columns:

- Weeks 5–7 (Sep): **H O L I D A Y**
- Weeks 12–13 (Nov): **H A L F   T E R M**
- Weeks 18–21 (Dec–Jan): **C H R I S T M A S   H O L I D A Y S**
- Weeks 27–29 (Feb–Mar): **H A L F   T E R M**
- Weeks 35–36 (Apr): **E A S T E R   H O L I D A Y S**
- Weeks 42–43 (June): **H A L F   T E R M**
- Weeks 48–49 (July–Aug): **S U M M E R   H O L I D A Y S**

N.B. It is necessary for tutors to adapt this layout according to their own school's circumstances and the dates of the year. This is just an example.

181

APPENDIX 5

SHEET 2 *Master Plan Chart* SIXTH FORM / SECOND YEAR 19_ _ – 19_ _

Subject	Level	Syllabus	Nature of Exam																									

APPENDIX 6

THE MASTER PLAN FACT-FINDER

Subject	Form of test (e.g. exam, assessment tests, presentation of a file of work, etc.,) and marks allocation	Important date or dates during lower and upper sixth	Date of decision for entry into exam	Date of final exam (if any)

Other Demands If you are involved or thinking of becoming involved with any school activities (e.g. sports teams, school trips abroad, music, drama, careers visits, work experience courses, etc.),

Activity	Write down here what is involved	Dates of activity

APPENDIX 7

THE MASTER PLAN CHECKLIST

From your chart of information answer the following questions in the spaces on this sheet.

1   Make a list of those subjects in which the exam will take place in two years' time.

2   Make a list of those subjects in which you will have regular assessment tests or exams, and say how often these will take place.

3   Make a list of those subjects which require a major piece of work, e.g. a file of essays, field-work, classwork, experiments, etc., some time before the end of two years, and say what is required.

4   List any subjects which do not have an exam. What tests do they have and when do they come?

5   Make a list of subjects which demand a certain minimum of course work, e.g. at least three completed woodwork projects, two completed needlework garments, four or more sketches for art, etc., and say what these requirements are.

6   Make a list of subjects which have special requirements and say what these are, e.g. overalls, ingredients, etc.

7   On which days of the week must these requirements be brought?

8   Is there anything else that has been forgotten and should be written down?

APPENDIX 8

NEWS LINE (Suggested tape recording)

Spoken items are given in inverted commas. Suitable background music may be put on the tape between the different items.

Instructions

'Each group will work as a team to prepare a three-minute news bulletin which will be read by one member of the group at the end of the session.

'You have thirty minutes of preparation time; your starting point is the fifteen newspaper cuttings in the envelope. You may select, edit and use these items in any way you choose. You must include one original item of news (fact or fiction) prepared from within the group. Extra items of news will be introduced during the preparation time.

'Here are the instructions again (repeat). You have thirty minutes of preparation time, starting now.'

Music.

After five minutes

'Reports of a large hotel fire have been received from Northern Ireland. Eye witnesses claim they heard a series of explosions before the fire started. More information will follow.'

After ten minutes

'The hotel fire in Northern Ireland is now thought to be much more serious than first reports indicated. The top three floors of the hotel are ablaze. Fire appliances from several forces have arrived at the scene. Ten people have been taken to the local hospital, including firemen overcome by smoke. Firemen using breathing apparatus are at the moment trying to reach a family of five believed to be trapped at the rear of the building. We will keep you informed as to any new developments.'

Music.

After fifteen minutes

'A statement from the Chief Fire Officer reads as follows:

"The fire is now under control. The family have been rescued unhurt from the hotel. Reports from the hospital indicate that none of the people admitted are seriously hurt, though some may have to stay overnight for observation. The cause of the fire is still thought to be an explosive device."'

Music.

After twenty minutes

A short, but very serious news item, either local or national (one minute duration).

After twenty-five minutes

'You have five minutes preparation time before you read your bulletin.'

APPENDIX 9

WHAT IS A FAMILY?

Example 1

ADULT MALE: Tom

Age: 49
Occupation: Teacher
Education: Grammar School
University
Income: £8,500
Favourite Newspaper: Express
Interests/Hobbies: Gardening, stamp
collecting

ADULT FEMALE: Joan

Age: 42
Occupation: Nursery Teacher
Education: Grammar School
Training College
Income: £5,000 approx.
Favourite Newspaper: Express
Interests/Hobbies: Sewing, knitting,
badminton.

TEENAGE SON: James

Age: 17
Occupation: Still at school
Education: Comprehensive School

Income: Casual
Favourite Newspaper: Times, Guardian
Interests: Pop music, sport

Example 2

HUSBAND: Bob

Age: 32
Occupation: Unemployed
Education: Secondary modern
Income: Social Security Benefit
and window cleaning
Favourite Newspaper: Daily Mail
Interests/Hobbies: Darts, computers

WIFE: Mary

Age: 35
Occupation: Supermarket assistant
Education: Secondary modern
Income: £60 per week

Favourite Newspaper: Daily Mail
Interests: Watching TV, knitting for third
child on the way, studying for Open
University degree.

SON: John

Age: 19
Occupation: Welder
Education: Local comprehensive
Income: £8,000 per annum

Newspaper: Angling Times
Interests: Fishing and poetry

DAUGHTER: Melanie

Age: 2½

APPENDIX 10

MASTER PLAN TIMETABLE – 'ACTIONS REQUIRED'

	Week One	Week Two	Week Three	Week Four
Monday				
Tuesday				
Wednesday				
Thursday				
Friday				

APPENDIX 11

CHECKLIST – 'ACTIONS REQUIRED'

1   Put up list to be signed by those interested in joining the outing and an outline of the day's programme (making alternatives clear). Add a break-down of costs.
   Make clear minimum numbers in order to benefit from block booking reductions.

2   Ring up Travel Enquiries and find out times and prices.

3   Get permission from Headteacher.

4   Invite members of staff.

5   Inform parents and get permission slips signed. Ask one or two to offer emergency telephone numbers.

6   Confirm bookings in writing and pay deposits.

7   Fix closing date for payments.

8   Open special account at bank.

9   Complete accounts book.

10   Investigate theatres, museums, eating places, etc.

11   Arrange transport to and from meeting point at home end of journey.

12   Fix final briefing meeting.

13   Find out if there is a buffet car on train.

14   Preliminary meeting of interested parties to draw attention to list.

15   Give details of programme to Headteacher.

16   Clear any timetable alterations that might be necessary. Discuss this checklist. Which items should be dealt with first, second, etc? Rearrange the above in the order agreed by the group.

APPENDIX 12

HOMEWORK TIMETABLE

Monday	Tuesday	Wednesday	Thursday	Friday	Saturday	Sunday	Monday	Tuesday	Wednesday	Thursday	Friday (x)
MP1	MP1	MP1 (boxed)									
MS1	MS1	MS1 (boxed)									
	F1 (boxed)										
	F2	F2	F2 (boxed)								
	Gm1	Gm1	Gm1 (boxed)								
		F3	F3	F3	F3	F3	F3 (boxed)				
		Gm2	Gm2	Gm2	Gm2	Gm2	Gm2	Gm2 (boxed)			
			MP2	MP2	MP2	MP2 (boxed)					
			MS2	MS2	MS2	MS2 (boxed)					
				Gm3	Gm3	Gm3	Gm3	Gm3	Gm3	Gm3 (boxed)	
					Gm4	Gm4	Gm4 (boxed)				
				F4	F4	F4	F4 (boxed)				

DEADLINES

Monday	Tuesday	Wednesday	Thursday	Friday	Saturday	Sunday
F3	F1	MP1	F2			MP2
Gm4	Gm2	MS1	Gm1			MS2
F4			Gm3			

(see notes APPENDIX 13)

APPENDIX 13

LOWER SIXTH HOMEWORK TIMETABLE

A lower sixth student was having trouble organising his work load which was taking up as much as four hours of his time on some evenings. He was very worried about his apparent inability to cope with the problem, and was rapidly losing confidence. The more worried he became, the worse the problem seemed to be.

Discussion with the student showed that the following points were essential features of his work schedule:

i) A clear exposition of work commitments was needed, setting out tasks for each evening as well as indicating 'deadlines' (i.e. the nights on which a given task *must* be completed to be handed in next day).

ii) The schedule should allow for reallocation of work if the student is engaged in an all-day visit, or attends an evening activity.

iii) Provision should also be made for extra projects, which may extend over a number of weeks.

iv) Because much of the students' homework is to be completed in the week following that in which it was set, a two-week schedule is necessary.

After the student had spent some time devising a complicated written homework schedule (a rather obscure document!) a more visual approach was suggested. The chart given on APPENDIX 12 was eventually designed.

Reading the chart

Read from the left:

a) Each set of work is first shown in the column representing the day of the week on which it was given.

b) It then reappears in every column until, the night before it should be handed in, it appears within a double rectangle.

c) It also appears on the *Deadlines* chart.

d) Once a task has been completed, it may be crossed off all ensuing columns and also the *Deadlines* chart.

This chart shows a complete week's homework as it is set, and when it should be handed in. 'Overlap' from week to week is not shown, e.g. on the second Monday MP1 and MS1 would appear again at the top of the column. Checking of the *Deadlines* chart with the main chart should clarify this point.

After the student was given a quantity of proformas such as the one attached, he soon learned to use them as an aid in clarifying his homework allocation and in planning his programme. His main source of worry disappeared, and his confidence was restored.

Key		
	MP1	– First Pure Maths homework
	MS1	– First Maths with statistics homework
	Gm2	– Second set of German homework
	F3	– Third set of French homework
Column Friday (x)		– Extra (long term) projects, etc.

190

APPENDIX 14

SIXTH FORM ISSUES

First Year Sixth

First term

1 Feel completely out of depth in early lessons of a subject you are normally good at and really enjoyed at 'O' level.

2 Spent most of a Saturday tackling your first essay at 'A' level. Where am I going wrong?

3 Have been asked to present a topic/take part in discussion or debate in General Studies. Do not feel able to do this in the mixed upper- and lower-sixth-form group.

4 Need to have extra lunch-time lessons in a particular subject I am re-sitting. Can I 'drop' an activity I am committed to, e.g. choir? Feel afraid to suggest.

5 Want to change from one subject to another, or from one group within a subject to another, for various reasons:
    i)   Maths makes Biology too difficult already;
    ii) Could go to History, but only had a low grade at 'O' level.
    iii) Prefer an alternative English 'A' level group – AEB/JMB.

6 I had Grade 4 CSE in English/Maths – need to get an 'O' level for my chosen career.

7 Embarrassed at changing for PE/games.

8 Changed career plans – find subjects chosen unsuitable.

9 Different teacher and approach for retake 'O' levels – feel more confused than ever.

10 Really cannot follow/understand one (or more) lecturer(s). Find their written criticisms on my work also confusing.

Second term

1 Parents insist I give up Saturday job after poor Christmas report. Enjoy it and need the money to pay debts.

2 Increasingly difficult to get books recommended. Local library and town library inadequate for needs of large 'A' level group.

3 Need to use Reference Library much more – problems of transport.

4 Think one of my year/tutor group is deliberately starving herself, although she denies this.

5   Good standard in essays when lots of time. Tests 'floor me' – cannot recall information quickly enough to analyse in these conditions.

6   Resit subjects seem to squeeze out 'A' level work. What do I do?

7   Met friends who are at tertiary/technical college. They have more freedom *re* uniform, private study, etc. Did I make the best choice for me?

8   What's the point of an organised games afternoon? I could use the time better at home doing jobs or catching up on work.

9   I still do not feel I really 'belong' to a group in the sixth form.

10 Had a Christmas job and enjoyed the 'world of work'. Did not want to return to school.

11 Had a Christmas job and hated it. Couldn't cope with the 'real world' outside school. Found it difficult to get on with fellow work mates.

Third term

1   Had an offer of job for July – tempting as I am not doing very well; *or* tempting even though I am doing well, but would like to be earning my own living and having more free time.

2   Need to get away on foreign holiday for my languages, but there are domestic problems – father unemployed, mother ill, etc.

3   Am interested in working abroad, preferably with children, or with others of my age. Where do I get information?

4   Teacher thinks I need to get into the environment of a French or German family this summer. Am really scared of 'going it alone'.

5   Increasing bulk of notes causes panic. How do I organise my revision?

6   Exam results out. Have been advised to repeat the year – what are the implications?

7   Sending for prospectus brings home the point that my course, in fact, necessitates my living away from home. Have not considered this. Should I choose another course?

Second Year Sixth

First term

1   Have not been made a prefect – feel humiliated.

2   Have been made a prefect – do not feel confident to exercise authority.

3   Evidence of glue sniffing, etc., amongst fifth form – threatened by the group responsible if I report.

4   Offered a job. Tempting, since I know or think I am borderline 'A' level.

5   UCCA form problems. What are they?

6   All my friends from lower-sixth days have left, and am finding it very difficult to break into established groups.

Second term

1   Approached by media to do interviews, photos, etc., anonymously on a political/controversial issue – local or national.

2   University acceptances, etc.: 'I've only had one offer!'

3   My revision completely ineffective for 'mocks' – staggered.

4   Met a boy at Christmas 'jollifications'. He has a less demanding job than my 'A' level course. Can't cope with 'A' levels and him.

Third term

1   Unable to work at home. Sister's family have had to come and live with us; I've lost my room, etc.

2   Other family problems which are worrying and demand time and energy, e.g. mother in hospital – running of the home falls on me.

3   Find the whole Nuclear Debate worrying – What can I do? Need to be better informed/need to get involved actively.

4   Am interested in SDP – would like to become involved. How do I go about it?

5   Was totally defeated during a recent debate of school Debating Society. Felt inadequate as main speaker – no confidence to speak in public in future.

6   My friend home from university – seems to have 'got in' with wrong crowd. Suspect already well into drugs.

APPENDIX 15

STUDY SKILLS

REVISION PLAN

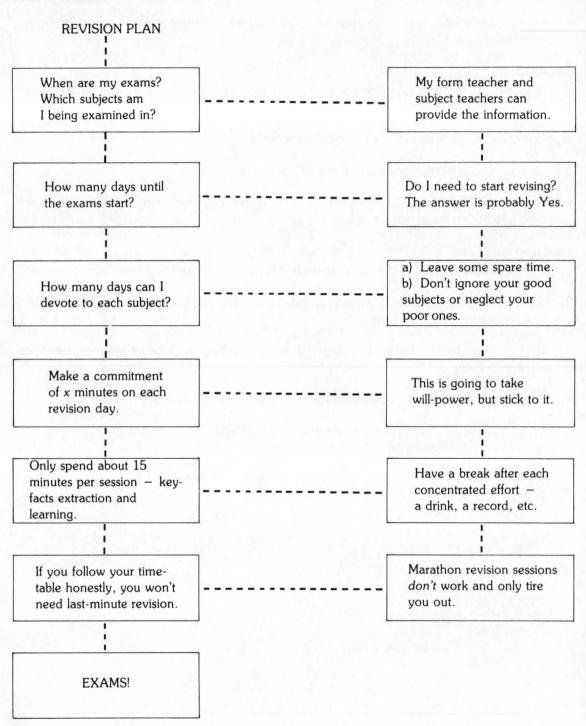

When are my exams? Which subjects am I being examined in?	My form teacher and subject teachers can provide the information.
How many days until the exams start?	Do I need to start revising? The answer is probably Yes.
How many days can I devote to each subject?	a) Leave some spare time. b) Don't ignore your good subjects or neglect your poor ones.
Make a commitment of x minutes on each revision day.	This is going to take will-power, but stick to it.
Only spend about 15 minutes per session – key-facts extraction and learning.	Have a break after each concentrated effort – a drink, a record, etc.
If you follow your time-table honestly, you won't need last-minute revision.	Marathon revision sessions *don't* work and only tire you out.
EXAMS!	

STORY

BROTHER OLIVER'S WINGS

The Abbot of Malmesbury was furious. 'You say you want to fly—like a bird?' he asked. And his voice shook with anger.

The monk to whom he spoke, smiled nervously. 'Yes, Reverend Father,' he said. 'Just like a bird.'

'But God meant birds to fly and He meant men to walk,' objected the Abbot. 'If He had wanted men to fly He would have given them wings.'

'But I have wings, Reverend Father,' said the monk.

The Abbot's eyes opened wide. 'You have wings?' he asked. 'You mean you have grown them—like an angel?'

'No, Reverend Father,' said the monk. 'I have made them!'

Now the monk, whose name was Oliver, really had made some wings. In the early Middle Ages the monks had time to read and study nature. Many times he had sat in the sun in the gardens of the Abbey watching the birds flying high above the trees and over the roofs of the little town nearby. 'If only I could fly like that,' thought Brother Oliver. 'How splendid it would be to soar over the trees and roof-tops like a bird.' He began to watch the birds more closely and saw that if they wanted to fly quickly they just flapped their wings and away they went, like arrows. If they wanted to circle round in one place, they just stretched their wings and glided. It looked very easy to Brother Oliver and he set to work to make a pair of wings for himself. He made them as like bird wings as he could and he fixed them to his arms so that he could flap them like a bird.

Now, although the Abbot of Malmesbury was angry when he first heard of Brother Oliver's idea, he soon calmed down. Monasteries were places of learning and it was right that the monks should learn about God's marvellous world. So the Abbot gave Brother Oliver permission to try out his wings from the top of the Abbey tower.

When they heard that a monk from the Abbey was going to fly, the people of Malmesbury town and the villages around gathered to watch the great event and soon there was a huge crowd waiting round the Abbey walls to see the monk who could fly. The tower of the Abbey was very tall—more than two hundred feet high—and all the way to the top went Oliver. Round and round the winding stone staircase he climbed—carrying his wings carefully folded under his arm. When the crowd saw him they craned their heads to get a better view. Whilst inside the Abbey, the Abbot and the monks made a little prayer to God to preserve Brother Oliver's life if his wings failed to work.

The crowd held its breath as Brother Oliver stood for a moment looking down at them. Then there was a gasp as the brave monk threw himself off the tower, his cloth wings spread wide.

For a moment it looked as though the monk really was going to fly for he did not fall straight to earth. The wings filled with air and Brother Oliver glided for over two hundred yards while the crowd watched spellbound. But then came disaster. Brother Oliver's arms were not strong enough to bear the weight of the wings. One wing collapsed and then the other. The poor monk crashed to the ground. But the prayers of the Abbot and his monks were answered for Brother Oliver was not badly hurt by the fall.

He said, afterwards, that his flight had failed because he had forgotten to make himself a bird's tail as well as wings. But he did not try to fly again. Perhaps the Abbot would not let him.

Read the passage on page 2 carefully and answer these questions with one word/one line answers.

You have 15 minutes in which to read and answer the questions.

1. *Where did the action take place?*

2. *When did the action take place?*

3. *Who were the characters?*

4. *What was the centre of the plot?*

5. *What were the main incidents?*

6. *What was the outcome?*

7. *How did this affect the characters?*

Now spend *ten minutes* in memorising the layout and contents of this sheet.
(Turn over only when you are told to do so.)

('Brother Oliver's Wings' is reproduced from the 'History Workshop 2' Sutton & Lewis by permission of Cassell Ltd.)

READ THIS PAPER CAREFULLY

Follow the instructions:

This story is set in Malmesbury Abbey during the early Middle Ages. It tells how a monk, Brother Oliver, persuades the Abbot to allow him to attempt a flight from the Abbey Towers. Unfortunately his home-made wings don't support his weight and he crashes to earth, unhurt, before a crowd of watching townspeople, never to fly again.

(58 words)

You have three minutes in which to read through the above passage twice.

Do not turn over until you are told to do so.

In 5 minutes

Write your version of Brother Oliver's story in approximately 50 words.

You may practice your answer in this space, if you wish.

Write your finished answer here:–

(OPEN YOUR PAPER OUT FLAT, WHEN YOU ARE TOLD TO DO SO.)

APPENDIX 17

THE STORY OF JESUS

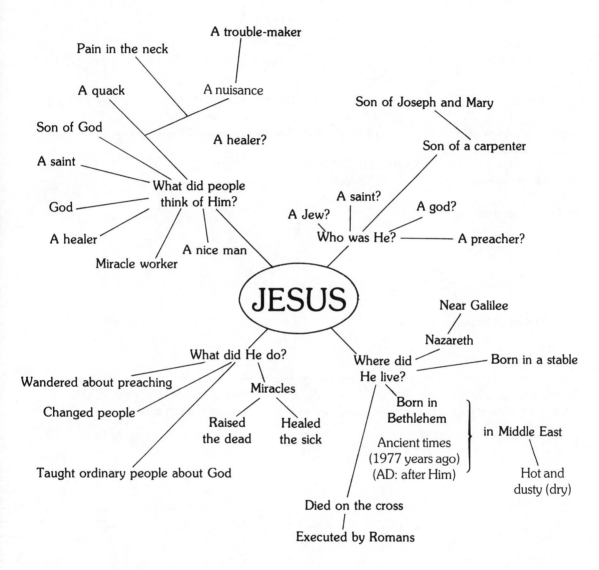

We started with one word, 'Jesus'.
From this, we've jotted down some rough ideas about the Story of Jesus; now let's sort them out.
  Which ideas join together nicely to make four or five interesting sentences (a paragraph)?
  Which paragraph (group of ideas) will make a start to the story?
  Which paragraph will make a good finish to it?
Now let's arrange the other groups of ideas into three other paragraphs to develop the middle part of the story.

APPENDIX 18

THE ROMANS

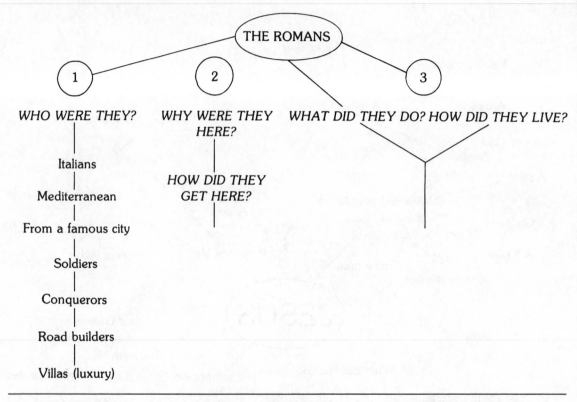

See if you can add ideas to columns (2) and (3), as has already been done in column (1).
Now write three groups of sentences (paragraphs) about the ideas in each column.

APPENDIX 19

HENRY'S FIRST CAR

Rearrange these extracts so that they make a logical story.

They lived in a house with a big coal shed in the back-yard. This shed became Henry's workshop and when he finished his day's work at the Edison Company, he began work on his horseless-carriage.

He had very little money and whenever possible he used scrap metal and bicycle parts to build his little car.

Then, climbing on to the bicycle saddle, he pulled back a lever and slowly the car moved. It bumped and clattered across the cobbled yard and then on to the road. The people of Detroit who were out early enough stopped to stare in amazement at the strange little car popping and spluttering as it went slowly through the streets.

'Our cars cost too much,' he told his men. 'Only rich people can afford to buy them. Let us make a car which costs so little that everybody can have one. Then, instead of selling thousands of cars, we shall sell millions!'

Ford Cars for Sale

Many other people in America were now building motor-cars and Henry soon found that his little car was not nearly good enough. In the year 1903, the Ford Motor Company was formed and, Henry began to build cars with proper steering-wheels, reverse gears and brakes.

It had four bicycle wheels fitted with John Dunlop's pneumatic tyres, and the driver sat on an old bicycle saddle fixed on top of the petrol tank. Part of the engine was made from a steam-engine exhaust pipe and instead of a steering-wheel the little horseless-carriage had a tiller as on a small sailing boat.

It broke down but Henry soon got it going again and he drove it back to Clara in triumph. The little horseless-carriage had no brakes, there was no reverse gear, and it could not go much faster than a man could walk. But it was Henry's first car and it worked!

In the beginning, the Ford Motor Company made three kinds of car. There was a big one which cost about £500, a middle-sized one costing £250 and a small one which cost about £150. All these cars sold well but not nearly quickly enough for Henry Ford.

It was a strange-looking vehicle that was pushed out of the back-yard workshop early one morning in May 1896. Clara Ford stood at the back door to watch while Henry started the engine.

When the other motor companies heard about Henry Ford's ideas they thought he was crazy. 'He will go bankrupt', they said. 'You wait and see!'

But Henry Ford paid no attention to what other people said. He had already thought of a way to make cars by the million.

Henry's First Car Motor Cars by the Million
In Detroit Henry Ford decided to build a horseless carriage of his own. Henry was now married and his wife, Clara, often helped him.

Story reproduced by kind permission of Cassell & Co. Ltd., from *History Workshop 6*, Sutton and Lewes

APPENDIX 20

MY FIRST HOLIDAY ABROAD

1   Weren't we glad when the coach slowed down at last and left the motorway, because now we knew we were heading towards the coast and the boat.

2   They were sometimes too high for the road to climb and we would disappear into long, dark tunnels.

3   Cable-cars, chair-lifts and tiny toy trains take people up to the top-most peaks of the mountains. We went by cable-car. It was like a tiny tram-car going through space on a long length of thread. Looking down, the houses looked like dolls' houses and the roads and rivers looked like ribbons. It was frightening but it was fantastic.

4   I hadn't actually been on a boat before and because of that I found the next bit, on the quay-side, exciting and annoying. I was dying to get on that ferry-boat but there seemed to be so much queuing and red tape.

5   We drove inland on a motorway, only they called it an *autobahn* and drove on the right instead of on the left like normal people. It was wide and it was fast – but oh! it went on and on, for hundreds of miles across the plains and the green, wooded, hills of southern Germany.

6   The mountains were divided by beautiful lakes and steep-sided valleys.

7   At first it was fun on the motorway and we stood up and cheered each time we passed another coach but we got fed up after a while and settled down to read our books and comics.

8   July, at last; Ian, Terry, Mick and I bagged the back seat as we had planned, waved goodbye to our parents, took out our lollies and waited for our holiday adventure to begin: fourteen days in Switzerland with my mates and plenty of spending money in my pocket.

9   The road wound this way and that as it climbed through these steep mountain sides passing beautiful wooden houses, called chalets, fields of flowers and cows with tinkling bells round their necks.

10 The hooter sounded and the strip of water between the boat and the dock grew wider; people shrank and lights dwindled to twinkling stars; suddenly it was colder than I expected – quite windy in fact. But I was afloat. I was a sailor, I was bound for foreign parts at last.

11 It was a bit slow at first as the coach wound its way out of town and through the narrow country roads. We were eager to get on to the M6 and the M1 to enjoy a bit of speed.

12 We all had our own ideas about which was the most exciting part of the trip – getting on the boat, stepping on to foreign soil for the first time or winding round those hair-pin bends in the coach. For me, that cable-car trip was out of this world: I really felt daring – an adventurer in space.

13 Across another frontier and into Switzerland we rode with real mountain peaks now coming into view.

14 Belgium looked a bit different from Britain; but not a lot. People spoke quickly as if they were excited. I couldn't understand the words on the signs, but I could understand their pictures. I was on foreign soil. In fact, I was a foreigner.

APPENDIX 21

FIRE – A DESCRIPTIVE PASSAGE

FIRE!

It was just an ordinary Sunday afternoon; I was walking along the High Street towards the corner of Market Street, when someone rushed past me shouting 'Fire!' Almost at the same time, I heard fire-engine sirens approach and die down. As I turned into Market Street I was confronted with a scene of great drama and excitement, as yet another fire-engine rushed by.

Already a crowd of onlookers was beginning to gather, and policemen were pressing them back to make more room for the firemen. Some firemen were handling ladders, whilst others were directing the hoses on to the flaming building. Hose-pipes writhed across the pavements like tormented serpents, and there was water everywhere. Yellow and orange flames leaped from every window of the old Market Hall, which was now well alight. More fire-engines arrived as, in the flickering light of the flames, the crowd pressed forward and policemen and firemen perspired in the heat and the strain.

The air was full of sound; the sound of crackling flames, the alarm bells and sirens of the fire-engines and ambulances against a background of excited cries from the crowd. Orders were shouted over loud-speakers to the firemen, whilst the police were constantly asking people to get out of the way. Next, there was more crashing of breaking glass, the groan of straining timbers and the thunder of falling masonry. An ambulance departed hurriedly, siren awail, and now there was a new sound, as steam rose hissing and sizzling as water began to win its battle against flame.

Our nostrils were filled with smoke, and some firemen were now wearing masks to avoid smoke-filled lungs and streaming eyes. It smelled like bonfire night at first, but then we could smell burning butter and bacon, and someone said it smelled like one great big camp breakfast. We were full of admiration for the firemen who were fighting the flames, and some people, particularly the older ones in the crowd, were concerned for their safety. I'd never seen anything like it; it was tense, it was exciting and, in a way, it was like a great big wonderful bonfire night and firework show.

At last the flames began to die down, and there was more smoke to be seen than flame. The air was hot and heavy as some of the weary firemen began to re-pack their equipment on the engines, whilst others still played jets of water on the smouldering rubble. It was time to leave, the excitement was over, and the scene looked more like the aftermath of a flood than a fire. There was water everywhere!

APPENDIX 22

FIRE – RANDOM IDEAS TO BE REARRANGED BY STUDENTS

FIRE

Here are some words and phrases which tell something about the progress of a fire. Each of these could be made into a sentence.

The ideas have been printed out of order, and even as sentences won't make a sensible story until they are re-arranged properly.

UNDERLINE IN RED   — all the ideas which would make a good opening paragraph (introduction).

UNDERLINE IN BLUE — all the ideas which would make a good closing paragraph (aftermath, conclusion).

Next, make three other groupings (paragraphs). They could perhaps be arranged around:

sight, the scene	— UNDERLINE IN GREEN
sounds	— UNDERLINE IN YELLOW
smell, atmosphere	— UNDERLINE IN BROWN

---

walking down street;   more fire engines;   smoky at first;   concern;   people rushing past;   police; ambulance;   coughing;   some fire engines leaving scene;   excitement;   growing crowds;   was someone hurt;   burning butter;   water everywhere;   steaming, blackened ruins;   sound of bells; fire-engine rushed past;   leaping flames;   bacon;   crackling of flames;   shouts of 'Fire!';   ladders; like one great big breakfast;   sizzle of water on fire;   firemen untangling hoses, etc.;   crashing of glass;   wonder;   admiration;   tangle of hoses;   colours;   market on fire;   keeping crowds back; flickers;   excitement;   shrieks;   cries of 'Help!';   cracking, creaking, crashing of timber and girders.

APPENDIX 23

FIRE – FOR THE TEACHER

Possible groupings of the random ideas in APPENDIX 22.

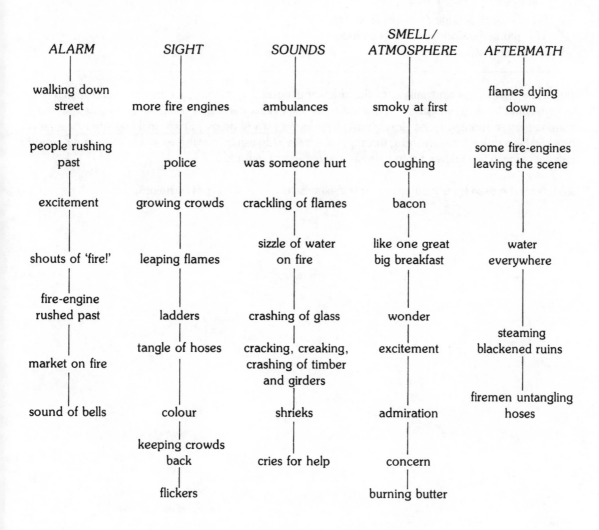

ALARM	SIGHT	SOUNDS	SMELL/ ATMOSPHERE	AFTERMATH
walking down street	more fire engines	ambulances	smoky at first	flames dying down
people rushing past	police	was someone hurt	coughing	some fire-engines leaving the scene
excitement	growing crowds	crackling of flames	bacon	
shouts of 'fire!'	leaping flames	sizzle of water on fire	like one great big breakfast	water everywhere
fire-engine rushed past	ladders	crashing of glass	wonder	steaming blackened ruins
market on fire	tangle of hoses	cracking, creaking, crashing of timber and girders	excitement	
sound of bells	colour	shrieks	admiration	firemen untangling hoses
	keeping crowds back	cries for help	concern	
	flickers		burning butter	

APPENDIX 24

THE JOURNEY OF A RIVER TO THE SEA

Break up the words and phrases below into three groups, so that they would help to tell the story of a river's journey to the sea, in three parts:

1   Where the river begins as a small stream
2   The middle (lowland) part of its course
3   Its meeting with the sea

---

rain; wider; river rises and falls with the tide; rippling and gurgling; merging of streamlets; passing through flatter land; no longer fresh, but salty; rushing over waterfalls; too wide even to cross by bridge; moorland bogs; running more slowly now; too deep to wade across; tiniest trickling streamlets; small ships slip in to unload; meandering through meadows; sluggish bigger fish to be caught; sandy, muddy shallows at low tide; children fishing, on narrow banks, for minnows

Colours can be used for underlining as in the exercise on 'Fire' if this will be helpful.

APPENDIX 25

THE LIFE OF A ROBIN

The beginnings of the reproductive cycle in robins can be regarded as when adult robins have completed their moults in July and August. After this period the cocks hold individual territories and begin to sing. A cock may try to defend a territory covering some hundred square yards or so. If threatened by other cocks, a cock may put on a threatening display, by singing, and may engage in actual fighting. The behaviour of the hens is slightly different; some hens might also try to hold individual, exclusive territories whilst others may migrate to and fro over an area of a few square miles. Yet other hens may leave England for the winter and return in spring. In January the cocks put on a determined song display to attract the hens and pair-bonding usually takes place between January and March when the two birds will share the same territory. Following this pairing, and by mid-March, the hen is responsible for building a well-hidden, cup-shaped nest, usually in a bank close to the ground. The nest consists largely of moss on a foundation of dead leaves, and lined with hair that has been foraged; the nest is completed within four days. The hen is careful not to draw attention to herself during this period, spending only a few hours each day in this activity; the cock does not take any part in nest-building.

Mating then occurs after the hen has built the nest, and then the hen may lay a clutch of five eggs over a period of five days. The eggs are normally white, speckled with small reddish-brown spots. The egg-shell is porous to allow gases like oxygen and carbon dioxide to diffuse through it. Indeed, there is an air-space within the egg between the two outer membranes. This air-space is located at the broad end of the egg. Also within the egg will be the young embryo and a yolk, both suspended by a string of mucus in the white of the egg which is a solution of protein albumen. Only the hen is responsible for sitting on and incubating the eggs, for a period of thirteen to fifteen days. The cock may attract the hen away from her eggs by his song and, once away from her eggs, the hen repeatedly calls to the cock to feed her. After hatching of the eggs, both parents remove the egg shells from the nest and the hen spends much time brooding the naked young for the first few days after hatching. The young robins are fed mainly on caterpillars supplied by their parents. After only a fortnight, the young robins may venture from the nest, returning to be fed by their parents. They do not start to forage for themselves for another week, and do not become completely independent for another twenty-one days. A mating pair of robins usually rear two broods before starting to moult again in July. The cock may still be feeding the fledgelings of the first brood as the female begins to lay a second clutch.

APPENDIX 26

LECTURE BOARD

SOLUTION	SOLUTION
	PROBLEM
SOLUTION	SOLUTION

APPENDIX 27

PROBLEM AND SOLUTION CARDS

Problems	Solutions
Content good Presentation confusing	Plan the day to maintain interest
Content not clear	Copy up work from other students
Poor note-taking Record of lecture incomplete	Talk it over with tutor group
Missed previous lecture Difficulty with new ideas	Allocate more time for the subject
Lecture late in the day Difficult to concentrate	Ask other students to explain difficult points
Failed to do last assignment Feel out of touch	Undertake extra to make up for lost work
Others in group may cause too many distractions	Talk it over with the tutor
Large group Not confident to ask questions	Approach the lecturer with the problem
No real interest in the subject	Work out way to concentrate more in lecture period
No opportunity to ask questions or discuss	Try and build up self-confidence to take more part in lecture

APPENDIX 28

PARTIALLY COMPLETED TIMETABLE

NOTE: Some students have more than the four free periods shown here. Some have as many as ten. Alter this timetable to reflect the situation which your own students will encounter. This will probably mean adjusting the time allocation in Pack A, APPENDIX 29.

	Monday	Tuesday	Wednesday	Thursday	Friday	Saturday	Sunday
1	'A'/'O' level lesson	'A'/'O' level lesson			'A'/'O' level lesson	Morning activities	Morning activities
2	'A'/'O' level lesson	General studies	'A'/'O' level lesson	'A'/'O' level lesson	'A'/'O' level lesson		
Lunch	Lunch	Lunch	Lunch	Lunch	Lunch	Lunch	Lunch
Lunch activity	Lunch activity	Lunch activity	Lunch activity	Lunch activity	Lunch activity		
3			Form RE / Games	'A'/'O' level lesson	'A'/'O' level lesson	Afternoon activities	Afternoon activities
4	'A'/'O' level lesson	'A'/'O' level lesson		'A'/'O' level lesson	'A'/'O' level lesson		
Evening activity	Evening activity	Evening activity	Evening activity	Evening activity	Evening activity	Evening activity	Evening activity
3.45 pm to 5.30 or 6.00 pm							
7.30 or 8.00 pm to 11.00 pm							

208

APPENDIX 29

ACTIVITY CARDS

Make sets of cards from the following. Each set consists of three packs, A, B and C, each with its own Instruction Card.

PACK A: Choose four of the following for the remaining four 'free' periods.		PACK B: Choose five of the following lunch-time activities.		PACK C: Choose sixteen of the following – each activity represents one evening or a morning or afternoon at weekends.	
Number of cards		Number of cards		Number of cards	
5	Private study	5	Sitting in common room	2	Church
1	Community service	5	Library – study	1	Sunday School teaching
1	Careers talks for sixth formers	2	House competition	1	Helping at school function/ planning house activity
1	Current affairs	2	Team practice	1	Reading newspaper
1	Additional 'A' level lesson	2	Library duty	3	Going out with friends
1	Secretarial skills	2	Choir	1	Evening at sports centre
1	Art as a hobby	2	Supervising quiet room	1	Duke of Edinburgh activity
1	Science for Arts sixth formers	2	Careers talks	2	Part-time job (evening or week-end)
1	Reading newspaper	2	Reading newspaper	10	Homework
1	Weekly interview with subject/ form tutor			2	TV/Radio
				2	Staying in bed

APPENDIX 30

BITS AND PIECES

The group is divided into five groups of five, and the materials divided up into envelopes as follows:

Allocation of equipment

Group 1   Sheet of blue paper
            Sheet of pink paper
            Scissors
            Money in the form of four cards lettered M

Group 2   Red pencil
            Blue pencil
            Piece of string 9 inches long
            Green pencil

Group 3   Sheet of white paper
            Blue pencil
            Red pencil
            Green pencil

Group 4   Sheet of pink paper
            Ruler
            Scissors
            String

Group 5   Sheet of blue paper
            Sheet of white paper
            Money (real coins) or sweets
            Ruler

Task sheet

Object: To produce the following items as quickly as possible.

1) A triangle with 10 cm. sides out of pink paper.
    Write the letter A on it in blue pencil.

2) An 8 cm. square cut out of white paper.
    Write the initials of each group member on it in green pencil.

3) A 5 cm. × 12 cm. rectangle out of blue paper.
    Draw a 4 cm. square on it in red pencil.

Instructions

These should be kept to a minimum and confined to going over the details of the task sheet and emphasising that not all the groups have the same materials. Give a final instruction that no materials of their own should be used. The yellow cards marked M are money cards and can be used for bartering as with the real coins or sweets if used.

APPENDIX 31

UNITED NATIONS DECLARATIONS AND CONVENTIONS
UNIVERSAL DECLARATION OF HUMAN RIGHTS

Adopted and Proclaimed by the General Assembly of the United Nations on
10th December 1948

PREAMBLE

Whereas recognition of the inherent dignity and of the equal and inalienable rights of all members of the human family is the foundation of freedom, justice and peace in the world,

Whereas disregard and contempt for human rights have resulted in barbarous acts which have outraged the conscience of mankind, and the advent of a world in which human beings shall enjoy freedom of speech and belief and freedom from fear and want has been proclaimed as the highest aspiration of the common people,

Whereas it is essential, if man is not to be compelled to have recourse, as a last resort, to rebellion against tyranny and oppression, that human rights should be protected by the rule of law,

Whereas it is essential to promote the development of friendly relations between nations,

Whereas the peoples of the United Nations have in the Charter reaffirmed their faith in fundamental human rights, in the dignity and worth of the human person and in the equal rights of men and women and have determined to promote social progress and better standards of life in larger freedom,

Whereas Member States have pledged themselves to achieve, in co-operation with the United Nations the promotion of universal respect for and observance of human rights and fundamental freedoms,

Whereas a common understanding of these rights and freedoms is of the greatest importance for the full realisation of this pledge,

Now, Therefore,

THE GENERAL ASSEMBLY

proclaims

THE UNIVERSAL DECLARATION OF HUMAN RIGHTS as a common standard of achievement for all peoples and all nations, to the end that every individual and every organ of society, keeping this Declaration constantly in mind, shall strive by teaching and education to promote respect for these rights and freedoms and by progressive measures, national and international, to secure their universal and effective recognition and observance, both among the peoples of Member States themselves and among the peoples of territories under their jurisdiction.

Article 1

All human beings are born free and equal in dignity and rights. They are endowed with reason and conscience and should act towards one another in a spirit of brotherhood.

Article 2

Everyone is entitled to all the rights and freedoms set forth in this Declaration, without distinction of any kind, such as race, colour, sex, language, religion, political or other opinion, national or social origin, property, birth or other status.

Furthermore, no distinction shall be made on the basis of the political, jurisdictional or international status of the country or territory to which a person belongs, whether it be independent, trust, non-self-governing or under any other limitation of sovereignty.

Article 3

Everyone has the right to life, liberty and security of person.

Article 4

No one shall be held in slavery or servitude; slavery and the slave trade shall be prohibited in all their forms.

Article 5

No one shall be subjected to torture or to cruel, inhuman or degrading treatment or punishment.

Article 6

Everyone has the right to recognition everywhere as a person before the law.

Article 7

All are equal before the law and are entitled without any discrimination to equal protection of the law. All are entitled to equal protection against any discrimination in violation of this Declaration and against any incitement to such discrimination.

Article 8

Everyone has the right to an effective remedy by the competent national tribunals for acts violating the fundamental rights granted him by the constitution or by law.

Article 9

No one shall be subjected to arbitrary arrest, detention or exile.

Article 10

Everyone is entitled in full equality to a fair and public hearing by an independent and impartial tribunal, in the determination of his rights and obligations and of any criminal charge against him.

Article 11

(1) Everyone charged with a penal offence has the right to be presumed innocent until proved guilty according to law in a public trial at which he has had all the guarantees necessary for his defence.

(2) No one shall be held guilty of any penal offence on account of any act or omission which did not constitute a penal offence, under national or international law, at the time when it was committed. Nor shall a heavier penalty be imposed than the one that was applicable at the time the penal offence was committed.

Article 12

No one shall be subjected to arbitrary interference with his privacy, family, home or correspondence, nor to attacks upon his honour and reputation. Everyone has the right to the protection of the law against such interference or attacks.

Article 13

(1) Everyone has the right to freedom of movement and residence within the borders of each state.

(2) Everyone has the right to leave any country, including his own, and to return to his country.

Article 14

(1) Everyone has the right to seek and to enjoy in other countries asylum from persecution.

(2) This right may not be invoked in the case of prosecutions genuinely arising from non-political crimes or from acts contrary to the purposes and principles of the United Nations.

Article 15

(1) Everyone has the right to a nationality.

(2) No one shall be arbitrarily deprived of his nationality nor denied the right to change his nationality.

Article 16

(1) Men and women of full age, without any limitation due to race, nationality or religion, have the right to marry and to found a family. They are entitled to equal rights as to marriage, during marriage and at its dissolution.

(2) Marriage shall be entered into only with the free and full consent of the intending spouses.

(3) The family is the natural and fundamental group unit of society and is entitled to protection by society and the State.

Article 17

(1) Everyone has the right to own property alone as well as in association with others.

(2) No one shall be arbitrarily deprived of his property.

Article 18

Everyone has the right to freedom of thought, conscience and religion; this right includes freedom to change his religion or belief, and freedom, either alone or in community with others and in public or private, to manifest his religion or belief in teaching, practice, worship and observance.

Article 19

Everyone has the right to freedom of opinion and expression; this right includes freedom to hold opinions without interference and to seek, receive and impart information and ideas through any media and regardless of frontiers.

Article 20

(1) Everyone has the right to freedom of peaceful assembly and association.

(2) No one may be compelled to belong to an association.

Article 21

(1) Everyone has the right to take part in the government of his country, directly or through freely chosen representatives.

(2) Everyone has the right of equal access to public service in his country.

(3) The will of the people shall be the basis of the authority of government; this will shall be expressed in periodic and genuine elections which shall be by universal and equal suffrage and shall be held by secret vote or by equivalent free voting procedures.

Article 22

Everyone, as a member of society, has the right to social security and is entitled to realisation, through national effort and international co-operation and in accordance with the organisation and resources of each State, of the economic, social and cultural rights indispensable for his dignity and the free developmnt of his personality.

Article 23

(1) Everyone has the right to work, to free choice of employment, to just and favourable conditions of work and to protection against unemployment.

(2) Everyone, without any discrimination, has the right to equal pay for equal work.

(3) Everyone who works has the right to just and favourable remuneration ensuring for himself and his family an existence worthy of human dignity, and supplemented, if necessary, by other means of social protection.

(4) Everyone has the right to form and to join trade unions for the protection of his interests.

Article 24

Everyone has the right to rest and leisure, including reasonable limitation of working hours and periodic holidays with pay.

Article 25

(1) Everyone has the right to a standard of living adequate for the health and well-being of himself and of his family including food, clothing, housing and medical care and necessary social services, and the right to security in the event of unemployment, sickness, disability, widowhood, old age or other lack of livelihood in circumstances beyond his control.

(2) Motherhood and childhood are entitled to special care and assistance. All children, whether born in or out of wedlock, shall enjoy the same social protection.

Article 26

(1) Everyone has the right to education. Education shall be free, at least in the elementary and fundamental stages. Elementary education shall be compulsory. Technical and professional education shall be made generally available and higher education shall be equally accessible to all on the basis of merit.

(2) Education shall be directed to the full development of the human personality and to the strengthening of respect for human rights and fundamental freedoms. It shall promote understanding, tolerance and friendship among all nations, racial or religious groups, and shall further the activities of the United Nations for the maintenance of peace.

(3) Parents have a prior right to choose the kind of education that shall be given to their children.

Article 27

(1) Everyone has the right freely to participate in the cultural life of the community, to enjoy the arts and to share in scientific advancement and its benefits.

(2) Everyone has the right to the protection of the moral and material interests resulting from any scientific, literary or artistic production of which he is the author.

Article 28

Everyone is entitled to a social and international order in which the rights and freedoms set forth in this Declaration can be fully realised.

Article 29

(1) Everyone has duties to the community in which alone the free and full development of his personality is possible.

(2) In the exercise of his rights and freedoms, everyone shall be subject only to such limitations as are determined by law solely for the purpose of securing due recognition and respect for the rights and freedoms of others and of meeting the just requirements of morality, public order and the general welfare in a democratic society.

(3) These rights and freedoms may in no case be exercised contrary to the purposes and principles of the United Nations.

Article 30

Nothing in this Declaration may be interpreted as implying for any State, group or person any right to engage in any activity or to perform any act aimed at the destruction of any of the rights and freedoms set forth herein.

APPENDIX 32

MEMBERSHIP FUNCTIONS

Some Task Functions

1) *Initiating*

   Proposed tasks or goals or actions; defining group problem; suggesting a procedure.

2) *Informing*

   Giving expression of feeling; giving an opinion.

3) *Clarifying*

   Interpreting ideas or suggestions; defining terms; making clear issues before the group.

4) *Summarising*

   Putting together related ideas; restating suggestions; offering a decision or conclusion for group to consider.

5) *Testing for reality*

   Making a critical analysis of an idea; testing an idea against some data; trying to see if the idea would work.

6) *Expediting*

   Prodding the group to action or decision; attempting to stimulate the group to 'greater' or higher quality activity.

Some Maintenance Functions

1) *Harmonising*

   Attempting to reconcile disagreements; reducing tension; getting people to explore differences.

2) *Gate keeping*

   Helping to keep communication channels open; facilitating the participation of others; suggesting procedures that permit sharing remarks.

3) *Consensus testing*

   Asking to see if a group is nearing a decision; sending up 'trial balloon' to test a possible conclusion.

4) *Encouraging*

   Being friendly, warm and responsive to others; indicating by facial expression or remark the acceptance of others' contributions.

5) *Compromising*

When his/her own idea or status is involved in a conflict, offering a compromise which yields status; admitting error; modifying in interest of group cohesion or growth.

6) *Process observing*

Watching how the group is operating and sharing these perceptions with the group.

7) *Standard setting*

Expressing standard(s) in the group to work by and/or testing its behaviour against such standard(s).

NOTE: It is not possible to make final distinctions between task and maintenance functions; it will be seen that there are areas of overlap in the suggestions given.

APPENDIX 33

Scene:	A march of extreme 'right-wingers' through an urban area with a high immigrant population. The police are lining the route to prevent any clash with 'left-wingers' standing behind barriers.
Props:	Two lines of chairs marking the path taken by right-wing marchers.
Characters:	1) *Chief constable and three or four police constables.* 2) *Leader of right-wing group (target for abuse and insults), with assorted lackeys! – four or five in number.* 3) *Spokesman for left-wing group assembled behind barriers, and ten assorted 'hangers-on' (i.e. should be the largest numerical group).*

The Role-Play

(Enter right-wing marchers along the route)

Spokesman LW:	Here they come – bloody Fascists! Let's get at 'em, lads, and show solidarity with our brothers in the area.
LW Hanger-on:	(*To policeman*) And whose side are you on then? You ought to be damn well marching with that crew – you're no better than them! *(Several LWs attempt to climb the barriers to approach RWs)*
Chief Constable:	(*To LW spokesman*) This organisation marching here have applied for and obtained permission for their activity. Any attempt by you to stir up this mob, and you'll be charged with inciting a breach of the peace.
LW Hanger-on:	Bloody typical! Our wonderful British policemen showing themselves in their true colour – blackshirts!
RW Lackey:	As usual, the communists are trying it on again!
Policeman:	If the Chief Constable weren't around, I'd soon teach all these yobbos the meaning of law and order! *(Finally, two or three LW members manage to scale the barriers)*
Chief Constable:	As expected. Get in there and arrest those men. *(Police grapple with LW members. Spokesman remains peacefully behind the barrier)*
Spokesman:	Those men are innocent – you blind idiot! Didn't you see the lump of concrete hurled at us by those b- - - - - - - -!

Chief Constable:	You've been warned once! Now disperse, – or else!
Spokesman:	I'm doing nothing you can do me for.
Leader of RW:	(*To Chief Constable*) I insist you protect us during our lawful pursuit.
Spokesman:	You'll need more than his protection! (*Hurls concrete lump into RW group*)
Chief Constable:	In and arrest that man!
Policeman:	I knew it would ruddy well come to this, and now it's going to be a hell of a job to get him into the van! (*Scuffle and general melee*)

APPENDIX 34

SCENARIO AND CHARACTERS

Scene: An industrial dispute. There is secondary picketing at another branch of a multi-group company which is not in dispute with its management. The union are seeking a wage rise comparable to the rise in inflation, but are faced with the threat of a lock-out and redundancy by management. A container lorry approaches the factory gates . . .

Props: Use a line of chairs to divide off the factory compound, with a gap for the entry of the lorry.

Characters:

1) **Lorry driver** seeking access (. . . might be played by tutor as a central character to keep the activity volatile!).

   The groups of four students are allocated one of the following roles, and are given five minutes to plan their strategy/dialogue. The following suggestions may be given to the individual groups as attitudes which might be adopted or points that might be tried to be made.

2) **Chief constable and policemen:**
   - maintenance of peaceful picketing
   - avoiding a breach of the peace or intimidation
   - general uncompromising and unsympathetic attitude in spite of need to be apolitical
   - over-zealous to apply picketing code of practice

3) **Official stewards of pickets and other pickets:**
   - reasonableness of furtherance of trade dispute
   - necessity to stop visitors for peaceful persuasion
   - disheartened by lack of loyalty of workers at picketed works

4) **Local councillors:**
   - of political leaning towards workers/management
   - indignation at behaviour of police inflexibility/inability to control situation
   - attempting to make political capital
   - member of the local Police Watch Committee

5) **Management:**
   - uncompromising attitude
   - bewilderment that previous small family business should be dragged into dispute
   - seeking political/industrial martyrdom
   - inherent belief in own right to manage

6) **Wives of workers not in dispute:**
   - contempt for persons creating confrontation
   - worry about prospective lack of income
   - anger at involvement of their husbands

APPENDIX 35

SOME 'LOADED' STATEMENTS

For use in 'Line Up' as material to stimulate changes in sympathy groups. Debriefing and discussion to follow each realignment of sympathies (to be spoken by the student remaining and representing each group, possibly).

For management: This lorry load is the essential consignment of raw materials that are needed to complete an export order. If we do not receive the materials, then the compensation we will have to pay will bankrupt us.

For councillors: If this firm goes bust, then we have to tell you that only a massive increase in the rates will enable us to support any workers' co-operative that may be set up.

For the lorry driver: I'm not even a member of any union, and I'm just trying to do my job. If I take this load back undelivered, my boss is likely to either dock my pay, or even sack me!

For pickets: They are not even paying us the agreed national rate for the job, and even if we got the full 20% we would only just have caught up with inflation.

For policemen: You're striking for 20% increase, but what you get already is as much as my salary. Look at the insults I have to put up with from everybody.

For wives: If our husbands join the strike for even a week, it'll take six months of higher pay to recoup the lost money.

These are some suggested pointers to help stimulate movement amongst the 'sympathy groups' – probably many more relevant ones will come to the notice of the tutor as the second role-play activity is acted out.

APPENDIX 36

ISSUE CARDS

Sheet 1

ONE

1 Nuclear disarmament is the only answer to world survival.
2 An elected president should be head of state.
3 Nationalised industries serve the whole community fairly.
4 Society does not have the legal right to a life for a life.
5 Closed shops deprive people of freedom of conscience.

TWO

1 Nuclear deterrents are essential for survival.
2 All the Conservative Party seems to care about is money.
3 Murderers should forfeit their own lives.
4 Culling of seals is essential for controlling fish stocks.
5 Nationalised industries serve the whole community fairly.

THREE

1 Murderers should forfeit their own lives.
2 All the Conservative Party seems to care about is money.
3 Nuclear disarmament is the only answer to world survival.
4 An elected president should be head of state.
5 Private enterprise stimulates competition and creates wealth.

FOUR

1 The monarchy preserves the stability of the country.
2 Society does not have the legal right to take a life for a life.
3 Culling of seals is essential for controlling fish stocks.
4 Comprehensive schools provide equal opportunities for all pupils.
5 All the Conservative Party seems to care about is money.

FIVE

1 Every woman has the right to an abortion.
2 Nationalised industries serve the whole community fairly.
3 Closed shops deprive people of freedom of conscience.
4 Culling of seals is essential for controlling fish stocks.
5 All the Conservative Party seems to care about is money.

SIX

1 The monarchy preserves the stability of the country.
2 Socialists want people to be equal whatever the cost.
3 Every woman has the right to an abortion.
4 Nuclear deterrents are essential for survival.
5 Comprehensive schools provide equal opportunities for all pupils.

SEVEN	EIGHT
1 The monarchy preserves the stability of the country.	1 Nationalised industries serve the whole community fairly.
2 Socialists want people to be equal whatever the cost.	2 A closed shop benefits all workers.
3 Every woman has the right to an abortion.	3 Parents should have the right to buy a good education for their children.
4 Nuclear deterrents are essential for survival.	4 The monarchy preserves a certain stability in the country.
5 Comprehensive schools provide equal opportunities for all pupils.	5 Nuclear disarmament is the only answer to world survival.

NINE	TEN
1 Private enterprise stimulates competition and creates wealth.	1 An unborn child has the right to live.
2 Blood sports inflict unnecessary cruelty.	2 Blood sports inflict unnecessary cruelty.
3 Socialists want people to be equal whatever the cost.	3 All the Conservative Party seems to care about is money.
4 Comprehensive schools provide equal opportunities for all pupils.	4 Parents should have the right to buy a good education for their children.
5 Murderers should forfeit their own lives.	5 Closed shops deprive people of freedom of conscience.

ELEVEN	TWELVE
1 Closed shops deprive people of freedom of conscience.	1 Private enterprise stimulates Competition and creates wealth.
2 Comprehensive schools provide equal opportunities for all pupils.	2 Every woman has the right to an abortion.
3 Every woman has the right to an abortion.	3 Murderers should forfeit their own lives.
4 Blood sports inflict unnecessary cruelty.	4 A closed shop benefits all workers.
5 Nuclear deterrents are essential for survival.	5 Socialists want people to be equal whatever the cost.

223

APPENDIX 37

THIS IS ME

```
┌─────────────────────────────────────┐
│              FLAMBOYANT              │
│                                      │
│                                      │
│                                      │
│                                      │
│                                      │
│                                      │
│                                      │
│                                      │
│                                      │
│                                      │
│                                      │
│                                      │
│              FLAMBOYANT              │
└─────────────────────────────────────┘
```

Make up one set of 62 playing cards, 3″ × 4″, for each groups, as shown opposite.

Using a felt-tip pen, print each of the 62 personal qualities listed below, on separate cards.

Adventurous	Consistent	Loyal	Self-reliant
Ambitious	Content	Mature	Sensitive
Amusing (Droll)	Disappointed	Moody	Shy
Anti-social	Dominating	Neat	Slapdash
Anxious	Enthusiastic	Noisy	Sociable
Apathetic	Extravagent	Obliging	Talkative
Bad-tempered	Flamboyant	Quiet	Thorough
Capricious	Forceful	Reliable	Thoughtful
Carefree	Fortunate	Responsible	Thrifty
Casual	Friendly	Retiring	Tough
Cautious	Gentle	Sad	Unlucky
Cheerful	Happy	Satisfied	Unobstrusive
Confident	Impulsive	Scatty	Untidy
Conforming	Indifferent	Sedate (earnest)	Worried
Conscientious	Industrious	Self-assured	
Considerate	Lazy	Self-centred	

APPENDIX 38

A PERSONAL PROFILE

This is a scale of opposing personal qualities with seven spaces separating them. Put a tick nearest to the one which is most like in each case. The nearer the tick is to the left, the more nearly you identify yourself with that quality, and so on.

Retiring								Self-reliant
Thorough								Slap-dash
Fortunate								Unlucky
Self-centred								Considerate
Extravagant								Thrifty
Enthusiastic								Apathetic
Shy								Confident
Self-assured								Anxious
Flamboyant								Unobtrusive
Worried								Carefree
Indifferent								Obliging
Anti-social								Friendly
Cheerful								Bad-tempered
Forceful								Gentle
Quiet								Noisy
Casual								Conscientious
Happy								Sad
Industrious								Lazy
Moody								Sociable
Capricious								Consistent
Adventurous								Conforming
Untidy								Neat
Cautious								Impulsive
Responsible								Scatty
Tough								Sensitive
Satisfied								Disappointed
Droll (Amusing)								Sedate (Earnest)
Ambitious								Content

APPENDIX 39

CHECK LIST FOR 'STARTING FROM SCRATCH'

Identifying Personal Qualities

Place a tick nearest to the description in each pair which applies most to you.

Enjoy working outside	Prefer being inside
Well organised	Tend to let things pile up
Neat and tidy	Untidy
Confident in speaking	Rather quiet and shy
Good with money and figures	Hopeless with figures
Work well with others	Prefer to work alone
Good at making things	Hopeless with hands
Good at paperwork	Better at practical work
Like organising others	Prefer to be organised
Enjoy taking responsibility	Prefer others to take responsibility
Patient	Impatient
Like freedom at work	Like regimented atmosphere
Like to work flexible hours	Like to work set hours
Don't mind heavy work	Dislike heavy work
Clear speaking voice	Tend to mumble
Like varied jobs	Like to stick to one set job

ATTRIBUTE CARDS

How Others See Us

Patient	Happy	Shy
Quiet	Friendly	Talkative
Kind	Thoughtful	Confident
Helpful	Capable	Enquiring
Generous	Gentle	Cheerful
Sensible	Serious	Fair
Polite	Carefree	Contented
Dependable	Trustworthy	Reliable

APPENDIX 40
STEREOTYPING

HAS A DARK SKIN	HAS A WHITE SKIN	WEARS OLD-FASHIONED CLOTHES
WEARS STYLISH CLOTHES	HAS WELL-STYLED HAIR	LIVES IN A SEMI-DETACHED HOUSE
LIVES IN A TERRACED HOUSE	LIVES IN A COUNCIL HOUSE	LIVES IN A BUNGALOW
LIVES IN A DETACHED HOUSE	MARRIES BEFORE 21 YEARS OLD	MARRIES AFTER 21 YEARS OLD
HAS A LARGE FAMILY	HAS A SMALL FAMILY	CHILDREN ATTEND LOCAL COMPREHENSIVE SCHOOL
CHILDREN ATTEND PRIVATE SCHOOL	IS WELL QUALIFIED	IS HONEST
IS FRIENDLY	IS BAD TEMPERED	DOES AN IMPORTANT JOB
IS RELIABLE	IS UNRELIABLE	ATTENDS SCHOOL PARENTS' EVENINGS
RIDES A MOTOR BIKE	HAS A SAILING DINGHY	TWO-CAR FAMILY
WATCHES BBC 2	WATCHES BBC 1	WATCHES ITV
GOES TO A DISCO	MUSICAL/DRAMATIC SOCIETY MEMBER	ATTENDS THE MAYOR'S BALL
HOLIDAYS IN BLACKPOOL	ATTENDS CHURCH	GOES ABROAD FOR HOLIDAYS
KEEPS PIGEONS	ENJOYS DO-IT-YOURSELF	LIBRARY MEMBER
PLAYS SQUASH	GOES TO THE BOOKIES	SMOKES A PIPE
SMOKES CIGARETTES	READS THE 'SUN'	READS 'THE GUARDIAN'
GOES TO THE LOCAL PUB	GOES TO THE WORKING MEN'S CLUB	DRINKS BEER
DRINKS SHORTS	MEMBER OF A GOLF CLUB	HELPS RUN THE YOUTH CLUB
IS VERY BOSSY	HELPS OTHER PEOPLE	

You may add others if you wish.

APPENDIX 41

YOU HAVE JUST ARRIVED AT COLLEGE

You have just arrived at college/university. You are to share a study-bedroom. The person with whom you are to share has not arrived. You have been given the following, rather sketchy information, which the warden has remembered from a previous interview. Your room-mate is:

    nineteen years old
    lives in the country
    enjoys the outdoor life
    likes pictures
    enjoys music
    has two 'A' levels
    attended a comprehensive school.

You have just arrived at college/university. You are to share a study-bedroom. The person with whom you are to share has not arrived. You have been given the following, rather sketchy information, which the warden has remembered from a previous interview. Your room-mate is:

    nineteen years old
    lives in the country
    enjoys the outdoor life
    likes pictures
    enjoys music
    has two 'A' levels
    attended a grammar school.

You have just arrived at college/university. You are to share a study-bedroom. The person with whom you are to share has not arrived. You have been given the following, rather sketchy, information which the warden has remembered from a previous interview. Your room-mate is:

    nineteen years old
    lives in the country
    enjoys the outdoor life
    likes pictures
    enjoys music
    has two 'A' levels
    attended sixth-form college.

You have just arrived at college/university. You are to share a study-bedroom. The person with whom you are to share has not arrived. You have been given the following, rather sketchy information, which the warden has remembered from a previous interview. Your room-mate is:

    nineteen years old
    lives in the country
    enjoys the outdoor life
    likes pictures
    enjoys music
    has two 'A' levels
    attended an independent school

APPENDIX 42

WHAT WILL YOUR NEW ROOM-MATE BE LIKE

Below is a list of alternative statements. Based on the information which you have been given, cross out one statement in each pair, i.e. the one which you think *least* likely to apply to your room-mate. Make a guess if you are not sure. Don't miss out any items.

1	Studies conscientiously.	Studies take second or third place.
2	Thinks no one needs to be unemployed.	Thinks unemployment is a national disgrace.
3	Careful with money.	Free-spending: careless with money.
4	Cheerful and optimistic.	Rather gloomy: pessimistic.
5	Upholder of law and order.	Critical of the police.
6	Untidy: disorganised.	Tidy: everything has a place and in its place.
7	Plans his career and the future.	Tomorrow can take care of itself.
8	Little interest in reading; it's a chore!	Enjoys reading.
9	Self-confident.	Unsure: needs the approval of others.
10	A gambler: takes chances.	Opposed to gambling: not a risk-taker.
11	Has concern for others.	Rather self-centred.
12	No strong religious beliefs.	Religious: church-goer.
13	Supports defence spending.	Supports CND and disarmament.
14	Left in politics.	Right in politics.
15	Extrovert.	Quiet and thoughtful.
16	Has limited spoken vocabulary.	Has extensive spoken vocabulary.
17	Lives in a small house.	Lives in a big house.
18	Slow and deliberate.	Impulsive.
19	Immigration should be curtailed.	There should be no limits on Commonwealth immigration.
20	Intensely patriotic.	Deplores nationalism.
21	Ambitious.	Not particularly ambitious.

APPENDIX 43

ANALYSIS OF RESULTS

Indicate below the total responses by your group for each item in the appropriate column.

Item	Left	Right	
1			Write here a brief summary of your impression of your room-mate, and include those items which you feel are of particular importance, (e.g. he is rather self-centred).
2			
3			
4			
5			
6			
7			
8			
9			
10			
11			
12			
13			
14			
15			
16			
17			
18			
19			
20			
21			
22			
23			

APPENDIX 44

WHO SAID IT

Take a statement like:

> If parents would use more firmness and discipline with their children, there would be less vandalism and violence

and print it on to six cards if you have six groups, five cards if you have five groups, and so on.

On each card attribute the statement to a different person, e.g.

Barbara Woodhouse	Sebastian Coe	John Wayne
Douglas Bader	Elton John	
Olivia Newton John	Kevin Keegan	

or others whom you feel would be known to your group.

Another example:

> A little sincerity is a dangerous thing.

Attributed to:

Oscar Wilde	Harold Wilson	Margaret Thatcher
David Bowie	Lord George Brown	
Barbara Castle	Debbie Harry	

or others of 'differing persuasion' who would be known to your group. You could make up other examples of your own or take examples from the news of the day.

APPENDIX 45

PREJUDICE

A

1 Lives in a large detached house
2 Likes playing
3 Enjoys many sports
4 Father is a doctor
5 Has a twin sister
6 Is not very clever
7 Parents are divorced
8 Likes reading
9 Is a German
10 Has been in trouble once with police for stealing

B

1 Enjoys cooking
2 Is very intelligent
3 Lives in America
4 Has two younger brothers
5 Loves swimming and has own pool in large garden
6 Has visited many other countries
7 Not sure what to do when leaves school
8 Likes inventing things
9 Father is in politics
10 Is black

C

1 Is one of four children
2 Has a part-time job to pay for trip
3 Lives in France
4 Is studying to be a lawyer
5 Is easy to get on with
6 Likes watching football
7 Goes to church regularly
8 Lives in a flat in a city
9 Father is a long-distance lorry driver
10 Is very attached to family

D

1 Has never been away from home before
2 Plays the violin
3 Lives in the country
4 Likes reading and writing to pen friends
5 Has long blond hair
6 Is an only child
7 Lives in Sweden
8 Would like to be a professional musician
9 Wears a leg caliper
10 Lives with grandparents as parents work abroad

APPENDIX 46

COMMUNITY CONCERNS PROBLEM CARDS

Instructions: These cards are spread on a table or sheet of paper, in no particular order or hierarchy.

MEALS ON WHEELS SERVICE NEEDS TO BE EXPANDED	COUNCIL HOUSES IN NEED OF REPAIR	LOCAL LEISURE CENTRE RUNNING AT A LOSS
MORE PARKING SPACE NEEDED IN TOWN CENTRE	WASTE FROM TIP BLOWING ON TO SURROUNDING AREA	THEATRE GROUP TO BE DISBANDED: NOT ENOUGH DEMAND IN THE AREA
FOOTBALL SUPPORTERS CAUSE DAMAGE IN AND AROUND THE GROUND	MORE ADVENTURE PLAYGROUNDS NEEDED	THE NUMBER OF UNEMPLOYED INCREASES
LOCAL MATERNITY WARD TO CLOSE. LACK OF MODERN FACILITIES	A NUMBER OF EVENING LEISURE CLASSES CUT	PLAYGROUND IN A DEPRIVED AREA TO CLOSE: NO BUILDING TO MEET IN
OLD COAL MINE SITE DANGEROUS	HISTORIC BUILDINGS DAMAGED BY TRAFFIC VIBRATIONS	TRANSPORT TO HANDICAPPED CENTRE TO BE CUT
MINI-BUS NEEDED FOR YOUTH SERVICE	YOUTH CLUB CLOSURES DUE TO LACK OF TRAINED LEADERS	LACK OF PLAYING FIELD FOR LOCAL SPORT
COST OF VANDALISM INCREASES	MORE PRIVATE HOUSES NEEDED	NO NEW INDUSTRIES BEING ATTRACTED TO THE AREA

APPENDIX 47

COMMUNITY CONCERNS SOLUTION CARDS

Instructions: a) One person holds the cards and the group discuss where to place each one. When agreed, the solution card is placed beside a problem card.

b) The solution cards may be dealt and the activity made into more of a game, with group members trying to use up their 'solutions' first. Cards may be used more than once, if necessary, and may also be replaced by better solution cards of students' own making. The tutor would have to give the latter a 'value'.

GIVE A GRANT TO VOLUNTARY ORGANISATIONS TO TAKE THE RESPONSIBILITY (5)	GIVE GRANTS TO TENANTS TO UNDERTAKE HOME IMPROVEMENTS (10)	SCHOOL CHILDREN TO PAY FOR SWIMMING LESSONS IN SCHOOL TIME (5)
BUILD A NEW CAR PARK (15)	PLANT TREES AS A WINDBREAK AND SCREEN (5)	CO-OPERATION WITH ADJOINING AREA TO SHARE EXPENDITURE (5)
BUILD A COACH PARK NEAR THE GROUND FOR VISITORS (10)	USE EXISTING MATERIAL AND WORK FORCE TO DO THE BUILDINGS (5)	GIVE GRANT TO LOCAL JOB-CREATION SCHEMES (15)
BRING FACILITIES UP TO REQUIRED STANDARDS (15)	INCREASE CLASS FEES (5)	GIVE GRANT TO HIRE CHURCH HALL (5)
DEMOLISH AND LANDSCAPE (15)	BUILD A BY-PASS ROAD (15)	REPLACE OLD SMALL VEHICLES WITH LARGER NEW ONES (10)
APPOINT A YOUTH WORKER WITH SPECIAL RESPONSIBILITY FOR TRANSPORT (10)	SET UP A LOCAL TRAINING PROGRAMME (10)	RENT LAND FROM ADJOINING AUTHORITIES (5)
APPOINT WARDENS TO PATROL DIFFICULT AREAS (10)	GIVE GRANTS TO HELP RESIDENTS TO CONVERT THEIR OWN PROPERTY (15)	APPOINT AN INDUSTRIAL OFFICER TO ATTRACT FIRMS TO THE AREA (10)

APPENDIX 48

VILLAGE PLAN

12" square – one for each group.

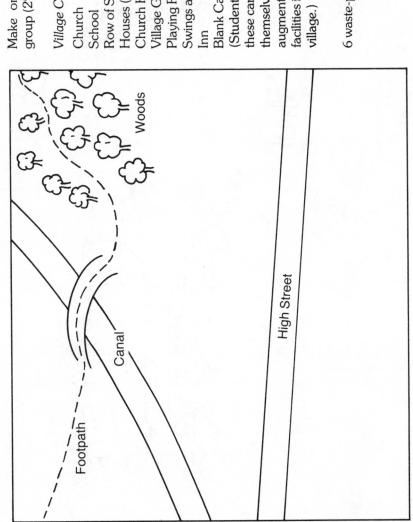

Make one complete set of cards for each group (2" × 1") as follows:

Village Cards (Green)	*Litter Cards (Red)*
Church	Confetti (×2)
School	Rusty Bike
Row of Shops (×2)	Chip papers (×2)
Houses (×6)	Old Bingo Cards (×3)
Church Hall	Tickets (×4)
Village Green	Sweet Wrappers (×4)
Playing Field	Old Mattress
Swings and Slides	Crisp Packets (×3)
Inn	Ice Cream
Blank Cards (×4)	Wrapper (×3)
(Students 'name'	Torn Fete Poster (×2)
these cards for	
themselves to	
augment the	
facilities in the	
village.)	

6 waste-paper bin cards (1" square, white)

APPENDIX 49

A LOCAL ISSUE

TRADE UNIONS
(Want more jobs)
Have persuasive arguments

TOWN HALL COUNCIL

Half left-wing beliefs

Half right-wing beliefs

Considers pros and cons

ENVIRONMENTALISTS

Protest

A FIRM

Has a proposal for a new development in an area

Has persuasive arguments for local council

Anticipates problems from residents

PRESS

Protest

Protest to Council

RESIDENTS AREA A
(Fear noxious odours)

Protest

RESIDENTS AREA B
(Fear noise and disturbance)

APPENDIX 50

ASSIGNMENT CARDS

1

What is a political party?

Which are the main parties in Britain?

Outline their principal aims and beliefs in not more than one hundred words.

2

What is meant by:

    government   in relation to the British
    opposition   system of government?

3

Which parties form part of your local council?

What is an Independent?

Could you make a brief case for and against
    a) parties?
    b) independents on local councils?

4

How are local councils organised?

How are they elected and by whom?

What is the role of the Mayor?

What is the difference between the Mayor and the Town Clerk (or Chief Executive Officer)?

5

What is a committee?

What part do committees play in local government? To whom are they responsible?

Where does real power reside – in the council or committee?

Which meetings can the press and public attend? Can they be excluded?

6

What is a pressure group?

How are they formed? (Give examples)

Is pressure sometimes legitimate?

Is it avoidable or is it always present in some form?

7

Local councils:

    Where does the money come from?

    How much power does the government have over local spending?

    How is this power exercised?

APPENDIX 51

FORMING ATTITUDES AND OPINIONS

This is the family which has surrounded me at different times in my life. One or two neighbours are included too. On this sheet 'I' tell you a little of the background of each of them; on the next sheet I want 'you' to write down your assessment of the probable attitudes and beliefs of each of them.

My dad   A highly skilled craftsman and trade union secretary; Sunday school superintendent; choirmaster; violinist-teacher and orchestral. Unemployed in the Great Depression – beat it by 'getting on his bike'. Alderman, mayor. Peace campaigner – League of Nations – yet joined the Home Guard without delay in 1940. Early motor cyclist – carried on until he was eighty-two. Didn't like crash helmets – loved the wind in his hair. Surprisingly, in his seventies watched 'Match of the Day', but used to think my time spent on sport in my youth was trivial and wasteful – I should be working/studying. The world's greatest optimist – every day was always good for something! Not a great gardener, but loved it nevertheless.

My mum   Attended local board school – paid a ha'penny per week for tuition; left at thirteen to work half time 'in't mill'. Stopped work on marrying – returned part-time during the war and carried on to sixty-five to 'get her stamps on'. Lifelong chapel-goer. Reticent; a reluctant mayoress. Loves all children, particularly in the family. Still lives in the house we moved into when I was five. Now widowed but insists on maintaining her own home amidst familiar people and places. Put her foot down once – made me apply for a job in the town hall when I was fifteen – for security!

My grandads: *Mum's father*   Gentle, bowed, pipe-smoking philosopher/gardener. A play-goer in the far-off days when the theatre was not respectable. At seventy he could recite Macbeth by heart. A highly skilled foundry worker from a poor, fatherless family; worked to keep his younger brother at school. His brother later became an industrialist out of the World War I boom but became 'distanced' from his family.

      Dad's father   Built like a mountain-side, hands like shovels – beaming, jovial. Shipyard-worker turned market-gardener – physically could move mountains! Bee-keeper, bandsman – his one day off per year was to the National Brass Band Contest at Crystal Palace. Had little schooling and his brothers ran off to sea. One became a beach-comber and the other a Salvation Army Officer. The beach-comber became the wealthiest of the three. Grandad died in modest circumstances, but his 'estate' was my Dad's first and only real capital. Grandad wheeled his produce round his village on a hand-cart; his only transport was his bicycle and the horse and trap which was his pride and joy. Grandad's education was through night school and self-tuition in his forties. I remember him reading to me, haltingly, from the newspaper, as I sat on his knee, and I still recall his pride that he had learned to read.

My wife   She was fourteen when we met at Sunday School. I was in scout uniform and she was the prettiest girl around. Now a grandma six times over, she still is a strikingly attractive woman. A good wife, good mum, lovely grandma – she's the hub around whom our family life revolves. Her father was a self-made man – literally rags to riches. My wife was 'paid' to the local grammar school but left early to assist in the family business due to war-time staff shortages. Even all those years back they lived in a 'big' house and had a car! Except for a few years in the seventies when she opened up a business of her own, she hasn't gone out to work since the children were born. Used to be sporty, lover of long moorland walks and a good dancer. Loves our garden, but the time and attention it demands conflict with a new and growing desire to travel.

My elder daughter   Married the boy she met in the fifth form and has three boys of her own under eight years old. She's petite, yet vigorous and business-like, and is still as athletic and sporty as she was at eighteen; went through the sixth form and trained to be a teacher for one year before giving it up to become qualified as a state registered nurse. Has not worked since the children came along until this year – now does a part-time job as a sports teacher in a local prep school. Has a good voice – formally in a good choir; plays the piano. Her husband has a good honours degree in physics. He trained originally for industry but teaches physics in a local comprehensive school.

My younger daughter   Was a tom-boy when she was younger. Went to the same grammar school as her brother and sister and through the sixth form and on to college for one year. Then started again and took a degree in horticulture at university. Good gymnast and all-round sports woman. Trekked overland and through the Khyber Pass to India when she was twenty. Later married an Indian student and has three children under seven years old. Has studied Urdu and Islam and writes children's books with multicultural backgrounds. Has drive and ambition; gregarious; a divergent thinker. Husband is in business in partnership with his brother.

My son   He loved Dublo trains, model-making and football; still good at sports – loves golf and tennis and swimming. He's outgrown trains but girl-friends still take second place to football. Passed his scholarship and later went on to the new sixth-form college. Not a high-flyer at school or college, but is, nevertheless, a bright lad. His physics degree took him into work in nuclear physics. His dislike of the latter and love for travel (caught perhaps from father and sister) led to work in Arabia for a Texas oil company. He'll be moving on again soon. Has visited USA, China, Malaysia, Egypt, Greece and Turkey, and many EEC countries. Fluent German. Unmarried; unhurried; quietly confident; a divergent thinker. Likes to meet his old pals and looks forward to settling down again in his home district eventually.

My favourite uncle   'Now this *is* a true story!' That's the line by which we all remember him. He left school at thirteen and worked 'in't mill'; was in the Royal Flying Corps in World War I, and a skilled fitter in World War II aircraft production. He was on first-name terms with bosses, foremen, work-mates and trade unionists alike, with a story for every occasion – it was his pilot who shot down the German ace, Baron von Richtofen!!!? He was, at times, 'no better than he ought to be' – all the family knew of his escapades, whilst he thought they didn't! A most infrequent chapel-goer, he would nevertheless turn up in the choir for special occasions and loved singing those ranting 'old-time religion' hymns. He was the family's lovable black sheep – how we miss him!

My neighbours   My most immediate neighbour, over the hedgerow to my right, is an accountant, with two grown-up children. He and his wife are locally born and educated. They live in a converted farm and have a few acres for their three horses. They're both keen on horses, but Mrs is fanatical – eats, sleeps, breathes them; rides regularly and attends show-jumping events every summer weekend. Her son has just taken finals as a solicitor.

My most immediate neighbour to my left is a young farmer who lives in the farm cottage. His sons are at a local comprehensive; the eldest one leaves soon and can't wait to get on the land. I remember the young farmer as a schoolboy – bright, keen, pleasant – no pretensions as a scholar, but a good little centre forward. His family own most of the land around us. It's pretty well all work – long hours and weekends.

My mother's neighbour   She lives 'next door above'. Both she and her husband are of the area – he was a senior school product and she attended the local grammar school. Her son is quiet, studious, a little withdrawn, and has a good honours degree but still no job, after a year. His step-father had an accident at work which has left him progressively more helpless physically. He'll never work again, and his wife has a full-time job looking after him. They can never go out together.

Now you've got to here – what about me? Just for fun, fill in the spaces below and on the next sheet. How old am I? Am I left, right, or centre in politics? Am I of strong convictions, easy going, or both? How might others (above, for example) have influenced me?

Me:

When you've completed APPENDIX 52, Attitudes and Opinions, using these sheets, take another three sheets of paper of this size and divide them into two columns. At the top of the first column write *Why?* and at the top of the second column write *Justification* on each sheet. Complete the *Whys?*, then change papers with another person. You will then be given further instructions.

APPENDIX 52

ATTITUDES AND OPINIONS

My dad

My mum

My Grandads

My wife

My elder daughter

My younger daughter

My son

My favourite uncle

My neighbours

My mother's neighbour

Me

APPENDIX 53

DEMOCRACY IN THE FACTORY

1 *Workers in industry*
   Six sets of cards:
   maintenance workers
   production line workers
   clerical/office workers
   foreman/engineers
   managers
   directors

2 *Job priorities*
   Twelve sets of cards (two per group):
   pay
   working conditions
   bonuses
   holidays
   the product(s)
   overtime
   status
   health/safety measures
   canteen facilities
   sport/social arrangements
   career opportunities
   production
   staff training
   dividends

APPENDIX 54

FRIENDSHIP PATTERNS

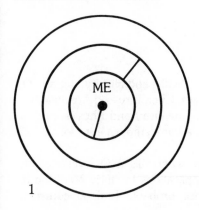

1

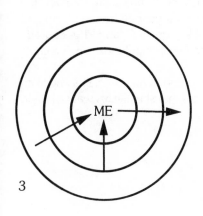

Arrows may be used to show
movement closer, or a friend
becoming more distant,
perhaps.

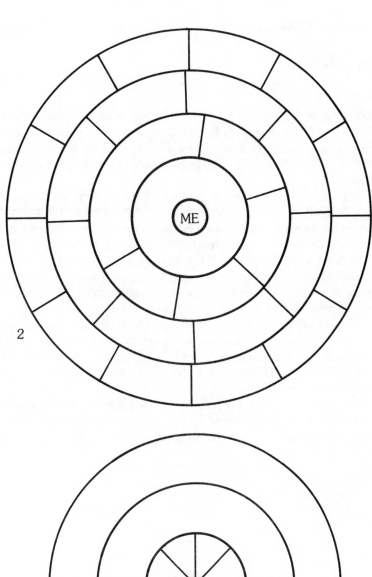

2

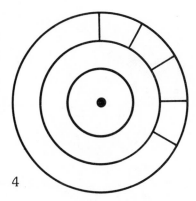

3

4

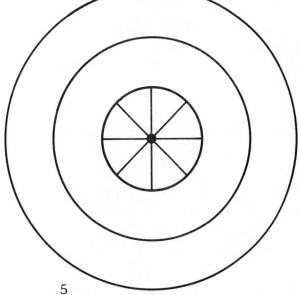

5

APPENDIX 55

Could this be you?

Julie

Julie entered the sixth form with six 'O' level passes and two subjects – Maths and History at grade D. The 'O' level passes include English Language, French, Biology, Physics, Chemistry and Art. Julie has been persuaded to do a science-based course of 'A' levels, Biology, Chemistry and Physics, and to repeat 'O' level Maths. She has been greatly influenced by her father, a bank employee, to follow this course.

At the end of the first year in the sixth form Julie double-enters in Maths and fails at 'O' level and gets a CSE grade 1. At the beginning of her second year she makes applications to study Medicine at university. Her tutor has advised her to apply for a broad-based science, probably, Biology, course at university. She receives no offers of places to study Medicine.

'A' level results bring the news that she has passed Biology with a grade C, and got 'O's in Physics and Chemistry. She is not interested in applying through the 'clearing-house' system for a possible university place nor does she make any applications to polytechnics. Instead she decides to return for a third year in the sixth form to repeat her 'A' levels.

There is still pressure from home for Julie to make a second application to university to study the Biological Sciences, but Julie seems to lack motivation throughout this third year in the sixth form and eventually the next round of 'A' level results find her with a pass in Biology, grade C, and Physics grade E and Chemistry 'O' level grade. She is persuaded by her career teacher to apply for a polytechnic course in Applied Biology.

After a term's work at the polytechnic, and disenchanted with having to look after herself away from home, she decides to leave the course. She arrives home and announces that she always wanted to do social work. Where does she go from here?

APPENDIX 56

'PROFILE' EXAMPLES

Could this be you?

Kenny

Kenny entered the sixth form with two 'O' level passes in Art and History. He was far from successful at Maths and English whilst at school and earned himself a bit of a reputation as a 'tearaway'. His immediate employment prospects were low and indeed he has made no effort to find a job. Instead he has turned up on the doorstep of the sixth form college on the first day of the new academic year seeking some course to occupy his time.

After a sympathetic hearing from the art teacher in college, Kenny has been persuaded to take 'A' level Art and 'A' level History of Art. The art teacher recognises that Kenny has some talent. During the course of his sixth form studies, and after repeated attempts, Kenny finally achieves a CSE grade I in English and Maths, and an 'O' level in Geography.

After achieving success in 'A' level Art, grade B, Kenny takes up the offer of a place at the local FE college to take a Foundation Arts course. His parents are sceptical as to his employment prospects but remain happy that their son is at last settling down and shows keen interest in his FE course. Shortly after the start of term the notices giving details of fees for tuition and materials are distributed to students. Kenny forwards this to his local education authority along with an application for a grant.

Towards the end of the first term Kenny receives the letter from his local education authority informing him that his course at the FE college is not covered by a mandatory grant nor is it possible for the authority to pay his tuition and materials fees. Luckily the FE college is able to offer Kenny a small amount from a scholarship to help him pay his fees. His parents interpret this as charity and pressurise Kenny into leaving the college and to sign on for unemployment benefit. Convinced of his own ability, Kenny turns up at the beginning of the next academic year at his previous sixth form college seeking some course to help his career/further education prospects, whilst also wishing to claim supplementary benefit under the 'twenty-one-hour' rule. Where does he go from here?

JAPANESE workers – the human ones – are having serious second thoughts about the 'robot revolution' sweeping Japanese industry.

Some 80 p.c. of all industrial robots of the world are at work in Japan, some 100,000 of them. In 1979, 14,500 new ones started on the job. Last year, there were 24,000 more, and this year there will probably be another 30,000 to 40,000.

To workers in the rest of the world, this presents a nightmarish threat – instead of competing with Japanese, which is bad enough, they will be trying to keep pace with clanking machines in Nagasaki or Nagoya which never sleep, never strike, never make a mistake, and ask for no more than an occasional wipe with an oily rag.

Now, for the first time, human Japanese workers are beginning to wonder whether they, too, may soon start to lose out in the race with tireless automatic machinery.

Japan is still a long way from the machine-smashing days of Ned Ludd, mythical leader of the movement by unemployed British handweavers to destroy the newly-invented automatic looms at the beginning of the Industrial Revolution.

Nevertheless, for the first time since Japan began to industrialise more than a century ago, the Japanese themselves are beginning to wonder where the robots are leading them.

'As the robot age arrives,' said the famous Tokyo daily newspaper Mainichi Shimbun, last week, 'we have to ask ourselves: "What useful work can human beings still do?"'

The Japanese are not, of course, worried about machines which fill beer bottles, fasten bolts or drill holes, which have existed in Japan, as in other industrial countries, for decades. Nor have Japanese engineers yet come up with a 'steel-collar' mechanical worker which can duplicate all the skills of its human counterpart, such as reading a drawing, or inventing a new process.

Check

However, in two different directions, robots are beginning to challenge human skills. One is in the nimbleness of human fingers. The Japanese are now making robots with 'five degrees of freedom' to carry out such operations as welding, operating lathes, and painting (engineers consider that a human hand has 'seven degrees of freedom').

The other breakthrough is the control of machines by sophisticated electronics, to the point that a machine can now (up to a point) check its own work, repair or reject mistakes, and, suitably programmed in advance, produce objects which are different from each other.

In turning out, for instance, cars of different specifications for different markets, or to suit individual customers' preferences, Japanese industrial robots are probably already superior to human workers, 'remembering' complex design changes without any mistakes.

FEAR

In the land of the rising robot

by MURRAY SAYLE

IN TOKYO

It is easy to see why the robot revolution has gone so far in Japan, the world leader in making both machine tools and cheap, serviceable electronics. Put these two together and you have a robot. And, for the first 20 years of the Japanese 'economic miracle' (when Japanese real wages increased ten times) there was no resistance, but rather a welcome from Japanese workers.

This was partly because the primary loyalty of a Japanese worker is to his company and, through the system of twice-yearly bonuses, he shares in the company's profits. The company in return promises the worker a job for life.

Consequently, when the new generation of industrial robots was first intro-duced, most Japanese workers stood to benefit and the unions, based on the companies (and often part of the company management), raised no objections. Workers used to tie ribbons to their robots and give them the names of Japanese girl pop stars. In good times, the robots threatened no one.

So while Japanese wages continued to rise, everyone was happy. The rapidly expanding postwar economy has had a perpetual shortage of skilled manual workers, especially fitters and turners, welders and painters – tough, skilled trades which robots can do as well as humans.

Japanese immigration policy allows no immigrants or 'guest workers' and so, from a company's viewpoint, a sophisticated robot costing £50,000 is a better bet than taking on a skilled craftsman who might well earn five times that much in a lifetime and expect a lump sum payment of anything up to £10,000 when compulsorily retired at 55.

Especially as a Japanese painting robot can do the work of 1.5 human painters, seven days a week, 24 hours a day.

As recently as last year, the general conference of the Japanese Confederation of Labour, Domei (set up with the support of the American occupation after World War II), devoted a day to speeches on the theme of 'how we can co-operate with the robot revolution'. Speakers urged that companies should retrain workers as and when their jobs were taken over by robots.

But now, as the Japanese Minister for International Trade and Industry, Shintaro Abe, warned last week: 'The honeymoon between workers and industrial robots may soon be over.' Domei and its rival trade union organisation Sohyo (also, ironically, set up with American support) have called for a three-way study by business, trade unions and government of the social and economic impact of the new machines.

A typically Japanese advisory council on the subject is due to hold its first meeting on March 18, the first official investigation of robots to be held anywhere in the world.

The world economic situation is behind the rethink. Japan continues prosperous in a world sliding into recession, but only just. Japanese unemployment is edging up, from 2 p.c. last year to 2.7 p.c. now.

Primitive

Japan's trade balance went negative in January, for the first time in nearly two years. The Japanese home economy is slowing down, and only exports are keeping the factories busy. In real terms, Japanese industrial wages barely keep pace with inflation. The 'economic miracle' is over.

The big, famous companies, like Toyota and Nissan, Honda and Sony, continue to do well. But some 70 p.c. of Japanese work for companies employing 50 or less, many of them subcontractors for the giant firms, are the ones who feel the pinch first when times go bad, and it is exactly these smaller companies – often operating in primitive sheds and shacks, in run-down suburbs – who are buying the new, cheaper robots.

Small firms employ casual workers, women, older men – all people who can be fairly easily made redundant, even in Japan.

It is hard to imagine Japanese smashing a machine. On the other hand, as the 1930's demonstrated, Japanese democracy is relatively new and untested and mass unemployment has already produced social chaos and one military dictatorship.

We may yet see a kamikaze version of Ned Ludd swinging a sledgehammer in a busy, unmanned factory, forcibly putting the robots out of work for a change.

From the Daily Mail, 10 March 1982

APPENDIX 58

LIFE STYLES

1   Living at home
    a)   Contributing to the budget at home
    b)   Provide own lunches from family stores
    c)   Buy own clothes, with possibility of subsidy from parents
    d)   Supervision of comings and goings and choice of friends
    e)   Sharing of chores
    f)   Limited use of car
    g)   Entertaining of friends: some restriction, e.g. on parties
    h)   Family support
    i)   Washing may be done for you
    j)   Meals cooked for you

2   *Living in digs*
    a)   Pay for board – possibly more than at home
    b)   No lunches provided
    c)   Responsible for buying own clothes
    d)   No real household chores other than keeping bedroom tidy
    e)   Supervision variable – could be more irritating than home, or completely free
    f)   No car unless running one's own: very expensive – problem of garaging
    g)   Entertaining friends – may be forbidden
    h)   Ready ear – possible, but it takes time to build up trust
    i)   Washing – may be done or not
    j)   Meals provided – often no choice of menu

3   *Living in a hall of residence (if in higher education)*
    a)   Pay termly according to set rate – direct debit from grant
    b)   Meals provided, lunches depending on distance of hall from lectures. What about week-end catering?
    c)   Buy own clothes
    d)   Free comings and goings within reason; 'ready made' friends – pros and cons; noisy corridors; possibility of having to share a room
    e)   Keeping own room tidy, or not; may be complaints about you from cleaners
    f)   No car unless own one
    g)   Parties within limits – in own room and communal rooms
    h)   Existence of a warden for problems; also friends around all the time
    i)   Do own washing

4   *Living in a bed-sitter (by yourself)*
    a)   Landlady may never be seen, or may be intrusive and nosey
    b)   Own meals to shop for, budget for and prepare
    c)   Own clothes, etc., to buy, plus bedding, table-linen, towels, cleaning materials, etc.
    d)   Free comings and goings, but there will be a necessity to make friends with the possibility of loneliness

e) Do all chores and odd jobs
f) No car unless own one; problem of garaging
g) Parties – remember neighbours and your belongings
h) Possibility of 'no shoulder to cry on'
i) Doing own washing

5 *Sharing a flat/house*

a) Contribute to rent and all over needs
b) Make own meals, or arrange with rest of the household
c) Buy own clothes
d) Shared chores
e) No supervision
f) No car unless shared
g) Parties within limits – breakages
h) Friends as 'shoulder to cry on'
i) Washing by arrangement
j) Cook in turn
k) Uncongenial companions – may lead to tension